Transmissions of Memory

The Fairleigh Dickinson University Press Series in Italian Studies

General Editor: Dr. Anthony Julian Tamburri,
Dean of the John D. Calandra Italian American Institute

The Fairleigh Dickinson University Press Series in Italian Studies is devoted to the publication of scholarly works on Italian literature, film, history, biography, art, and culture, as well as on intercultural connections, such as Italian-American Studies.

On the Web at http://www.fdu.edu/fdupress

Recent Titles

Patrizia Sambuco, *Transmissions of Memory: Echoes, Traumas, and Nostalgia in Post-World War II Italian Culture* (2018)

Thomas Cragin and Laura A. Salsini (eds.), *Resistance, Heroism, Loss: World War II in Italian Film and Literature* (2018)

Catherine Ramsey-Portolano, *Performing Bodies: Female Illness in Italian Literature and Cinema (1860–1920)* (2018)

Ryan Calabretta-Sajder, *Pasolini's Lasting Impressions: Death, Eros, and Literary Enterprise in the Opus of Pier Paolo Pasolini* (2018)

Robert Pirro, *Motherhood, Fatherland, and Primo Levi: The Hidden Groundwork of Agency in His Auschwitz Writings* (2017)

Theodora D. Patrona, *Return Narratives: Ethnic Space in Late-Twentieth-Century Greek American and Italian American Literature* (2017)

Ursula Fanning, *Italian Women's Autobiographical Writings in the Twentieth Century: Constructing Subjects* (2017)

Gabriella Romani and Jennifer Burns (eds.), *The Formation of a National Audience in Italy, 1750–1890: Readers and Spectators of Italian Culture* (2017)

Lisa Sarti and Michael Subialka (eds.), *Pirandello's Visual Philosophy: Imagination and Thought across Media* (2017)

Elena Borelli, *Giovanni Pascoli, Gabriele D'Annunzio, and the Ethics of Desire: Between Action and Contemplation* (2017)

Gregory M. Pell, *Davide Rondoni: Art in the Movement of Creation* (2016)

Sharon Wood and Erica Moretti (eds.), *Annie Chartres Vivanti: Transnational Politics, Identity, and Culture* (2016)

Flavio G. Conti and Alan R. Perry, *Italian Prisoners of War in Pennsylvania: Allies on the Home Front, 1944–1945* (2016)

Graziella Parati (ed.), *Italy and the Cultural Politics of World War I* (2016)

Susan Amatangelo (ed.), *Italian Women at War: Sisters in Arms from the Unification to the Twentieth Century* (2016)

Alberica Bazzoni, Emma Bond, and Katrin Wehling-Giorgi (eds.), *Goliarda Sapienza in Context: Intertextual Relationships with Italian and European Culture* (2016)

Transmissions of Memory

Echoes, Traumas, and Nostalgia in Post–World War II Italian Culture

Edited by
Patrizia Sambuco

FAIRLEIGH DICKINSON UNIVERSITY PRESS
Vancouver • Madison • Teaneck • Wroxton

Published by Fairleigh Dickinson University Press
Copublished by The Rowman & Littlefield Publishing Group, Inc.
4501 Forbes Boulevard, Suite 200, Lanham, Maryland 20706
www.rowman.com

Unit A, Whitacre Mews, 26-34 Stannary Street, London SE11 4AB

Fairleigh Dickinson University Press gratefully acknowledges the support received for
scholarly publishing from the Friends of FDU Press.

British Library Cataloguing in Publication Information Available

Library of Congress Cataloging-in-Publication Data Available

ISBN 9781683931430 (hardback : alk. paper) | ISBN 9781683931447 (electronic)

∞™ The paper used in this publication meets the minimum requirements of American
National Standard for Information Sciences Permanence of Paper for Printed Library
Materials, ANSI/NISO Z39.48-1992.

Printed in the United States of America

Contents

Acknowledgments

It is a truth universally acknowledged that a scholar in possession of a project for an edited volume must be in want of much patience; such are the unpredictable turns that projects of this kind are subjected to. Yet this was not the case for *Transmissions of Memory: Echoes, Traumas and Nostalgia in Post–World War II Italian Culture*. Thanks are due to several people who made my work possible and the process enjoyable.

I wish to thank the contributors for their endeavors in producing the chapters published in this volume. I am grateful to the staff of Fairleigh Dickinson University Press (FDUP) and Rowman & Littlefield for their efficiency, accuracy, and kindness. I thank in particular the FDUP director Harry Keyishian for his ever-prompt response to all my queries, the editor of the Italian Studies Series Anthony Tamburri for his support, and both for believing in the project. I also thank Zach Nycum and Darren Williams for their help through the details of the final submission.

This project is the result of more research activities and has come together also thanks to the advice of several colleagues. I thank Zygmunt Baranski, Martin McLaughlin, and David W. Ellwood for their suggestions that helped to shape the volume as it is today. The project would have not existed, had I not met the encouragement of John Gatt-Rutter at a very early stage, when my ideas were blurry and incoherent. I am indebted to him for the many conversations, first in Melbourne and later across the oceans; I also thank him for his suggestions on my chapter. I am grateful to Gavin Bowd for his advice on my chapter and to Alessandra Manca for carefully proofreading it.

I thank the following publishers who granted copyright permission for the reproduction of poetry and fiction. All quotations from Eugenio Montale's works in Italian are reproduced by kind permission of the publisher Mondadori (© 1984, Arnoldo Mondadori SpA, Milano; © 2015, Mondadori Libri

SpA, Milano). All quotations from Claudio Magris's *Blameless*, translated by Anne Milano Appel (2017, Yale University Press) are reproduced by kind permission of Yale University Press, © 2017 Yale University Press.

Putting together this volume coincided with a period of my life that can only be defined as *challenging*. If everything proceeded smoothly, it is thanks to a small group of extraordinary people who made their presence significant at that time. I am very grateful to Mirna Cicioni who provided shelter, conversations, and silence, and even came up with the title for this volume, putting an end to months of failed attempts on my side. I thank Jessica Chakowa for her warm pragmatism and beneficial influence. I am deeply grateful to Gildo and Maria Tilli whose kindness touched me beyond words. A big thank you to Alberto and to Raymond for their cunning ability to appear always at the right moment knowing how to say the right thing. Of all of them Jane Austen would have said, "There is no charm equal to tenderness of heart."

Introduction

Transmissions of Memory: Echoes, Traumas, and Nostalgia in Post–World War II Italian Culture is concerned with cultural memory, and hence with transforming cultures, within post–World War II Italy. It deals with narrative, poetic, filmic, computer-based, and architectural products of cultural transmission taking an encompassing view on what constitutes memory. The "turn toward memory" that has characterized the research interest of several disciplines over the last few decades has produced a proliferation of works, branching out to the analysis of personal and national memory, of psychoanalysis and history, and of medical approaches and literature. As Elisabeth Krause says, reporting the words of both Wulf Kansteiner (2002) and Geoffrey White (2006), a myriad of analyses have been conducted under the umbrella of memory studies, yet their approach is so diversified that what is intended by memory becomes blurred.[1] Antonio Traverso and Mick Broderick complain of the same difficulty when facing the overwhelming literature on trauma studies, which is indeed deeply connected with, deriving from, and at times muddled with memory studies.[2] *Transmissions of Memory: Echoes, Traumas, and Nostalgia in Post–World War II Italian Culture* considers the interplay between past and present at the core of any revisitation of the past as crucial for agency, both individual and collective. Memory here is not to be intended exclusively within the social framework of Eric Halbawchs's collective memories, that is, as societal remembrance. The essays in this volume discuss memory as a cultural phenomenon where literature, architecture, and films shape its meanings. Therefore the discourse on memory here shifts toward cultural memory, another much debated term. From Aby Warburg's concept of cultural symbols as subject of transforming interpretations in history to Jan Assman's definition of cultural memory as a society's construction of identity, where the selection of which past and heritage to carry forward tell "much about the constitution and tendencies of a society,"[3] to a more transcultural articulation of cultural memory as advocated by Peter Carrier and Kobi Kabulek in a recent work,[4] the understanding of cultural memory has been multidirectional. The interpretation of literary critic Mieke Bal, who thinks that memory has to be studied through culture because it "can be understood as a cultural phenomenon as well as an individual or social one,"[5] echoes best the directions taken by *Transmissions of Memory: Echoes, Traumas, and Nostalgia in Post–World War II Italian Culture.*

Literary and artistic revisitations and indeed any revisitations of the past involve an interplay of past and present and of truth and fiction, that is in fact not only pertinent to memory but also to history. The multidirectional interpretations of memory are parallel to a reframing of the meaning of history that has also been conspicuous over recent decades. Carlo Ginzburg (2012) has established that discussions on the perception of historical truth, and therefore on the perception of the past, are to be traced back to a much earlier time, indeed to antiquity. In the contemporary period, the move from macrohistory to microhistory, with its emphasis on oral history and the disenfranchised, has reshaped many hitherto dominant concepts of history. In literary studies, Linda Hutcheon's "historiographic metafictions" clarified the influence of the postmodern on historical fiction in order to assert that history and fiction are both constructs with their "claim to truth."[6]

To say that *Transmissions of Memory: Echoes, Traumas, and Nostalgia in Post–World War II Italian Culture* has at its core the sense of agency that revisitation of the past may endow means that the volume focuses on the sense of empowerment, resilience, and on the enriched perspectives that the cultural products considered convey. Both ideas of continuity with the past, clearly visible in the first section of essays dedicated to cultural transmission, and ideas of fragmentation, emerging from the second and third sections, concerned with divided memory and nostalgia, are considered for what they generate in terms of the enrichment of the perception of personal and collective power in the present and future.

The interplay of past and present has much in common with a gender approach. As Marianne Hirsch and Valerie Smith (2002) have shown, memory and gender are two analogous lines of research, equally focused on transformed and revised visions of history and narratives, as well as on challenges to preestablished knowledge. Narrations, revisions, and transmissions of tradition and culture are all part of the shaping and reshaping of individual and national memory. Revisions or rewriting of traditions, of national and personal narratives, are also the core interest of feminist and gender studies where new readings aim at constructing new perceptions and new subjectivities. This volume has in a gendered approach one of its focuses; the methodological similarities between revisitations of the past and gendered revisitations solicit such emphasis, but the volume intends also to propose an all-encompassing study on the topic of cultural transmissions.

In this volume the discussions of cultural transmissions in Calvino and Eco, through to Moravia, Montale, and Scego testify to the use of literary and cultural heritage as a means to acquire new literary interpretations. These head toward different personal directions as in the case of Calvino and Eco, or toward socio-political and personal criticism, as in the case of Moravia. Literary and cultural heritage provide a framework to define alternative views of female figures, as in the case of Montale, and a means to see the shortcomings of a translated Somali culture into the Italian context, as in Scego. Cultural transmission is intended therefore as a tool for personal and collective assertion. Even the case of the Foibe di Basovizza, which opens the second section, with its intricate and complex history, does not pay tribute so much to the healing of the divided memory to which it testifies, but rather to the empowerment of the different parties who see it as a symbol of their own memory. This is echoed in local Triestine literature and in the projected, perhaps utopian, vision in Magris's latest novel, as the essays on Triestine literature and on Magris show. A gendered reading of the Allies presence in Italy highlights the endurance of suffering by the local people, their resilience, rather than a glorified representation of liberation. The relational psychoanalytic framework of post-trauma in Ferrante as well as the discussions on nostalgia in Di Pietrantonio's depiction of Abruzzi, in the history and memory of Italian feminism and in the social media engagement of the "Ambasciatrici del Buon Gusto" developed in the last section, hint at the desire for affirmation, both personal and political, that comes from the re-elaboration of the past. In the cluster of essays collected in this volume, cultural memory in all its forms of divided memory and nostalgia, hints at a sense of transformation and often enrichment or resilience, individual or collective, that appreciates the present and the future more than the past.

The volume is divided into three sections: cultural transmission, fractured memories, and nostalgia. The first section opens with Martin McLaughlin's analysis of the works of Italo Calvino and Umberto Eco, which makes us appreciate how transmission of cultural memory was at the heart of the work of two giants of Italian literature. McLaughlin takes us on a magisterial journey covering Graeco-Roman times, the Medieval-Renaissance period, and modern times to show how the critics Calvino and Eco have turned literary appreciation into a source of inspiration for their own fiction, and how literary influences, and therefore the interplay between past and present were at the foundation of their novels. Although Calvino at the beginning of his career was inspired by modern literature, he referred back to the classics throughout his writing life, and not only as a critic for his *Why Read the Classics?*, as McLaughlin points out. Eco, on the other hand, finds in Aristotle's *Poetics* both a text for critical analysis and an inspiration for fiction. Calvino's and Eco's interests as writers and critics reach from Dante to Marco Polo, from the classics of French literature to literature in English such as Edgar Allan Poe, Stevenson, and Hemingway for Calvino, and Joyce for Eco. Throughout their life-long engagement with literature of different epochs, both Calvino and Eco have distinguished themselves in giving us a continuous dialogue with authors of the Graeco-Roman times, of the Medieval and Renaissance period, and of modern times. In making sure that this dialogue opened up new perspectives, they showed how cultural memory could be an essential element of inspiration and progress.

In chapter 2, Adele Bardazzi revisits the categorization of Eugenio Montale's female figures by considering his revision of two great myths of Western culture: the myth of Orpheus and Eurydice, and the myth of Persephone. By looking at what she calls the Eurydice-Persephonean archetype, Bardazzi demonstrates how the Montalean female figures depart substantially from the traditional classification of angelic versus monstrous and companion-like woman. Bardazzi argues that within the idea of a chthonic femininity, not previously analyzed in Montale, the figure of Mosca has to be revalued as the central female figure among Montale's muses.

Focusing on *Xenia*, Adele Bardazzi looks at Mosca as a figure of superior powers. Through the revisitation of the Eurydice-Persephone archetype, justified by Bardazzi by the recurrence of characteristics related to Mosca, she demonstrates that echoes of the two classic myths are key to the construction of Mosca as a female figure who encompasses dichotomies, but confirms Cavarero's critique of the author as the only voice for the absent, dead woman.

Charles Leavitt's chapter on Alberto Moravia's novel *The Woman of Rome* develops an analysis of the author's critique of the bourgeoisie, taking into account both a traumatic encounter narrated by Moravia himself, and his essays on Fascism and the bourgeoisie, as well as the very vivid echoes of Guy de Maupassant's short story "Boule de suif." Leavitt's reading offers a prismatic effect, where each side of the analysis illuminates the topic to persuasively demonstrate how prostitution exemplifies for Moravia, the hypocrisy of bourgeoisie under Fascism. Moreover, Leavitt argues that Moravia's revisitation of his encounter with a prostitute in Rome ten years before is layered with his experience of the trauma of contemporary Italian history, adding to his reflections on the Fascist bourgeoisie, on anti-Fascism and the role of literature. It is through this complexity that Leavitt underlines Moravia's self-criticism for his own bourgeois anti-Fascism, but also, through the prostitute Adriana, Moravia renews his commitment to the representation of an uncensored reality. The thorough and sharp criticism of the Italian sociopolitical context is unfolded and can be understood by us only thanks to the literary echoes that pervade and construct the novel.

In chapter 4, Maria Cristina Seccia takes the discourse of transmission of memory into the twenty-first century with her analysis of Igiaba Scego's memoir *La mia casa è dove sono*. Seccia looks at Scego's book through the lens of translation studies criticism, with a particular focus on the maternal transmission of memory. She reads therefore the representation of the mother's story by the narrator as a form of cultural translation, meaning a transfer of aspects of Somali culture into Italian culture for an Italian readership. Yet she argues that the narrator's representations of two key events, the mother's infibulation and the birth of her first child once in Italy as a refugee, reveal domesticating strategies on the part of the narrator, where the mother is represented from a Western perspective. Pain, suffering, and victimization are the emotions connected to these life events that thereby emphasize a Western point of view of women's agency and not a sense of agency perceived from a Somali perspective. Through her cultural translation approach, Seccia demonstrates that in Scego's *La mia casa è dove sono*, transmission of memory is tinged by manipulation and intervention and in part supports the established belief of Italian readership about Somali culture.

The second section opens with John Foot's analysis of the extraordinary battle of memory experienced in the northeastern borders of Italy. Foot takes us through the complexity of the history and memory of this part of Italy, and by taking the Foibe di Basovizza as an emblematic example unlocks for us the details of the historical events that affected the area since the fascist period, their contradictory interpretations, and the present irreconcilable memory.

Foot argues that, in relation to the killings that occurred in September 1943 in Istria and in May-June 1945 between Trieste and Gorizia (*infoibati*), the search for correct historical data (number of deaths and the nationalities involved) does not help to understand the complexity of the situation of that area where memory, suffering, trauma have much more to say than History. As Foot emphasizes, numbers do not help to understand a "purging" directed not exclusively against Fascist Italians and fail to make a link between those events and the *grande esodo* (mass exodus) of Italians from Istria to Italy. On the other hand, the lack of historical data also leads to explanations that see the killings of Italians as dictated by merely ethnic reasons, disregarding therefore the previous ferocious twenty years of abuse against the Slavs. From the 1990s on the *foibe* have become the event which has most problematized the history of liberation: a symbol of revisionism for the right-wing parties in government as Foot explains, and a symbol of their separation from a certain type of Communism for the left-wing party. From the institutionalization of a day of memory for the *foibe* in 2004, the occasions for conscious memory creation have increased consistently. From Foot's analysis of the complexity of the northeastern borders, the Foibe di Basovizza emerge as an emblem of that divided memory. Yet with all its limitations, Basovizza has become the memorial for each of the parties involved.

In chapter 6, Sandra Parmegiani continues the discussion about the fragmented history of the northeastern borders, by analyzing *Blameless*, Claudio Magris's most recent novel. As Parmegiani states, Magris continues his post-millenium focus on the fragmented nature of memory and its interrelation with history, expressed through polyphonic narration. In *Blameless*, a complex narrative structure elaborates the real story of the fire that destroyed Diego de Henriquez's warehouse and collection of war memorabilia, and took his life. De Henriquez's collection included sensitive materials on the Risiera di San Sabba, the Nazi extermination camp, operational at the outskirts of Trieste from September 1943 to April 1945.

Magris's fictionalization of the event creates a sophisticated interplay of stories: the story of the collection curator and that of the woman who is taking care of the collector's materials in view of a planned new museum, together with four other sections that appear completely unrelated to the main events. As Parmegiani argues, the various sections, in particular the ones apparently unrelated to the central plot, and the story of the woman curator—she is the daughter of a Triestine Jewish woman and an Afro-American soldier—all contribute to the creation of collective and individual memories that are interdependent on other memories. Magris constructs what Parmegiani defines as a form of multidirectional memory that goes across time and space, acknowledging a variety of stories. In this sense Parmegiani's analysis of Magris's book dovetails perfectly with Foot's chapter on the fragmented memories of the Foibe di Basovizza, where the Trieste memorial is a symbol of the diverse interpretations of history and memory, Magris's text intends to overcome the fractured memory of the Italian northeast.

The discussion on the city of Trieste as an emblematic place of traumatic and divided memories is continued by Katia Pizzi in chapter 7. She looks at a wide range of examples of cultural memory, from memorial sites to Triestine literature, highlighting the contribution of women writers of the area, and discusses contemporary transnational writers. Pizzi's chapter opens with an overview of the theorization around memory and sites of memory and focuses on the metaphors deriving from such theories. She then uses these to unpack memory perceptions within the Triestine cultural landscape.

In Pizzi's analysis, Andreas Huyssen's idea of memory as palimpsest and Michael Baxandell's suggestion of the memorial process as comparable to the wearing down of sand dunes are keys to understanding the divided memory of the city of Trieste. In the first cluster of literary works on the *foibe* considered by Pizzi, representations of memory proceed with no transcultural exchange but as multi-layered or "laminated" narratives that the metaphors described above imply. According to Pizzi, a similar rendition of memory can be seen in the Risiera di San Sabba monument by architect Romano

Boico. This highlights the isolation of the Risiera, its detachment from any surrounding context. The complex and traumatic experiences of this part of the country continue to create divided memory through cultural products that highlight particularity, not sharing. However, a number of writers have produced exceptions to this rule, especially women writers who in recent years have created a discourse that offers a transnational perspective, one which is missing from the concepts of sand dunes and palimpsests applied to most of the cultural memory produced in Trieste.

Chapter 8 by David W. Ellwood takes us into a revisitation of one of the most enduring myths of Italy's wartime period, the role of the Allies. In John Foot's chapter, we already see the importance of memorials in the legacy of World War II and its divided memory. David W. Ellwood begins his discussion noting that for all the dominant narratives that up until the present day have symbolized them as the saviours of Italy, "no-one has ever proposed erecting a monument to the Allies." As Ellwood explains, it is probably Italian women's experience of the liberation/occupation that lies at the core of this apparent paradox.

Combining literature and films of the postwar period, recent historical research on the violence suffered by Italian women during the liberation/ occupation experience, and direct witness accounts, Ellwood reconstructs a gendered history of Italian liberation that reveals long-term silences and overturns the joyous representation of the Allies most commonly offered by the media. Many Italian novels and films focus on the ability of the local people to endure the suffering of the war, including the period of liberation, and pay no attention to the role of the Allies in all this. It is thanks to the most recent research on rape, prostitution, and violence that a gendered memory of the war years can now help to create an encompassing history of that period.

In the last chapter of this second section, chapter 9, the topics of traumatic experiences and of the fragmented memory they generate, so far seen mainly within a sociopolitical context are discussed by Torunn Haaland within a literary and psychoanalytic framework. Haaland's chapter suggests an overall conclusion on the strategies of post-traumatic narratives. She looks at Elena Ferrante's *La figlia oscura* and develops an interpretation that allows us to see liminality as a dialogic structure of post-traumatic narratives.

La figlia oscura presents some of the familiar themes of Ferrante's narrative: the return to the native city in the south of Italy, a troubled mother-daughter relationship, and the rupture between the female protagonist's emancipated life in the present and a repressive, often violent, past. Haaland shows that the main protagonist, Leda, is a character in-between social classes, languages, and experiences of time—where in her narrative, past memories often intrude on her present. It is such a liminal position that makes her unable to clearly step outside her past. The revisitation of the past and of the protagonist's life requires an engagement with her internal Other, but also the external Other, a possibility available from her liminal position. As such, the protagonist of Ferrante's novel offers a relational perspective, one that does not resolve her personal trauma but suggests connection rather than division.

Haalad's theorization of a relational perspective takes us into the third section on nostalgia. From this group of chapters there emerges a concept of nostalgia that expresses the need to negotiate past and present; in this sense it acquires a distinctive relational flavor. Nostalgia is not intended therefore as a desire to return to the past. My chapter opens this section with a discussion of Donatella Di Pietrantonio's *Mia madre è un fiume*. Emerging as one of the most interesting voices of the contemporary Italian literary scene, Di Pietrantonio in her first novel presents us with a remote agricultural Abruzzi setting and a difficult mother-daughter relationship. Her handling of the theme allows a discussion of nostalgia as an emotion that helps renegotiate past and present.

The onset of Alzheimer's disease is the daughter's initial reason to tell the story of her mother, which turns out to be a narrative of the life in a small, isolated foothills village near Teramo, in a period of history spanning several decades, from the World War II to the present. Unlike many mother-daughter narratives, the mother figure, although belonging to a different era of strenuous daily toil when duty always had priority over family pleasure, is not presented as part of a linear development of history where the mother is confined within an antiquated but emotional time. Mother and daughter are both part of a progressive development of history. It is the daughter-narrator's re-elaboration of the rural setting that allows some closure in the troubled relationship with her mother and generates nostalgia as a valid tool to bring the past forward into the present.

In chapter 11, Andrea Hajek argues that both the history and memory of feminism are normally interpreted through a framework that implies a linear time development, from past to present. This has repercussions for interpretations of nostalgia, as any looking back would seem to imply a nostalgic sense of loss. Hajek establishes a distinction between nostalgia for feminism and feminist nostalgia: the former implies regret for a loss of the golden period of feminism symbolized by the 1970s movement; the latter departs from this negative view and aims at utilizing feminist values from the past within the present.

In her analysis of nostalgia, Hajek takes into consideration two texts dealing with Italian feminism and its memory: *Fra me e te: Madre e figlia si scrivono: Pensieri, passioni, femminismi* by Mariella Gramaglia and Maddalena Vianello, and Marina Santini and Luciana Tavernini's *Mia madre femminista: Voci di una rivoluzione che continua*. Both are structured as a dialogue between mother and daughter, and therefore as a generational confrontation. The two texts provide opposite outcomes and, in fact, illustrate Hajek's categorization of nostalgia for feminism and feminist nostalgia. The chapter concludes not only by advocating the end of linear descriptions of feminism but also opens up the prospect of a united feminism that takes advantage of an active intergenerational relationship.

The last chapter, by Incoronata (Nadia) Inserra, applies the discourse about nostalgia as a way to negotiate cultural memory to the field of social media and blogging, and in so doing opens up perspectives that in some respects are very different from the feminist versions explored in chapter 11. Inserra's text is based on her observations and interviews with the all-female Facebook group and cooking blog called "Le Ambasciatrici del Buon Gusto: Donne Italiane nel Mondo." Her analysis focuses on the representation of Italian food culture visible on the transnational platform and on the self-representation of Italianness performed by the bloggers.

Despite the transnational dimension of the platform examined, and notwithstanding the transnational interpretations of Italian food culture on display in the blogs, Inserra shows that nostalgia for the image of simple, genuine Italian food is a striking element of the discourse created by "Le Ambasciatrici del Buon Gusto." This nostalgic revisitation of Italian food traditions has problematic repercussions on the bloggers' projections of their own gender identity. Inserra argues that although successful professionals, for "Le Ambasciatrici" their self-representation as traditional women around the family table ends by endorsing many of the stereotypes that have grown up around Italian food culture. It also shows the complexity of asserting Italianness through social media. Inserra's discussion concludes our journey through cultural memory within the Italian context. Through the variety of perspectives included here, a vision of memory transmission appears that emphasizes empowerment, endurance, and agency as key concepts for approaching and understanding present and future.

NOTES

1. Elizabeth L. Krause, "The Turn toward Memory: From History's 'Little People' to Anthropology's 'Others,'" *Social Science History Association* (2007): Available at http://works.bepress.com/elizabeth_krause/12/.

2. Antonio Traverso and Mick Broderick, "Interrogating Trauma: Towards a Critical Trauma Studies," *Continuum: Journal of Media and Cultural Studies* 24 (2010): 8.

3. Jan Assman, "Collective Memory and Cultural Identity," *New German Critique* 65 (1995): 133.

4. Peter Carrier and Kobi Kabalek, "Cultural Memory and Transcultural Memory—a Conceptual Analysis," in *The Transcultural Turn*, edited by Lucy Bond and Jessica Rapson (Berlin: De Gruyter, 2014), 39–60.

5. Mieke Bal, "Introduction," in Mieke Bal, Jonathan Crewe, and Leo Spitzer *Acts of Memory: Cultural Recall in the Present* (Hanover, NH, and London: University Press of New England, 1999): vii.

6. Linda Hutcheon, *A Poetics of Postmodernism:History, Theory, Fiction* (New York and London: Routledge, 1988), 93.

WORKS CITED

Assman, Jan. "Collective Memory and Cultural Identity." *New German Critique* 65 (1995): 125–33.

Bal, Mieke. "Introduction." In *Acts of Memory: Cultural Recall in the Present*, edited by Mieke Bal, Jonathan Crewe, and Leo Spitzer, vii–xvii. Hanover, NH, and London: University Press of New England, 1999.

Carrier, Peter, and Kobi Kabalek. "Cultural Memory and Transcultural Memory—a Conceptual Analysis." In *The Transcultural Turn*, edited by Lucy Bond and Jessica Rapson, 39–60. Berlin: De Gruyter, 2014.

Ginzburg, Carlo. *Thread and Traces: True False Fictive*. Translated by Anne C. Tedeschi. Oakland, CA: University of California Press, 2012.

Hirsch, Marianne, and Valerie Smith. "Feminism and Cultural Memory: An Introduction." *Signs, Gender and Cultural Memory Special Issue* 28 (2002): 1–19.

Hutcheon, Linda. *A Poetics of Postmodernism: History, Theory, Fiction*. New York and London: Routledge, 1988.

Krause, Elizabeth L. "The Turn toward Memory: From History's 'Little People' to Anthropology's 'Others.'" *Social Science History Association* (2007): Available at http://works. bepress.com/elizabeth_krause/12/.

Traverso, Antonio, and Mick Broderick. "Interrogating Trauma: Towards a Critical Trauma Studies." *Continuum: Journal of Media and Cultural Studies* 24 (2010): 3–15.

Section I

Memory as Cultural Transmission

Chapter One

Calvino, Eco, and the Transmission of World Literature

Martin McLaughlin

This volume's overarching theme is that of transmissions of memory in its broadest sense. In this chapter, I consider transmissions of culture and literature, with a particular emphasis on the interplay between the past and the present, in two of the most important Italian writers of recent times, Italo Calvino (1923–1985) and Umberto Eco (1932–2016). Both writers were highly conscious of the way past literature could shape what contemporary authors write today, and both wrote in a modern, at times postmodern, way but with an awareness of what the literature of previous times and other cultures could offer to today's writers and readers. They composed many essays on world literature (mainly Western texts), so much so that they would both have been major literary critics even if they had not written any fiction. They were also influenced by many non-Italian writers in their creative works. However, the way they interpreted and were inspired by texts from other literatures was different. This chapter seeks to compare these two major Italian writers in terms of both their critical writings on world literature and the different ways their fiction was transformed by it. We will see that what they have in common is their capacity to draw creative inspiration even from texts that are very remote in time and place from their own poetics. To structure the chapter, I will examine three chronological fields of comparison: firstly, texts of classical antiquity; secondly medieval and Renaissance works; and finally, the literature of the nineteenth and twentieth centuries.

In what follows I will concentrate largely, though not exclusively, on two major collections of essays: Calvino's *Why Read the Classics?*, a posthumous collection from 1991,[1] and Eco's *On Literature*, published a decade later in 2002.[2] Naturally, since these two collections simply form the tip of the iceberg of essays written by the two authors, I will also take into consideration several other essays about world literature written by Calvino and Eco.

THE FIRST PERIOD: GRECO-ROMAN ANTIQUITY

Our two authors, like many writers of their generation, had had a solid classical education in a *liceo classico*, so it is not surprising to find many references to ancient texts, especially in their essays. For Calvino in particular, we must first note the five essays on the Greco-Roman classics from around 1980, from the wonderful title essay *Why Read the Classics?* (1981) to the four articles on specific authors such as Homer (1981), Xenophon (1978), Ovid (1979) and Pliny (1982), in other words two poets and two prose writers. Calvino had begun his literary career with a graduating thesis on Joseph Conrad, and in his early fiction his major model was Ernest Hemingway, so his debut in the early postwar years was as a writer totally imbued with modern literature. However, in the course of his literary career, he turned back in time toward the classic texts of the past—not just to his beloved Ariosto, but also to the classical past, as in these essays from the late 1970s.

But Calvino does not relate to such texts just as a reader and critic. Some aspects of these classical works also resurface in his creative writings. A striking example of how he blends the ancient with the very modern in a work of fiction is in *Mr Palomar*, where one can see that some of the key ideas held by the eponymous protagonist derive from those of Pliny the Elder: this paradoxical fact is not in the end so surprising, since Calvino had written the essay on Pliny's *Natural History* in 1982 just as he was completing the final chapters of *Palomar*.[3] Thus in the Pliny essay Calvino had referred to the ancient writer's ideas on childbirth and the period that precedes one's birth:

> Pliny shares the view that death is followed by another non-existence which is equivalent and symmetrical to the non-existence before birth. . . . "Model your own peace of mind on your experience before birth," he says: in other words, project yourself into contemplating your own absence, the only secure reality both before we came into the world and after we die.[4]

In the final chapter of *Mr Palomar*, "Learning to Be Dead," written in 1983, the year after the Pliny essay, we find the protagonist expressing exactly the same ideas as Pliny regarding the period before being born: "First of all, you must not confuse being dead with not being, a condition that occupies the vast expanse of time before birth, apparently symmetrical with the other, equally vast expanse that follows death."[5] Throughout *Mr Palomar* the eponymous protagonist seems to be a very contemporary figure, who tries to defend himself from the general neurasthenia that afflicts his own times, but his ideas on death and on nonexistence clearly derive from an ancient Latin text.

Later in the Pliny essay, Calvino describes the way the classical writer organizes his chapters on animals in book 8: "The survey of land animals moves on—as in a child's visit to the zoo—from the elephant to the lions, panthers, tigers, camels, giraffes, rhinoceroses and crocodiles. Following a decreasing order of size, we then come to the hyenas, chameleons, porcupines, animals with lairs, and so on down to snails and lizards."[6] It is no accident, then, that in the section in *Palomar* titled "Palomar at the Zoo," where the protagonist takes his own child to the zoo, we find that the three sections dealing with three animals are also in descending order of size, just as in Pliny: the giraffe, a gorilla, and an iguana.[7] Again themes from Calvino's critical essays mingle creatively with the thematics of his fictional works.

In the excellent essay on Ovid's *Metamorphoses* one can again see how the work of the critic is connected to that of the fiction writer. Talking of Baucis and Philemon, the elderly couple whose story appears in the middle of the central book of Ovid's epic (book 8), Calvino explains how the Latin poet decides at this midpoint to slow down his otherwise very rapid narration and to describe all the details of the couple's poor house as they offer some food to the two gods who are visiting them in disguise:

> There are also times . . . when the pace of the narrative has to slow down, switch to a calmer rhythm, give the feeling of time being suspended, almost veiled in the distance. What does Ovid do at such times? To make it clear that the narrative is in no hurry, he stops to dwell on the smallest details. . . . It is by continuing to add to the detail of the picture that Ovid obtains an effect of rarefaction and pause.[8]

Ovid's story ends with the town where the old couple lived disappearing into a swamp. Calvino's description of the central city in *Invisible Cities* (1972) is in fact called Baucis: being supported on stilts, it too is invisible from the earth, but is described in detail in rhythmic, poetic prose, which like Ovid's technique in book 8 also represents a moment of rarefaction and pause:

> There are three hypotheses about the inhabitants of Baucis: that they hate the earth; that they respect it so much they avoid all contact; that they love it as it was before they existed and with spyglasses and telescopes aimed downward they never tire of examining it, leaf by leaf, stone by stone, ant by ant, contemplating with fascination their own absence.[9]

Once more, a postmodern creative work is enriched by narrative qualities identified by the author in a classical text.

If one considers the classical works read and exploited creatively in a similar way by Umberto Eco (in other words, texts that are not just the object of an analysis in an essay, but that also offer the modern writer fictional inspiration), one immediately realizes that the most stimulating ancient text for Eco is Aristotle's *Poetics*. His most substantial essay on the centuries-long influence of the *Poetics* was written in 1992,[10] but twelve years earlier this famous Aristotelian work had played a vital role in Eco's first novel. Toward the end of *The Name of the Rose* (1980) the detective figure, William of Baskerville, finally reads what purports to be the opening of the lost second book of Aristotle's *Poetics*:

> "In the first book we dealt with tragedy and saw how, by arousing pity and fear, it produces catharsis, the purification of those feelings. As we promised, we will now deal with comedy (as well as with satire and mime) and see how, in inspiring the pleasure of the ridiculous, it arrives at the purification of that passion."[11]

In this passage the novelist invents and quotes from a forged text (and influential forgeries would remain a life-long passion for Eco, from the lost book of the *Poetics* to the *Protocols of the Elders of Zion*), but he bases it precisely on the famous definition of tragedy in the genuine first book of the *Poetics* (1449b), a definition which is actually preceded by Aristotle's promise to provide a study of epic and comedy in the second book: "We shall later discuss the art of mimesis in hexameters, as well as comedy. . . . Tragedy, then, is mimesis of an action which is elevated, complete, and of magnitude; in language embellished by distinct forms in its sections; employing the mode of enactment, not narrative; and through pity and fear accomplishing the catharsis of such emotions."[12]

Thus Eco, like Calvino, turns a famous ancient text into something very modern, indeed postmodern, and he notes the influence of the *Poetics* on other favorite modern writers of his including Joyce, who quoted the philosopher several times.[13] Paradoxically Eco considers Aristotle's classic work a revolutionary text, something ultramodern, "the first appearance of an aesthetics of reception or reader-oriented theory."[14]

Eco the critic makes a similar ancient/modern claim for another classical text often coupled with the *Poetics*, namely the treatise *On the Sublime*, attributed to Longinus. Here too he interprets this critical work in very contemporary topical terms, regarding it as one of the texts that first launched the notion of "close reading."[15] Eco also quotes on several occasions from another ancient critic, the Latin rhetorician Quintilian, but he does so in essays relating to modern authors such as Joyce, T. S. Eliot, and Robbe-Grillet.[16]

Thus both Calvino and Eco consider the transmission of certain ancient texts as fundamentally relevant to the modern age, but one key point of difference between our two authors emerges even here, in that while Calvino privileges poets and scientific writers such as Ovid and Pliny, Eco turns more often to the essayists and critics of the ancient world, such as Aristotle, Longinus and Quintilian.

SECOND PERIOD: MIDDLE AGES AND RENAISSANCE

As far as this period is concerned, one could in very general terms note that Eco is more a reader of medieval texts, while Calvino prefers works from the Renaissance period. Certainly one could not say of Calvino, as Eco said of himself, that the Middle Ages were his "day-to-day fantasy."[17] However, the situation is more complex than this generalization would lead us to believe. First of all, Calvino does devote space in his essays to Dante and Boccaccio. In the 1960s, he claims that Dante's *Comedy* evinces "a deep-rooted vocation in Italian literature, handed on from Dante to Galileo: the notion of the literary work as a map of the world of the knowable,"[18] and it is no surprise then that it was in the 1960s and 1970s that Calvino began to write totalizing works that contain entire universes, such as *Cosmicomics, Invisible Cities,* and *If on a Winter's Night a Traveller.* And Dante's name often crops up in the late essays of the 1980s: we find numerous references to the poet in Calvino's posthumous Harvard lectures, *Six Memos for the Next Millennium,* especially in the essays on "Lightness" and "Visibility";[19] and another essay of 1985, on chivalric literature, closes with a mention of the episode of Paolo and Francesca in *Inferno* 5 as "the first vertiginous move towards metaliterature."[20] But Dante's *Commedia,* like all the texts that are most significant for Calvino, supplies moments of inspiration for his creative works as well. Already in 1947 he writes a short story on the partisan war, titled "One of the Three Is Still Alive," which is closely modeled on Dante's own *descensus ad inferos.*[21] And at the other end of his career, the last book of fiction published in his lifetime, *Mr Palomar,* with its tripartite structure, presents itself as a kind of modern, secular version of the *Commedia,* but written in prose, as a kind of summa or encyclopedia or indeed Plinian *Natural History* for our time.[22] So from 1947 to the mid-1980s Dante's poem remains a key intertextual resource for Calvino's fiction.

Another founding text of Italian literature, Marco Polo's *Il Milione,* turns out to be one of the inspirations behind that ultramodern work, *Invisible Cities.* Here Calvino transforms the centuries-old work into a contemporary, metaliterary text by substituting contemplation for Polo's action, changing the mercantile descriptions of objects into accounts of mental conditions, and replacing the irregularity of Polo's rambling account of his travels into the perfect, diamond-shaped symmetry formed by the chapters of *Invisible Cities*.[23]

The third great medieval Italian writer, Boccaccio, is mentioned in several Calvino essays, while the *Decameron*, that prototype of modern narrative with its mixture of frame and embedded stories, acts as the structural model for that masterpiece of contemporary storytelling that is *If on a Winter's Night a Traveller* (1979). Calvino even claims Boccaccio as a modern writer, one who creates "a clean stylistic split" between the frame-narration and the *novelle* in the *Decameron*.[24] Just like his medieval predecessor, in this work Calvino tries to write in many different styles in the various micro-novels and in the frame narration of the 1979 novel. These observations on the *Decameron* are contained in a 1978 essay titled "Levels of Reality in Literature," a study that analyses the various levels of narrative present in classic texts from *The Odyssey* to *Madame Bovary*, and which seems to be the theoretical basis behind the novel that he was writing in that same year, *If on a Winter's Night*. Calvino's hypernovel is a homage to the novel, so it is no surprise that he turns to the wellsprings of Western fiction for inspiration, both to the *Decameron* and to its oriental equivalent *The Arabian Nights*, which also has a structure of frame story and embedded narrations.

So Calvino's triad of medieval authors differs in one author from the three that are usually seen as the canonical founders of Italian literature, the Tre Corone Fiorentine, Dante, Petrarch, and Boccaccio. Instead the modern novelist privileges Dante, Polo, and Boccaccio, with the prose writer Marco Polo replacing the poet Petrarch: this should not surprise us since Calvino was always more interested in prose than in poetry.

Nevertheless, although Calvino was interested in Dante, Polo, and Boccaccio, he never possessed that profound knowledge of medieval culture that characterizes Eco's works, fiction and nonfiction. For Eco the critic, his most significant medieval writer is of course St Thomas Aquinas: he had graduated with a thesis on Aquinas's aesthetic theories, and throughout his literary career he would constantly quote the great medieval theologian. Eco the critic also refers to other canonical authors of the Middle Ages, such as Boethius, Saint Augustine, Abelard, and so on.

For Eco the novelist, on the other hand, the most important medieval author is Dante. The whole plot of *The Name of the Rose* is set in Dante's world (the poet had died only six years before the year 1327 in which the destruction of the library occurs),[25] and the poet of the *Comedy* is the object of study in several essays by Eco, including a fine reading of the *Paradiso* written in 2000 for the centenary of the fictional date of Dante's great poem. This essay provides several reasons for the modern author's interest in the medieval poem. First of all, the critic tries to explain why the *Paradiso* is the most beautiful cantica of the entire poem, and he attacks the prejudices of the Romantic and post-Romantic age that saw true poetry only in episodes like that of Paolo and Francesca. Thus he disagrees with the Romantic critic De Sanctis, for whom the monotony of the *Paradiso* was unrelenting, while the entire cantica was, according to the nineteenth-century critic, nothing but "a series of questions and answers between a teacher and pupil."[26] Instead, argues Eco, there is also a poetry of the intellect, which today's reader is capable of appreciating after having read works by the likes of Donne, T. S. Eliot, Valéry, and Borges. Like Calvino, Eco manages to read Dante in a totally modern key, especially as regards the poet's imagery of light, and concludes that the *Paradiso* "is anything but doctrinal poetry and debates between teacher and pupil!"[27]

Another reason for Eco's fascination with Dante is linked to Calvino's pleasure in finding in the *Comedy* a map of the cosmos: Borges's idea and story of *The Aleph*, in other words a single point that also contains the whole universe, actually derive—according to Eco—from the first Aleph in literature, namely the one described by Dante when he says at the end of *Paradiso* that he saw "bound by love in one volume, whatever is scattered throughout the universe, substances and accidents and their ways of interacting."[28] For Eco, in short, "Dante's *Paradiso* is the apotheosis of the virtual world. . . . The *Paradiso* is more than modern."[29]

A third reason resides in the fact that Eco is fascinated by Dante's search for a universal language, and the poet's linguistic theories surface often in Eco's essays on Joyce. In fact the Italian critic is fond of Dante also because the medieval poet was championed by two of his favorite modern authors, Joyce and Borges. In any case, Eco had already initiated another campaign in favor of the *Paradiso* before this essay of 2000: in one of his brief, humorous reports in his first *Diario minimo* (1972) a literary agent from the Middle Ages is purportedly writing a report to his publisher about the possibility of buying the rights to Dante's *Comedy*. He tells the publisher that Dante's epic will go down well with their early fourteenth-century readers, particularly for the *Paradiso*'s astronomical descriptions and learned theological discussions, whereas the most difficult part to "sell" to readers will certainly be the *Inferno*, with its scenes of low eroticism and scurrility. Another problem the agent sees is Dante's choice of that "Tuscan dialect" instead of the Latin used by all serious writers: Eco jokes that this was a linguistic move that was typical of the avant-garde but which would not go down well with the wider public and in any case the Italian vernacular would never catch on![30]

Thus both Calvino and Eco often invoke Dante, and find in his works many contemporary elements that are relevant to the writers and readers of today. On the other hand, if we move to the Renaissance period, we note that Calvino's love for Ariosto finds no counterpart in Eco, indeed the poet is never mentioned in the eighteen essays *On Literature*. Perhaps the only early modern author that both modern writers engage with substantially is the polymath Jesuit, Athanasius Kircher. Eco names him several times, especially in the essays dedicated to the search for the perfect language, and cites a long passage from the *Oedipus Aegyptiacus* in his essay "On Symbolism" (1994).[31] Thus the aspect of the Jesuit's work that Eco finds most significant is his critical-interpretative work. Calvino, on the other hand, is fascinated by his treatise on optics, the *Ars magna lucis et umbrae*, and by his work on combinatory art, *Ars magna sciendi, sive Combinatoria*: in fact the protagonist of one of the micro-novels in *If on a Winter's Night* models himself on the German Jesuit.[32] Kircher is also a figure invoked on countless occasions by Borges, so it is not surprising that he appeals also to Eco and Calvino.[33]

To conclude this section, we must briefly consider Calvino's favorite text from this period, Ariosto's *Orlando furioso*—briefly because much has already been written about Calvino and the *Furioso*.[34] This was by far the most influential older text on Calvino, but it finds little resonance in Eco. Calvino's interest in the genres that preceded and gave rise to the modern novel also explains his love for Renaissance chivalric poems, especially his beloved *Orlando furioso*. In fact the Italian word for novel, *romanzo*, is also the term used to describe the genre to which the *Furioso* and similar poems belonged, the *romanzo cavalleresco*. The contemporary novelist devoted several essays to Ariosto's epic, produced a shortened version of it, and was constantly inspired by the poem in his fiction, notably in *The Non-Existent Knight* (1959) and *The Castle of Crossed Destinies* (1973).[35] Calvino often linked Ariosto to another favorite Renaissance writer, namely Galileo. Toward the end of an essay written in 1967, he had actually claimed that Galileo was the greatest prose writer in Italian: "As soon as Galileo, the greatest prose-writer in Italian literature in any century, starts to talk about the moon, he raises his prose to prodigious levels of precision, clarity and lyric rarefaction."[36] In a follow-up essay he would remark that "Galileo admired and wrote marginal comments on that cosmic, lunar poet, Ariosto," and that the Ariosto-Galileo-Leopardi line was "one of the mainstreams in our literature."[37] By contrast, Galileo does not often appear in Eco's pages, though he does crop up in an aside in his favorite topic of out-of-date thought-systems and forgeries.[38] We might conclude this section by noting that Eco's fascination for Dante is matched by Calvino's love for Ariosto, and both modern writers regularly write about and draw inspiration from these two earlier ones.

THIRD PERIOD: THE MODERN AGE

When one turns to the nineteenth and twentieth centuries, one is struck immediately by the fact that both our authors greatly admire the major French exponents of the nineteenth-century novel, such as Stendhal, Balzac, and Flaubert, and that, if there is a difference here, this resides in the fact that

Calvino does not exhibit that obsession with one particular text as evinced by Eco in his enthusiasm for Nerval's novella *Sylvie*, an enthusiasm that is expressed in his translation of the novella and in his many perceptive analyses of the work. [39]

One poet of this period greatly admired by both authors is Leopardi, but despite their admiration, he exerts little creative influence on either of them. [40] The other great canonical author of nineteenth-century Italian literature is Manzoni, but while Calvino dedicates just one essay to his famous novel, *The Betrothed*, [41] Manzoni was one of Eco's favorite authors, someone to whom he returned time and time again: he declares that he loves Manzoni's novel, [42] and even the subtitle of *Il nome della rosa—Storia italiana del XIV secolo* was a quotation from the subtitle of *I promessi sposi*. [43] Eco sees meta-narrative elements in Manzoni's masterpiece and the allusion contained in the title of the first chapter of Eco's novel (*Naturalmente, un manoscritto*) is a homage to the Milanese author and his claim that he had based his novel on a story he found in a manuscript. [44]

When it comes to foreign writers, both Calvino and Eco agree on the greatness of Edgar Allan Poe, but with a difference. Calvino often talks of the American writer's fiction:[45] he claims that throughout one stage of his life Poe was the storywriter who reigned supreme in his Pantheon;[46] *Gordon Pym* was one of the most memorable and terrifying stories he had ever read. [47] While in a late interview, in 1984, Calvino even declared that the author who had most influenced him had been Poe. [48] Eco, on the other hand, devotes considerable attention not just to the story of *Gordon Pym*, but also to Poe's critical essay *The Philosophy of Composition*, an essay that explains the rhetorical strategies and effects in his poem *The Raven*, and which Eco analyzes both in his footnotes to *The Name of the Rose* and in his essay on Aristotle's *Poetics*. [49] What particularly endears Poe to Eco is that like Joyce he is an Aristotelian. Thus in his essay on "The *Poetics* and Us" he says of *The Philosophy of Composition*, "The extraordinary thing about this text is that its author explains the rule whereby he managed to convey the impression of spontaneity, and this is the same message as is transmitted by the *Poetics* and goes against any aesthetics of ineffability."[50] Here we notice two constants in Eco: first that he often prefers the writer as critic to the creative writer, and second that he admires modern writers who adopt the transmitted heritage of his favorite ancient writers: Eco loves Aristotle, so he embraces Aquinas and more modern Aristotelians such as Poe and Joyce.

Turning now to the twentieth century, one could say instantly that our two writers are particularly inspired by both French literature and works written in English. Both authors often invoke Proust, while Calvino has a special fondness for Queneau (on whom he writes three essays, and he also translates the French writer's *Les fleurs bleues*, just as Eco had translated *Sylvie*) and Perec (on whom he composes two substantial essays). [51] As for literature in

English, we should note first of all that Eco does not appreciate as much as Calvino the authors that played such a role in the latter's early formation such as Conrad (on whom he writes not just his graduating thesis but also another three essays)[52] and Robert Louis Stevenson (on whom Calvino writes four articles);[53] nor does Eco write so many essays on American authors as Calvino, whose range goes from Washington Irving, Mark Twain, and Henry James between the nineteenth and twentieth centuries, to Sherwood Anderson, Richard Wright, Ernest Hemingway, and Gore Vidal nearer our own times, not to mention a fine essay on Marianne Moore.[54]

But perhaps the most revealing area of difference regarding modern authors is the attitude of the two writers toward James Joyce. For Eco, the Irish writer's works are an influential model right from the time of his early work *Opera aperta* (1962), and the Irish writer is the subject of several essays including one titled "A Portrait of the Artist as Bachelor" of 1991.[55] Calvino, on the other hand, initially reacted negatively to Joyce and this negativity only began to change in the 1960s, just at the time when Eco starts to praise the Irish novelist in *Opera aperta* and in the articles he writes for the journal run by Vittorini and Calvino, *Il menabò della letteratura*. Since it was only after this time that Calvino's attitude turned to one of positive enthusiasm for *Ulysses*, it is perhaps not an exaggeration to say that Eco played a crucial role in the "conversion" of Calvino from an anti-Joycean to an enthusiastic reader of *Ulysses* and *Finnegans Wake*.[56]

In fact, in a famous essay written in 1962, "The Challenge to the Labyrinth," published in *Il Menabò*, Calvino hints that his stylistic hero hitherto, Hemingway, is no longer satisfactory and states that he feels the need for more complex literary models and here Joyce would have been the most obvious choice. But at this point Calvino does not care much for the Irish writer for a number of reasons: Joyce's interest in the physiological, his blasphemous Catholicism, and his Irishness.[57] However, in that same issue of the journal, Eco published an article that praised the Aeolus chapter of Joyce's *Ulysses* as well as *Finnegans Wake*, an essay which Calvino read and commented on in a letter to Eco of May 1962.[58] Five years later, in 1967, in an article on "Philosophy and Literature" for the *Times Literary Supplement*, Calvino would write about Joyce for the first time in positive terms. Talking of how when philosophy enters literature it can either confirm or put into crisis what we know, Calvino writes,

> It all depends on how the writer penetrates below the surface of things. Joyce, for example, projected onto a desolate beach all the theological and ontological conundrums he had learned at school, things very far from his concerns at the time of writing. Yet everything he touched—old shoes, fish eggs, pebbles—was utterly transformed to the very depths of its being.[59]

The precise details chosen by Calvino in this essay here show that he had in mind the beach scene that takes place in chapter 3 ("Proteus") of *Ulysses* where Stephen walks along the shore thinking of theological and ontological problems, and seeing in fact fish eggs, an old shoe, and pebbles.[60] Calvino imitates this scene in the opening episodes of *Mr Palomar*, which are set on an Italian beach every bit as squalid as the one in *Ulysses*, and one where Calvino's protagonist also reflects on existential problems. The final list of items on Palomar's beach confirms this Joycean intertext since the list echoes the items seen by Stephen in the Proteus chapter.[61] Thus *Mr Palomar* is a work that looks backward to Pliny the Elder's ancient encyclopedia (as we saw at the outset) but it also takes inspiration from a modern encyclopedic classic, Joyce's *Ulysses*.

As confirmation of the idea that Calvino converts to being a fan of Joyce in the second half of his literary career, there is also the fact that even before writing *Mr Palomar* he had justified his choice of the many different styles in the micro-novels in *If on a Winter's Night a Traveller* by citing the example of other "hyper-novels" and specifically *Ulysses*: "Pursuing complexity by means of a catalog of different linguistic possibilities is a procedure that characterizes a whole swathe of literature in this century, starting with the novel that recounts an ordinary day in the life of a Dublin man in eighteen chapters, each one of which has a different stylistic set-up."[62] Thus at the end of his career as a creative writer Calvino becomes a convinced aficionado of the Irish writer, so it is no surprise to find this reflected in his later critical essays: his final lecture in the *Six Memos*, the one on "Multiplicity," singles out for great praise that encyclopedia of styles that Joyce embraces in both *Ulysses* and *Finnegans Wake*.[63]

If Calvino converted to Joyceism only in the second half of his career, Eco was always a faithful fan of the Irish writer right from the start. Joyce had in a sense been the hero of *Opera aperta*, and the author of the *Name of the Rose* readily admitted that dividing up the novel into the canonical church hours was done in imitation of the cast-iron structure of the tolling of the hours in *Ulysses*.[64] Another reason for Eco's admiration for *Ulysses* and *Finnegans Wake* was because his other favorite prose writer, Borges, also thought so highly of them, and he admits that these are the two writers who influenced him most: "Why do I mention Joyce? Perhaps and above all because, along with Borges, he is one of the two contemporary writers I have most loved and who have most influenced me. . . . Joyce played with words, Borges with ideas."[65] Our survey of transmissions of cultural memory in Eco and Calvino ends here, since although both writers admired Borges, much has already been written on the Argentinian's influence on the two Italian authors, and in any case Borges died only in 1986 and was more an older contemporary of Calvino and Eco than an object of cultural or literary memory.[66]

What we have been looking at in this chapter are two avid readers of texts of all ages and countries, two prolific writers and critics, and two authors devoted to the constant transmission of literary culture of all ages to today's readers. As essayists, they cover most periods of world literature, from classical antiquity through the Middle Ages and Renaissance down to our own age; as novelists they both find inspiration in any work, picking out modern elements of content and structure in ancient texts, and seeing classical constants in contemporary works. What strikes one most of all is the acuity of their analyses, and their ability to find creative inspiration in texts that seem at first sight remote from their own poetics.

In terms of comparison, as far as their relationship to classical works are concerned, Eco turns more often than Calvino to the works of critics such as Aristotle, Quintilian, and Longinus, authors who are rarely cited by Calvino. By contrast, Eco sees himself as a descendant of that line of great critics. This difference is reflected also in their attitude to E. A. Poe: while Calvino is influenced by the American writer's stories, Eco was entranced by Poe's critical work, *The Philosophy of Composition.*

As for other periods, we have seen that Eco is inspired more by the Middle Ages, Calvino by the Renaissance (Ariosto, of course but also Galileo, Cardano, Cyrano de Bergerac, and so on). When it comes to the modern age, both are inspired particularly by works written in English: Calvino's adoration of Stevenson, Conrad, and Hemingway is paralleled by Eco's love of Joyce, but Calvino had read more literature in English than Eco and was more creatively inspired by it than any other Italian writer.

However, I want to end by stressing something that the two Italian writers have in common. Both admired the traditional nineteenth-century novel, but Calvino identified in the works of Balzac and Stevenson a formula for a successful novel that would be used by both writers. He notes that a sure-fire subject for attracting readers was the idea of a secret worldwide conspiracy:

> The murky conspiracy that spreads its tentacles everywhere will become a half-serious, half-playful obsession for the most sophisticated English novelists of the turn of the nineteenth century and will reemerge in the serial production of violent spy-thrillers in our own times.[67]

This formula that links high and popular culture underlies all ten micronovels in *If on a Winter's Night a Traveller,* but it is also the basic ingredient in most of Eco's lengthy fictional works.

This idea of the continuity of plots between the nineteenth and twentieth centuries brings us back to the subject of cultural transmission. We saw that both Italian authors would not have been as successful without their engagement with the literature of other times and other cultures. The secret of their creativity lies in the fact that they are both willing to change as writers, though in one sense we might see Calvino as more prone to being transformed by what the past transmits. Thus we witnessed the gradual move from his early cult of Hemingway's stark simplicity to his need for Joycean complexity and his embracing of the idea of writing works that encompassed whole universes. Eco on the other hand, while admiring Borges, admits that he could never adopt the Argentine writer's minimalist brevity and stays faithful to his own notion of narrative abundance.[68] Still the two writers' engagement with what the past transmits is never passive. Their critical essays provide us with a rear view into the everyday workshop of two great critics and creative authors: one of the secrets of their creativity is that what they read was often metamorphosed creatively, intertextually into what they wrote.

NOTES

This is a revised and expanded version of my chapter "Calvino, Eco e il canone della letteratura mondiale" in *Tra Eco e Calvino: Relazioni rizomatiche*, Atti del convegno "Eco & Calvino. Rhizomatic Relationships," University of Toronto, April 13–14, 2012, ed. Rocco Capozzi (Milan: EncycloMedia, 2013), 41–67.

1. Italo Calvino, *Perché leggere i classici* (Milan: Mondadori, 1991), appeared in English as *Why Read the Classics?*, trans. Martin McLaughlin (London: Jonathan Cape, 1999). References to the essays will be given in the form *WRC*, followed by the page number. References to Calvino's other essays not in this volume will be to Italo Calvino, *Saggi*, ed. Mario Barenghi, 2 vols. (Milan: Mondadori, 1995), henceforth Calvino, *S*, with volume and page number.

2. Umberto Eco, *Sulla letteratura* (Milan: Bompiani, 2002), was published as *On Literature*, trans. Martin McLaughlin (London: Secker & Warburg, 2005). References in what follows will be in the form *OL*, followed by page number.

3. Italo Calvino, *Palomar* (Turin: Einaudi, 1983), appeared in English as *Mr Palomar*, trans. William Weaver (London: Secker & Warburg, 1985). For the chronology of the composition of the individual chapters of *Palomar*, see Italo Calvino, *Romanzi e raccconti*, ed. Claudio Milanini, Mario Barenghi and Bruno Falcetto, 3 vols. (Milan: Mondadori, 1991–1994), vol. 2, 1402–36: 1436 (future references to this edition will be in the form *RR*, followed by volume and page number).

4. Italo Calvino, "The Sky, Man, the Elephant" (1982), *WRC*, 43–44.

5. *Mr Palomar*, 108.

6. *WRC*, 46.

7. *Mr Palomar*, 71–79.

8. "Ovid and Universal Contiguity" (1979), *WRC*, 31–32.

9. Italo Calvino, *Invisible Cities*, trans. William Weaver (New York-London: Harcourt, Brace, Jovanovich, 1974), 77.

10. Umberto Eco, "The *Poetics* and Us," *OL*, 236–54.

11. Umberto Eco, *The Name of the Rose. Including the Author's Postscript*, trans. William Weaver (San Diego–New York–London: Harcourt, Brace & Company, 1983), 468.

12. I quote from the Loeb volume: Aristotle, *Poetics*, ed. and trans. Stephen Halliwell; Longinus, *On the Sublime*, trans. W. H. Fyfe, rev. Donald Russell; Demetrius, *On Style*, ed. and trans. Doreen C. Innes, based on W. Rhys Roberts (Cambridge, MA–London: Harvard University Press, 1995), 47–49.

13. *OL*, 238.

14. *OL*, 242.

15. Umberto Eco, "On Style" (1995–1996), *OL*, 179.

16. Umberto Eco, "A Portrait of the Artist as Bachelor," *OL*, 96; "*Les sémaphores sous la pluie*," *OL*, 180–84, 194.

17. Eco, *The Name of the Rose*, 510.

18. Calvino, "Two Interviews on Science and Literature," in *The Literature Machine. Essays*, trans. Patrick Creagh (London: Secker & Warburg, 1986), 32.

19. Calvino, *Six Memos for the Next Millennium*, trans. Patrick Creagh (London: Jonathan Cape, 1992), 14–16, 81–83.

20. *S*, vol. 2, 1700–1701.

21. The English version is in Calvino, *Adam, One Afternoon and Other Stories*, trans. Archibald Colquhoun and Peggy Wright (London: Picador, 1984), 74–82. For an analysis of the Dantesque structure underlying the story, see Martin McLaughlin, *Italo Calvino* (Edinburgh: Edinburgh University Press, 1998), 13–14.

22. For Dantesque echoes in *Palomar*, see McLaughlin, *Italo Calvino*, 137–39.

23. For details, see my chapter, "Calvino's Rewriting of Marco Polo: From the 1960 Screenplay to *Invisible Cities*," in *Marco Polo and the Encounter of East and West*, ed. Suzanne Conklin Akbari and Amilcare A. Iannucci (Toronto: Toronto University Press, 2008), 182–200.

24. "Levels of Reality in Literature," in *The Literature Machine*, 101–21: 117.

25. See Sven Ekblad, *Studi sui sottofondi strutturali nel* Nome della rosa *di Umberto Eco. Parte I:* La Divina Commedia *di Dante* (Lund: Lund University Press, 1994).

26. Quoted in "A Reading of the *Paradiso*," in *OL*, 16–22: 16.

27. *OL*, 20.

28. "*legato con amore in un volume / ciò che per l'universo si squaderna / sustanze e accidenti e lor costume*" (*Paradiso*, 33.86–88), quoted in *OL*, 22.

29. *OL*, 22.

30. Umberto Eco, "Dolenti declinare *(rapporti di lettura all'editore)*," in *Diario minimo* (Milan: Mondadori, 1988), 150–51.

31. *OL*, 148–51.

32. *If on a Winter's Night a Traveller*, trans. William Weaver (London: Minerva, 1992), 162.

33. Eco points out that he was interested in Kircher even before reading Borges: Umberto Eco, "Osservazioni conclusive," in *Tra Eco e Calvino: Relazioni rizomatiche*, 325.

34. See, for instance, Stefano Verdino, "Ariosto in Calvino," *Nuova Corrente* 100 (1987): 251–58; Wiley Feinstein, *Humility's Deceit: Calvino Reading Ariosto Reading Calvino* (West Lafayette, IN: Bordighera, 1995).

35. For Calvino's essays on and rewritings of the *Furioso*, see Martin McLaughlin, "'C'è un furto con scasso in ogni vera lettura': Calvino's Thefts from Ariosto," *Parole Rubate/Purloined Letters* 7 (June 2013): 139–63: http://www.parolerubate.unipr.it/ (accessed February 22, 2017).

36. Calvino, "Il rapporto con la luna," in *S*, vol. 1, 228 (my translation).

37. "Two Interviews on Science and Literature," in Calvino, *The Literature Machine*, 32.

38. Eco, "The Power of Falsehood," *OL*, 275.

39. Gerard de Nerval, *Sylvie: Ricordi del Valois*, traduzione di Umberto Eco (Turin: Einaudi, 1999); "The Mists of the Valois," *OL*, 28–61; see also Eco, *Six Walks in the Fictional Woods* (Cambridge, MA: Harvard University Press, 1994), passim.

40. To take just one example from each writer: Calvino mentions Leopardi's literary qualities three times in his essays on Lightness, Quickness and Exactitude: *Six Memos for the Next Millenniums*, 24–26, 41–42, 57–64; Eco mentions the poet several times and discusses his best-known poem "L'infinito" in the essay "On Symbolism," (1994), *OL*, 158–59.

41. Calvino, "Manzoni's *The Betrothed*: The Novel of Ratios of Power," in *The Literature Machine*, 196–212.

42. Eco, *Six Walks in the Fictional Woods* (Cambridge, MA: Harvard University Press, 1994), 52.

43. Eco, "Borges and My Anxiety of Influence," *OL*, 130.

44. "Intertextual Irony and Levels of Reading," *OL*, 213, 216. See Renato Giovannoli, "Manzoni e Pierre Menard. L'influenza di Borges sulla letteratura italiana intorno al 1960 e *Diario minimo*," *Tra Eco e Calvino: Relazioni rizomatiche*, 221–50.

45. "Poe tradotto da Manganelli," in *S*, vol. 1, 930–35.

46. "Dino Buzzati," in *S*, vol. 1, 1012–15: 1013.

47. *S*, 1733–34.

48. "My City Is New York," in *Hermit in Paris: Autobiographical Writings*, trans. Martin McLaughlin (London: Jonathan Cape, 2003), 236.

49. On *Gordon Pym* see also Eco, *Six Walks in the Fictional Woods*, 17–21. Eco mentions Poe's essay "The Philosophy of Composition" in his postscript to his first novel: *The Name of the Rose*, 508–9; and in more detail in "The *Poetics* and Us," *OL*, 238–40, 249–50.

50. *OL*, 239.

51. For one of the essays on Queneau, see "The Philosophy of Raymond Queneau," *WRC*, 245–60. The essays on Perec can be found in *S*, vol. 1, 1388–92, 1393–1400.

52. See *S*, vol. 1, 808–10; 811–13; 814–19.

53. See *S*, vol. 1, 967–71, 972–76, 977–80, 981–88.

54. For these essays see *S*, vol. 1, 861–66, 867–70, 993–98, 1283–85, 1463–65, 1312–20, 1455–62, 1343–49. For an overview of Calvino's essays on writers in English, see Martin McLaughlin, "Calvino saggista: Anglofilia letteraria e creatività," in *Italo Calvino Newyorkese*, ed. Anna Botta and Domenico Scarpa (Cava de' Tirreni: Avagliano, 2002), 41–66; for a detailed account of the importance of British writers to Calvino, there is an excellent recent thesis by Giulia Bassi, *Italo Calvino e la letteratura inglese* (Tesi di laurea, University of Rome, La Sapienza, 2015–16).

55. *OL*, 84–103.

56. For a more detailed study of Calvino's gradual "conversion" to Joyceism, see Martin McLaughlin, "Calvino and Joyce on the Beach: The Story of a Conversion," in *Twenty Years After: An Irish Calvino?*, ed. Roberto Bertoni (Dublin-Turin: Department of Italian, Trinity College, Dublin – Trauben, 2007), 47–63.

57. "La sfida al labirinto," *S*, vol. I, pp. 105–23: 114.

58. Eco's article was titled "Del modo di formare come impegno sulla realtà" ("Form as Social Commitment"), in *Il Menabò* 5 (1962): 198–237 (the praise of Joyce was on pp. 227, 236). For Calvino's letter to Eco, see Italo Calvino, *Letters 1941–1985*, ed. Michael Wood, trans. Martin McLaughlin (Princeton, NJ: Princeton University Press, 2013), 227–28. On the context of these exchanges, María L. Calvo Montoro, "Le 'lezioni americane' di Umberto Eco e i 'boschi narrativi' di Italo Calvino," in *Tra Eco e Calvino. Relazioni rizomatiche*, 83–97: 83–84.

59. "Philosophy and Literature," *Times Literary Supplement*, September 28, 1967, 871–72: 871. Actually the English translator of the article had translated Calvino's "ciottoli" [*S*, vol. 1, 192] as "old pots and pans," presumably mistaking "ciottoli" [pebbles] for "ciotole" [pots, bowls].

60. "[S]easpawn and seawrack, the nearing tide, that rusty boot . . . squeaking pebbles, that on the unnumbered pebbles beats": James Joyce, *Ulysses*, ed. with an introduction and notes by Jeri Johnson (Oxford: Oxford University Press, 1998), 37–41.

61. *Mr Palomar*, 14–15.

62. First published in *Alfabeta*, 1.8 (December 1979), 4–5, now in *RR*, vol. 2, 1392 (my translation).

63. *Six Memos for the Next Millennium*, 117.

64. Eco, *The Name of the Rose*, 516.

65. Eco, "Between La Mancha and Babel," *OL*, 104–17: 110, 113.

66. Amongst the many items on the enthusiasm of Calvino and Eco for Borges, see Jorge J. E. Gracia et al. (eds.), *Literary Philosophers: Borges, Calvino, Eco* (New York-London: Routledge, 2002); Cristina Farronato, *Eco's Chaosmos. From the Middle Ages to Postmodernity* (Toronto-Buffalo-London: University of Toronto Press, 2003), 113–22.

67. Calvino, "The City as Novel in Balzac" (1973), in *WRC*, 139. He uses a very similar phrase about the basic plot in one of Stevenson's tales, in a preface written in the same year, 1973: "the elusive conspiracy that spreads its tentacles everywhere, a theme which has never

been out of fashion from the nineteenth century to our own day ("Robert Louis Stevenson, *The Pavilion on the Links*," *WRC*, 170).

   68. *OL*, 133–34.

WORKS CITED

Aristotle, *Poetics*. Edited and translated by Stephen Halliwell; Longinus, *On the Sublime*. Translated by W. H. Fyfe, revised by Donald Russell; Demetrius, *On Style*. Edited and translated by Doreen C. Innes, based on W. Rhys Roberts. Cambridge, MA-London: Harvard University Press, 1995, 47–49.

Bassi, Giulia. *Italo Calvino e la letteratura inglese*. Tesi di laurea, University of Rome, La Sapienza, 2015–2016.

Calvino, Italo. *If on a Winter's Night a Traveller*. Translated by William Weaver. London: Minerva, 1992.

———. *Invisible Cities*. Translated by William Weaver. New York-London: Harcourt, Brace, Jovanovich, 1974.

———. *Letters 1941–1985*. Edited by Michael Wood, translated by Martin McLaughlin. Princeton, NJ: Princeton University Press, 2013.

———. *The Literature Machine. Essays*. Translated by Patrick Creagh. London: Secker & Warburg, 1986.

———. *Mr Palomar*. Translated by William Weaver. London: Secker & Warburg, 1985.

———. *Palomar*. Turin: Einaudi, 1983.

———. *Perché leggere i classici*. Milan: Mondadori, 1991.

———. *Romanzi e raccconti*. Edited by Claudio Milanini, Mario Barenghi, and Bruno Falcetto, 3 vols. Milan: Mondadori, 1991–1994.

———. *Saggi*. Edited by Mario Barenghi, 2 vols. Milan: Mondadori, 1995.

———. *Six Memos for the Next Millennium*. Translated by Patrick Creagh. London: Jonathan Cape, 1992.

———. *Why Read the Classics?* Translated by Martin McLaughlin. London: Jonathan Cape, 1999.

———. "The City as Novel in Balzac." In Calvino, *Why Read the Classics?*, 139–43, 139.

———. "Dino Buzzati." In Calvino, *Saggi*, vol. 1, 1012–15.

———. "La sfida al labirinto." In Calvino, *Saggi*, vol. 1, 105–23.

———. "Levels of Reality in Literature," in Calvino, *The Literature Machine*, 101–21.

———. "Manzoni's *The Betrothed*: The Novel of Ratios of Power." In *The Literature Machine*, 196–212.

———. "My City Is New York." In Calvino, *Hermit in Paris. Autobiographical Writings*. Translated by Martin McLaughlin. London: Jonathan Cape, 2003, 235–39.

———. "One of the Three Is Still Alive." In Calvino, *Adam, One Afternoon and Other Stories*. Translated by Archibald Colquhoun and Peggy Wright. London: Picador, 1984, 74–82.

———. "Ovid and Universal Contiguity." In Calvino, *Why Read the Classics?*, 25–35.

———. "Perec, *La vita istruzioni per l'uso*." In Calvino, *Saggi*, vol. 1, 1393–1400.

———. "Philosophy and Literature." *Times Literary Supplement*, September 28, 1967, 871–72.

———. "The Philosophy of Raymond Queneau." In Calvino, *Why Read the Classics?*, 245–60.

———. "Poe tradotto da Manganelli." In Calvino, *Saggi*, vol. 1, 930–35.

———. "Ricordo di Georges Perec." In Calvino, *Saggi*, vol. 1, 1388–92.

———. "Robert Louis Stevenson, *The Pavilion on the Links*." In Calvino, *Why Read the Classics?*, 169–72.

———. "*Se una notte d'inverno un narratore*." *Alfabeta* 1.8 (December 1979), 4–5. Later in Calvino, *Romanzi e raccconti*, vol. 2, 1388–97.

———. "The Sky, Man, the Elephant." In Calvino, *Why Read the Classics?*, 37–46.

———. "Two Interviews on Science and Literature." In Calvino, *The Literature Machine*, 28–38.

Calvo Montoro, Maria L. "Le 'lezioni americane' di Umberto Eco e i 'boschi narrativi' di Italo Calvino." In *Tra Eco e Calvino. Relazioni rizomatiche*, 83–97.

De Nerval, Gérard. *Sylvie: Ricordi del Valois*. Traduzione di Umberto Eco. Turin: Einaudi, 1999.

Eco, Umberto. *The Name of the Rose: Including the Author's Postscript*. Translated by William Weaver. San Diego–New York–London: Harcourt, Brace & Company, 1983.

———. *On Literature*. Translated by Martin McLaughlin. London: Secker & Warburg, 2005.

———. *Six Walks in the Fictional Woods*. Cambridge, MA: Harvard University Press, 1994.

———. *Sulla letteratura*. Milan: Bompiani, 2002.

———. "Between La Mancha and Babel." In Eco, *On Literature*, 104–17.

———. "Borges and My Anxiety of Influence." In Eco, *On Literature*, 118–35.

———. "Del modo di formare come impegno sulla realtà." *Il Menabò* 5 (1962): 198–237.

———. "Dolenti declinare (rapporti di lettura all'editore)." In Eco, *Diario minimo*, 147–57. Milan: Mondadori, 1988.

———. "Intertextual Irony and Levels of Reading." In Eco, *On Literature*, 212–35.

———. "*Les sémaphores sous la pluie*." In Eco, *On Literature*, 180–200.

———. "The Mists of the Valois." In Eco, *On Literature*, 28–61.

———. "On Style." In Eco, *On Literature*, 161–79.

———. "On Symbolism." In Eco, *On Literature*, 158–59.

———. "Osservazioni conclusive." In *Tra Eco e Calvino. Relazioni rizomatiche*, 325–34.

———. "The *Poetics* and Us." In Eco, *On Literature*, 236–54.

———. "A Portrait of the Artist as Bachelor." In Eco, *On Literature*, 84–103.

———. "The Power of Falsehood." In Eco, *On Literature*, 272–301.

———. "A Reading of the *Paradiso*." In Eco, *On Literature*, 16–22.

Ekblad, Sven. *Studi sui sottofondi strutturali nel* Nome della rosa *di Umberto Eco. Parte I:* La Divina Commedia *di Dante*. Lund: Lund University Press, 1994.

Feinstein, Wiley. *Humility's Deceit: Calvino Reading Ariosto Reading Calvino*. West Lafayette, IN: Bordighera, 1995.

Giovannoli, Renato. "Manzoni e Pierre Menard. L'influenza di Borges sulla letteratura italiana intorno al 1960 e *Diario minimo*." In *Tra Eco e Calvino. Relazioni rizomatiche*, 221–50.

Farronato, Cristina. *Eco's Chaosmos: From the Middle Ages to Postmodernity*. Toronto-Buffalo-London: University of Toronto Press, 2003.

Gracia, Jorge J. E., et al. (eds.). *Literary Philosophers: Borges, Calvino, Eco*. New York-London: Routledge, 2002.

Joyce, James. *Ulysses*. Edited with an introduction and notes by Jeri Johnson. Oxford: Oxford University Press, 1998.

McLaughlin, Martin. "Calvino and Joyce on the Beach: The Story of a Conversion." In *Twenty Years After: An Irish Calvino?*, edited by Roberto Bertoni. Dublin-Turin: Department of Italian, Trinity College, Dublin – Trauben, 2007, 47–63.

———. "Calvino, Eco e il canone della letteratura mondiale." In *Tra Eco e Calvino. Relazioni rizomatiche*, 41–67.

———. "Calvino saggista: Anglofilia letteraria e creatività." In *Italo Calvino Newyorkese*, edited by Anna Botta and Domenico Scarpa. Cava de' Tirreni: Avagliano, 2002, 41–66.

———. "Calvino's Rewriting of Marco Polo: From the 1960 Screenplay to *Invisible Cities*." In *Marco Polo and the Encounter of East and West*, edited by Suzanne Conklin Akbari and Amilcare A. Iannucci. Toronto: Toronto University Press, 2008, 182–200.

———. "'C'è un furto con scasso in ogni vera lettura': Calvino's Thefts from Ariosto." *Parole Rubate/Purloined Letters* 7 (June 2013): 139–63: http://www.parolerubate.unipr.it/ . Accessed February 28, 2017.

———. *Italo Calvino*. Edinburgh: Edinburgh University Press, 1998.

Tra Eco e Calvino. Relazioni rizomatiche, Atti del convegno "Eco & Calvino. Rhizomatic Relationships," University of Toronto, April 13–14, 2012, edited by Rocco Capozzi, 41–67. Milan: EncycloMedia, 2013.

Verdino, Stefano. "Ariosto in Calvino." *Nuova Corrente* 100 (1987): 251–58.

Chapter Two

Montale's *Xenia*

Between Myth and Poetic Tradition

Adele Bardazzi

Montale's poetic female figures have often been understood as belonging to specific categories, of which there have traditionally been three. First, the superior and transcendent angelic woman, who is set against a much less celestial, if not to say monstrous, second woman, and thirdly, a companion-like woman that seems to synthesize the two former antithetical typologies.[1] Despite their evident uses, these categories are bound to inevitable failure when it comes to capturing some more individual meanings of the object in and of itself—something unavoidably lost in the process of categorization. As a result, readings of Montale's female beloveds all share a very similar bias that excludes other interesting perspectives. In order to comprehend the nature and complexity of Montale's female figures fully, I believe it is necessary to overcome this tendency toward categorization. This becomes possible when one takes into account Montale's not much studied rewriting and revision of two of the most influential myths in Western culture and lyric poetry in particular: the myth of Orpheus and Eurydice and the myth of Persephone. In so doing I aim to address an aspect of the feminine in Montale—the darker and feral essence of some of his female figures—that has passed unnoticed until now. I will do so by focusing on Montale's most complex embodiment of what I will refer to as the Eurydice-Persephone archetype: the figure of Mosca.[2] Mosca is the affectionate name used by Montale for his wife Drusilla Tanzi, who was known for her tiny frame and near-blindness. By looking at Mosca, I will argue that the feminine in Montale departs from the kind of femininity that has been previously emphasized within Montalean criticism. Other female figures share important affinities with Mosca, especially Esterina and Arletta/Annetta. However, Mosca is the one that most clearly shows the way the two mythical figures of Eurydice and Persephone intertwine with each other. This is because in her being the poet(ic subject)'s wife, she powerfully embodies Persephone's transformation into the dreadful queen of the underworld, an aspect not present in the figure of the young Eurydice.

The figures of Eurydice and Persephone and the way they have been reinterpreted throughout the centuries are key to shedding further light on this unexplored chthonic and feral femininity of Montale's poetic world. In fact, Eurydice and Persephone have given rise to what can be called the Eurydice-Persephone archetype, which represents the influential and long-standing model of the virginal young woman with whom the male subject initiates a dialogue *in absentia*: Eurydice, the "moritura puella,"[3] and the young Persephone, the soon-to-be dreadful queen of the underworld. This chapter will reveal how some of Montale's female figures are ascribable to the archetype of the "fanciulla morta" (dead girl), which in turn is the modern paradigm of Eurydice-Persephone archetype. This is the same archetype that can be found in Leopardi's Silvia, and even before that in Petrarch's Laura; indeed, both, as we will see, are fundamental models for Montale's elaboration of his own chthonic female figures. From this standpoint, I suggest that Montale does not challenge the archetype of the young woman who undergoes a premature death; rather, he preserves this tradition that is so profoundly embedded in lyric discourse. The figures of Eurydice and Persephone converge into a synchronic mythologeme that functions as the pretextual essence of the female figure's textual existence. Moreover, as is proper to the poetic code, the evocation of the dead through dialogue *in absentia* with the female beloved allows a form of communication to be preserved and recovered not only with the departed female beloved, but also with the beyond: the afterlife. Herein lies the nature of this archetype. Echoes of both these myths have been highlighted in Montale before, but have been mainly circumscribed to his first poetic collection and limited to the figure of Arletta, and have thus never been put forward in order to reach a larger, coherent vision of his female figures and the feminine more broadly.[4] The core aim of this chapter is to highlight the much darker and chthonic femininity, compared to what previous studies have presented, that violently erupts from Montale's poetic underworld. Moreover, focusing on Mosca will allow a reevaluation of what I see as a key figure in Montale's poetry. Criticism has tended to position her erroneously in the category of the companion-like woman and has perceived her as not being a central female figure among Montale's female muses and thus as not worthy of further investigation. On the contrary, I see Mosca as the most significant figure that allows us to enter Montale's underworld, where many other figures redolent of Eurydice and Persephone dwell (e.g., the fearless diver of "Falsetto"—Esterina; and the Montalean Silvia—Annetta/Arletta).

Specifically, I will focus on *Xenia* and some other key poems from *Satura* written in memory of Mosca and directly addressed to her. *Xenia*, first published in 1966 after ten years of poetic silence that followed the publication of *La bufera e altro*, sees, for the first time, the exclusive presence of Mosca. In 1968 Montale published a second series under the title *Altri Xenia*, comprising again fourteen poems, which were eventually reunited under the titles *Xenia* I and *Xenia* II in *Satura*, his fourth poetic collection, published with Mondadori in 1971. *Xenia* is Montale's *canzoniere in morte* and it is this poetic genre of the *canzoniere in morte*, a poetry collection written by the poet for his or her dead beloved, a genre at the heart of the Western poetic tradition, that can guide us toward a better understanding of what occurs in *Xenia*. In the *canzonieri in morte* the subject, caught in a state of mourning and trying to re-elaborate the loss experienced, attempts to order the scattered fragments of memory by arranging them into a highly organized and structured work, the *canzoniere in morte*.[5] One of the most celebrated mythical couples of tragic lovers of all times, Orpheus and Eurydice, lead the reader along a path that in the Italian literary canon starts with Dante and Petrarch, passes through Leopardi, and eventually reaches the voice of Montale. Approaching *Xenia* as a *canzoniere in morte* requires one brief clarification in terms of methodology. Although in its final publication *Xenia* does not stand as an autonomous book, but rather represents the first two sections of a longer book, and regardless of the fact that there are other poems scattered throughout *Satura* outside the two series of *Xenia*, it is possible to consider it as a *canzoniere* for three reasons. Firstly, it maintains a certain autonomy from the rest of *Satura*; secondly, it was previously published as an autonomous work; and lastly, it possesses a strong structured form.[6]

It is noteworthy that Mosca's *nomignoli* (nicknames; e.g., "moschina," "mouche," "moscerino," "insetto," "grillo," "musclin," etc.) all belong to what Maria Antonietta Grignani rightly sees as an "idioletto diminutivo . . . [che] porta completamente fuori dai prodigi cliziani" (diminutive idiolect . . . that takes us far away from Clizia's miracles).[7] Not surprisingly, the subjects of *Xenia* are the banalities of everyday life: "le coincidenze, le prenotazioni, le trappole, gli scorni" (the coincidences, the bookings, the traps, the flops) (*Xenia* II.5, 5–6)[8] —none of which have anything transcendental or salvific about them. This is a book written "in pigiama" (in pajama) within the domestic walls of his later years with Mosca, and not "in frac" (in white tie) as his early poetry might have been.[9] This statement by Montale is also important as a way of highlighting how myth is reappropriated by the poet and transposed into a different setting: the intimate and private setting of his own house where he shared his life with Mosca. For all these reasons, Mosca cannot be classified as Montale's classical transcendent angelic figure together with Clizia. Traditionally, Mosca has been presented as a domestic angelic figure: an undersized Clizia sharing with Montale's *donna angelo* similar salvific characteristics, but limited to the sphere of everyday life. However, this is a reductive and erroneous reading that does not account for Mosca's complexity. Mosca shares some of the salvific features of Clizia, but she is much more bound to earthly reality rather than a celestial plane: Mosca has "ali . . . | solo nella fantasia" (wings . . . only in one's imagination) (*Xenia* I.2, 2–3). Nonetheless this "piccolo insetto | che chiamavano mosca" (tiny insect | that they used to call fly) (*Xenia* I.1, 1–2) is endowed with superior powers:

> Per gli altri no, eri un insetto miope
> smarrito nel blabla
> dell'alta società. Erano ingenui
> quei furbi e non sapevano
> di essere loro il tuo zimbello:
> di essere visti anche al buio e smascherati
> da un tuo senso infallibile, dal tuo
> radar di pipistrello.
>
> (Not for others, you were a short-sighted insect
> lost in the blah blah of high society.
> Naive were those sly ones who did not know
> that *they* were your laughing stock:
> they were seen even in darkness and unmasked
> by your never-failing sense, by your
> bat's radar.)
> (*Xenia* I.5, 4–11)

Regarding the third category of the female companion that Giusi Baldissone and Riccardo Castellana, among others, argue to be illustrated by Mosca, I maintain that, although she is the woman who is represented as sharing her life with Montale in their later years together, Mosca cannot be reduced to a domestic figure whose role is merely to accompany the male poetic subject and whose nature is still understood as angelic and salvific.[10] On the contrary, Mosca has superior powers: she is Montale's "vere pupille" (true pupils) (*Xenia* II.5, 11) and is the only one able to deconstruct the oxymoron-ic nature of reality by her being mysteriously connected with the earthly (and chthonic) reality more than anyone else.[11] Mosca is a hybrid between the traditional categories according to which Montale's figures have typically been pinned down. She is neither a Clizia-like salvific figure, nor her anti-thetical erotic counterpart as represented by Volpe, nor does she belong to the third category of the companionable female figure. In transcending easy categorization, Mosca brings about a *cortocircuito* (short circuit) to the re-solved picture of Montale's female figures as easily classifiable in separate boxes and demands a reevaluation of the classical categories into which Montale's female poetic figures have been enclosed so far.

Following the poetic tradition of the absent *fanciulla morta*, Montale's female figure stands as the only medium to give access to that "Niente" ("Violoncelli," *Poesie disperse*, 20–23), with which the poetic subject seeks to be put in dialogue. In that "beyond," however, the female beloved is condemned to disappear, to reside, and eventually she becomes its custodian. Herein lies her Persephonean nature. From this standpoint, Mosca allows us to step into the darker abyss of Montale's poetic underworld where the much more gloomy essence of the feminine—also embodied by Montale's other female figures like Esterina and Arletta/Annetta—resides. In so doing, Mosca enables us to blur the traditional antithetical categories within which Montale's female figures have thus far been enclosed, at times even erroneously, and highlights the way Montale revisits two of the most influential myths of Western culture and traditional lyric discourse.

There are three main aspects that allow us to trace the way Mosca embodies the Eurydice-Persephone archetype and on which this chapter focuses: firstly, images in which the female beloved is represented as enveloped by fog, a fundamental element that belongs to the *aldilà* (underworld) not just in Montale but also in Virgil and Petrarch; secondly, episodes in which Mosca is herself shown to belong to the underworld; lastly, instances representing the act of descending toward lower places that are essentially Mosca's *katabases*. In her journey toward the underworld the female beloved loses herself and becomes the custodian of this "beyond" within which she is now confined.

Mosca thus emerges as a propitiatory figure toward an "oltre" (beyond), which the male poet-creator yearns to enter in order to dialogue with it. Here lies her Eurydice-Persephone nature. What we therefore find is a male(-poet) creator making the fundamental element of his own existence, as well as of his oeuvre, out of the interest in entering in contact with the "Niente" that lies beyond the tangible world. This echoes what takes place in the myth of Orpheus. My reading of the myth of Orpheus and Eurydice draws on the political philosopher Adriana Cavarero's groundbreaking interpretation of this myth as she presents it in her *Tu che mi guardi, tu che mi racconti*. Following Cavarero, I reject the principal traditional understanding of this myth and Orpheus's fatal turning back as an act of excessive love that tends to position him as the victim. On the contrary, I share Cavarero's view that "[t]raendo da Euridice ormai morta la sua ispirazione, Orfeo canta appunto di lei ma non *a* lei. Forse per questo, maliziosamente, si volta" (Drawing his inspiration from the now-dead Eurydice, Orpheus sings *of* her but not *to* her).[12] Cavarero develops her view of Orpheus's not so innocent act of turning back, highlighting that in the moment of his turning backward he abruptly pushes Eurydice back to the underworld in order to enter, himself and his poetry, into the myth:

[S]e si fosse voltato *dopo*, infatti—fuori dalla bocca degl'Inferi dove il vedere Euridice, ormai salva, era concesso—avrebbe dovuto raccontare proprio a lei quella storia di lei che gli aveva aperte anche le porte dell'Inferno. Se si fosse voltato dopo, insieme a un improbabile *happy end*, avremmo potuto godere di un amore ricondotto alla scena d'amore alla portata di tutti, un amore dei giorni di festa. Invece, come sappiamo, si è voltato *prima*: ricacciandola indietro per entrare nel mito. [13]

(If he had turned around *afterwards*—outside the mouth of Hell, where seeing Eurydice, by then safe, was allowed—he would have had to tell her the story *about* her that had opened the doors of Hell for him. If he had turned around afterwards, along with an improbable happy ending, we would have been able to enjoy a love brought back to the narrative scene of the relationship—a banally happy love, a love accessible to all).

This reading of the myth of Orpheus is crucial to an understanding of the Eurydice-Persephone archetype and the origins and essence of that prolific and long-lasting lyric model of the absent female beloved whose death is lamented by the male poetic subject. The male poet-creator's song depends on its being bereaved, just like Orpheus: his poetry comes from an irremediable loss—that of his beloved. In other words, the female beloved must inhabit the world of the dead, just like Eurydice, in order for Orpheus to create his enchanting poetry that has the magic power of drawing the trees of the forest to him. Orpheus inaugurates what Cavarero sees as a persistent tradition that wants the loved woman to be a dead woman, something that remains traceable in Montale's poetry: "[i]n quanto simbolo della poesia d'amore, Orfeo inaugura l'ostinata tradizione che vuole nella donna amata una donna morta" (As the symbol of the poetry of love, Orpheus inaugurates the stubborn tradition, which wants the loved woman to be a dead woman). [14] Hence, Orpheus's story, just like Montale's *Xenia*, finds its legitimization in the absence of the female other. It is from this loss that the mourning Orpheus's song springs, and it is through this loss that the poet-lover Orpheus enters into the myth. Moreover, Cavarero's reading of the myth highlights another crucial element of this archetype: the female beloved is silenced, without voice; Orpheus sings not only of her, but also for her, and this is also what, as I will show in the last part of this chapter, takes place in Montale's *canzoniere in morte* to Mosca. In *Xenia* Mosca becomes the pretext for some of the most powerful and poignant of Montale's texts. The female poetic beloved, as is traditional in lyric poetry, becomes a *pretext* for the development and articulation of the poet's *text* (and self). [15] It is through the monologue (or dialogue *in absentia*) that the poet establishes with the *other* woman that a process of elaboration of his own self becomes possible. In losing Mosca, the *io* loses a crucial figure, who also represents his main medium of communication between himself and the world. In Montale, each female inspiration, each imagined interlocutor—whether distant or a lost love, or the heartless *belle dame sans merci*—represents the pretext for a new poetic and stylistic adventure: a pretext for a renewal of the poetic word.

"Un ciclo di poesie dedicate a una defunta non era davvero una novità nella poesia italiana; neanche in quella di Montale" (a cycle of poems dedicated to a dead woman was far from being a novelty in Italian poetry; including in the one by Montale).[16] With these words Franco Fortini opens his lecture on *Satura* for Guido Almansi's students at the University of Kent in 1971, soon after Montale's fourth poetic collection had been published. A novelty, however, is present in so far as wives are much less present in the courtly love tradition.[17] Mosca in fact enters Montale's poetry only in the poet's later years and in particular circumstances: "nel solco dell'emergenza" (in the wake of emergency) ("Ballata scritta in una clinica," *La bufera e altro*, 1). This is the only poem that sees Mosca at its center before *Xenia*. The specificity of the context in which Mosca enters Montale's poetry is worth noting as it is an element that clearly links her to both Eurydice and Persephone in so far as also the crucial part of their narratives similarly begin in the moment their life is threatened and when their journey to the "beyond" takes place. Here, in the underworld, they are condemned to dissolve and eventually, for Persephone, to become its custodian. In Montale's poetry, there is a motif of how this situation of emergency is repeatedly identified: the *topos* of the crevasse (*Xenia* II.4, 8). Montale's female figures are often desired precisely in the moment they move from one element to another; hence the significance of the topical image of the crevasse whose form inherently suggests the moment of standing in balance between one level and a lower one, something that recalls Esterina's *esitare/esistere* (hesitating/existing) while standing on the springboard.[18] Just like Mosca, Montale's female figures are desired precisely "[n]el solco dell'emergenza" (in the wake of emergency): in the moment right before their transitioning into the "Niente" with which the male poet seeks to dialogue. Here in this transition they dissolve into nothingness, the element to which they ultimately belong.

Mosca in *Xenia* visits the poet in the form of a shadow, and without her characteristic "grossi | occhiali di tartaruga" (big tortoise glasses) that at night Montale used to take off her and place near her analgesics: "che a notte ti tolgo e avvicino | alle fiale della morfina" (that at night I remove for you and put close | to your morphine's phials) ("Ballata scritta in una clinica," *La bufera e altro*, 16–19). Now Mosca appears without her glasses: "sei ricomparsa accanto a me, | ma non avevi occhiali" (you reappeared beside me, | but you did not have glasses) (*Xenia* I.1, 5–6). Without this symbol of identification, they cannot see each other: "non potevi vedermi | né potevo io senza quel luccichìo | riconoscere te nella foschia" (you couldn't see me | nor could I, without that sparkle, | recognize you in the haze) (*Xenia* I.1, 7–9). Here the dead Mosca emerges from some other unspecified place enveloped by a mist that recalls the bride of Hades. This fog is also the fog into which Petrarch's Laura vanishes in "Canzone delle visioni" (*Canzone* 323) enveloped "d'una nebbia oscura" (of a dark fog) in the so-called "stanza di Euridice" ("Standomi un giorno solo a la fenestra," *Canzoniere*, 68).[19] Eurydice herself in Virgil's *Georgics* was enveloped by darkness and condemned to disappear into shadow: "ex oculis subito, ceu fumus in auras | . . . fugit diversa" (*Georgics*, IV, 499–500). Montale himself reminds the reader that "c'è nebbia e fumo nell'aldilà" (there is fog and smoke in the underworld) ("Tergi gli occhiali appannati . . . ," *Altri versi*, 2). Furthermore, it is noteworthy that "afterlife"—"aldilà"—is one of the main lemmas in *Xenia*. Mosca-Eurydice is here summoned up to earthly life, but the poet soon becomes aware that the death of his beloved is final. Mosca, just like the other feral female figures, belongs to the underworld, that "oscura regione ove scend[ono]" (the dark region where they descend) ("Delta," *Ossi di seppia*, 8).

That Mosca belongs to this dark region is suggested throughout *Xenia*, as well as in other poems outside the two series included in *Satura*. One interesting case is to be found in the *xenion* II.6 where Montale reports an ironic exchange between Mosca and a "vinattiere" (barkeeper):

> Il vinattiere ti versava un poco
> d'Inferno. E tu atterrita: "Devo berlo? Non basta
> esserci stati dentro a lento fuoco?"

> (The barkeeper was pouring a little bit
> of Hell. And you petrified: "Should I drink it? Is it not enough
> to have been inside on slow fire?")
> (*Xenia* II.6)

"Inferno" is the name of a wine from Valtellina, a valley in the north of Italy at the border with Switzerland. On one level the *calembour* recalls Montale's conception of the "morte-in-vita" (death-in-life), something that is in tune with Mosca's health issues as presented in "Ballata scritta in una clinica." On another level, however, the reader cannot stop reading those lines a second time resulting in a much more literal interpretation: Mosca and the underworld are not strangers to each other. Mosca is a chthonian maiden. A second instance where Mosca emerges as a feral maiden is to be found in "Luci e colori," which does not belong to *Xenia*, but nevertheless belongs to what I would call a third series of *Xenia* traceable in the remaining two sections of *Satura* as well as part of the final triptych dedicated to Mosca formed by "Nel silenzio," "Luci e colori," and "Il grillo di Strasburgo nottuno col suo trapano."[20] In "Luci e colori," Mosca is said to have "gli occhi un po' gonfi di chi ha veduto" (swollen eyes of someone who has seen [line 2]). Clearly, these swollen eyes are those of someone who has seen the underworld.[21] In this poem it is also possible to find again the "foschia" (mist [line 5]). Once more, Mosca is presented to the reader as belonging to that "oscura regione" (obscure region) as do Esterina, Arletta, as well as other well-known Eury-dice-Persephone figures such as Petrarch's Laura, herself a contradictory figure who defies categorization.

Just as one finds a modern transposition of these chthonic muses descend-ing into the underworld through the "scale automatiche" (escalators) ("Gli uomini che si voltano," *Satura*, 15),[22] so the fog and mist that belong to that "oscura regione" (obscure region) are evoked by the "fumo" (smoke) in the train station ("Nel fumo," *Satura*), which is perhaps the same smoke of "Tergi gli occhiali appannati" ("Tergi gli occhiali appannati . . . ," *Altri versi*, 2). Here, two observations are necessary: first the railway is a theme directly linked to Mosca throughout *Satura*;[23] second, and most importantly, the train stands for a means of transition from one place to another: perhaps to an *aldilà*? Mosca, just like Esterina and Arletta, is caught and desired in that very moment of transition from one place to another. Here, at the train station, the poetic subject is awaiting Mosca "nel freddo, nella nebbia" (in the cold, and in the fog) ("Nel fumo," *Satura*, 2). The view of the train as a way of reaching the underworld is offered by Montale himself in one of his prose works. It is with a "tranvai" (tram) that in the short story "Sul limite" in *Farfalla di Dinard* the protagonist reaches the *aldilà* after dying in a car accident.[24] Here Montale even offers the reader a well-defined topography of the afterworld.

Mosca is also evoked in the act of descending to lower places, something that indirectly echoes the descent into the underworld:

> . . . e m'interruppi quando
> tu scivolasti vertiginosamente
> dentro la scala a chiocciola della Périgourdine
> e di laggiù ridesti a crepapelle.
>
> (. . . and I stopped when
> you slid down dizzily
> inside the Périgourdine's spiral stairs
> and from down there you bent over with laughter)
> ("La morte di Dio," *Satura*, 3–6)

With her characteristic laughter Mosca slides down. This "laggiù" (down there [line 6]), beneath the "scala a chiocciola" (spiral staircase [line 5]), can be associated with another lower place: the underworld. What emerges is that Mosca is either portrayed as descending to some obscure place, or, alterna-tively, she is represented on the threshold between life and death, in that space of transition between one place and another, in the "solco dell'emergenza" (in the wake of emergency) or "sul ciglio del crepaccio" (at the edge of the crevasse), where the crevasse stands for the doorstep that separates life from death (*Xenia* II.4, 8). Both scenarios bear the mythical *katabasis* of both Eurydice and Persephone, as well as their own. As a final note on "La morte di Dio," it is in the image of dying laughing, and the word "crepapelle" (dying skin) in particular ("La morte di Dio," *Satura*, 6) that it is possible to find a further feral element of this poem. The idiomatic expression of "ridere a crepapelle" (to split one's sides laughing/bend over with laughter) is synonymous with "morire dal ridere" or "scoppiare dal ridere" (to kill oneself laughing), and has an interesting etymological nature: it is composed by "crepare" (to die or to crack) and "pelle" (skin). Eating or, as in this case, laughing "a crepapelle" (oneself silly) means being unable to bear that act anymore. Here, the memory of Mosca's laughter, paradoxically a sign of her tireless vitality, is presented, masked by an idiomatic expression, as something that brings her close to death: to die laughing.[25]

One of the most celebrated poems that is rarely missing in any anthology is the *xenion* "Ho sceso, dandoti il braccio, almeno un milione di scale . . ." (*Xenia* II.5), where again one finds Mosca in the act of descending into lower places, but this time she is not alone, she is accompanied by her beloved Montale. Unlike our shared imaginary, with all its ideas of progress and life where that "lungo viaggio" (long voyage) (*Xenia* II.5, 3) could be more commonly pictured as a progressive movement upward toward higher places, here Montale and Mosca are trapped in following the path of their lives by descending millions of stairs. The poem opens with the image of the poetic subject giving his arm to Mosca suggesting a source of support: "dandoti il braccio" (giving you my arm [line 1]). Soon, however, it emerges that the real guide is not the poetic subject, but Mosca herself and now that she is not there with him any longer it is "il vuoto ad ogni gradino" (emptiness at each step [line 2]). Or similarly as the poem closes:

> Ho sceso milioni di scale dandoti il braccio
> non già perché con quattr'occhi forse si vede di più.
> Con te le ho scese perché sapevo che di noi due
> le sole vere pupille, sebbene tanto offuscate,
> erano le tue.

> (I went down a million stairs, giving you my arm
> not because with four eyes perhaps we see better.
> With you I descended those stairs because I knew that of the two of us
> the only true pupils, though so clouded over,
> were yours.)
> (*Xenia* II.5, 8–12)

Regardless of her strong myopia, her "grossi | occhiali di tartaruga" (big | tortoise glasses) ("Ballata scritta in una clinica," *La bufera e altro*, 16–17), and regardless of how much her eyes are "offuscat[i]" (clouded over [line 11]), it is Mosca who has the power of vision, the "vere pupille" (true pupils [line 11]). There is a tendency to read all this in mere contrast with the almost divine "chiaroveggenza" (clairvoyance) of Clizia as opposed to Mosca's more earthly faculty of vision.[26] I would argue instead that the much more earthly figure of Mosca as compared to the angelic figure of Clizia has a power of vision not just of earthly reality, but of the underworld as well. Caught in all her oxymoronic essence, which is also a constitutive element and marks the stylistic specificity of *Xenia* as well as some parts of *Satura* as a whole, Mosca appears as the embodiment of contradiction itself as well as being able to deconstruct the tangles of reality: "Ti piaceva la vita fatta a pezzi, | quella che rompe dal suo insopportabile | orbito" (You liked life in pieces | the one that breaks at its unbearable | sphere) (*Xenia* II.12, 9–11). All this leads to elevating the ordinary Mosca to a superior being, and it is no surprise that without her it is "vuoto ad ogni gradino" (emptiness at each step) (*Xenia* II.5, 2). It is her, the regal Persephone, who can guide by holding the poet who entrusts his arm to her in this feral descending of "almeno un milione di scale" (at least one million stairs) (*Xenia* II.5, 1). In the mythical dimension within which the *io*-Orpheus and the Mosca-Eurydice find themselves, the female figure and the poet are united in the same Orphic action of descending. The female beloved then emerges as an indispensable companion for the poet in order to be able to undertake his own "altro cammino" (other path) ("Incontro," *Ossi di seppia*, 50), his *katabasis* into the underworld.

What emerges from Mosca's oxymoronic and chthonic nature is that she is clearly not a small-scale Clizia endowed with less remarkable capabilities. Even more evident now is how Mosca is not ascribable to the traditional category of the companion-woman into which she has often been dismissed. In her transcending of the traditional antithetical binary of transcendent/immanent woman that so profoundly characterizes the lyric tradition, Mosca represents for critics a chance to supersede this tendency toward categorization implicitly informed by some level of teleological urgency—that in this case echoes a Hegelian-like dialectical process. It is through the figure of Mosca that Montale opens up spaces for less linear, non-binary representations of female identity that transcend the traditional antithetical angelic/terrestrial dichotomy that goes back to Dante's Beatrice *versus* Petra and partly finds its modern reactivation in Clizia *versus* Volpe. With Mosca Montale embraces such contradiction. Mosca is a figure that guides the poetic subject similarly to Clizia, but she is also bound to earthly reality. Mosca's darker and more gloomy feminine essence is linked to the place in which she is condemned to reside: the underworld. Here lies her Eurydice-Persephone chthonic and feral nature.

By the time we turn to the third *xenion*, any possibility of a direct exchange or conversation with the deceased beloved is evidently no longer possible. The poetic subject becomes aware that Mosca can come back to life only in the moment of recollection, in the moment where her gestures and the places that are still instilled by her presence are remembered. It is in this way

that the past and its memories become the one and only possible dimension
to live in and it is in these memories that the poetic subject's object of love
can be found. The poetic subject searches for the past in the present of that
absence or in the absence of that present. It is in this way that poetry eventually becomes the only possible medium to invoke the female beloved's presence, something that necessarily ends in re-affirming her absence. It is precisely because of the impossibility of being in contact once again with the
object of love that the poetic subject is eventually marked, and profoundly
so, by the absence of his female beloved:

> . . . Forse che
> te n'eri andata
> così presto senza parlare?
> Ma è ridicolo
> pensare che tu avessi ancora labbra.
>
> (Could it be that
> you left
> so soon without saying a word?
> But it is absurd
> to think that you would still have lips.)
> (*Xenia* I.2, 7–10)

The poet here expresses his surprise at Mosca's too hasty visitation, without
even saying a word: "te n'eri andata | così presto senza parlare?" (you left | so
soon without saying a word? [lines 8–9]). Where she has gone is clear by
now: she went back to where she belongs, the *aldilà*. The poetic subject has
now recognized, with sorrow, that it is no surprise that the dead beloved did
not speak a word: she no longer has substance, she does not have lips to
voice herself, she is now pure essence. The poetic subject returns to this idea
in the concluding *xenion* of the first series: Mosca is now "non . . . più forma,
ma essenza" (no . . . longer form, but essence) (*Xenia* I.14, 4).

Mosca is now voiceless. The poetic subject will no longer hear Mosca
lamenting the antibiotics she has to take or the pain of her femur, nor the
everyday logistical problems of how to plan the summer holidays. These,
however, as the poetic subject highlights in *Xenia* I.12, will be the banal
things that he misses so strongly now that spring slowly approaches and it is
through the evocation of them that her presence emerges through a sort of
"reliquario privato" (private reliquary) that served as an "inventario dei [loro]
ricordi, l'unico filo che [li] lega dopo tant'acqua . . . passata sotto i ponti"
(inventory of [their] memories, the only thread that keeps [them] connected
after so much water passed under the bridge), something that we read in the
farfalla "Reliquie", but which so perfectly fits the two protagonists of *Xenia*
as well.[27] It is in fact precisely at this point when the poetic subject becomes
aware that Mosca's death is final that his loss too becomes permanent and the

io-Orpheus can finally mourn and lament to us, his readers, through his verses. Here lies the Orphic quality of Montale's *canzoniere in morte*.

Mosca no longer has "labbra" (*Xenia* I.2, 10): inevitably then, as the poetic subject highlights, her voice has "mutato l'accento" (changed accent) (*Xenia* I.8, 3):

> La tua parola così stenta e imprudente
> resta la sola di cui mi appago.
> Ma è mutato l'accento, altro il colore.
> Mi abituerò a sentirti o a decifrarti
> nel ticchettìo della telescrivente,
> nel volubile fumo dei miei sigari
> di Brisago.
>
> (Your word so weak and reckless
> remains the only one I can trust.
> But it changed its accent, altered its color.
> I will get used to hearing you and deciphering you
> in the ticking of the teletype,
> in the fickle smoke of my cigars
> of Brisago.)
> (*Xenia* I.8)

Montale will then not only write and speak *of* her, but *for* her: his writing is the way to give voice to her, to hear her voice one more time. This is the reason why Mosca's voice enters Montale's poetic voice. But this is also the reason why the reader will never be able to hear Mosca-Eurydice, but only Montale-Orpheus retelling her story, voicing her: there is no possibility of hearing Mosca's voice. Mosca cannot speak herself, and it is important to see this within Cavarero's already-mentioned interpretation of the myth of Orpheus and Eurydice especially as it allows us to shed further light on the gender dynamics at play in this myth. This is something that will be preserved in lyric poetry for centuries from Dante, Petrarch, and Leopardi to Montale, and beyond. It is noteworthy that Mosca is here evoked by the persistent repetition of the pronoun "tu" (you) and the sound of this pronoun itself functions as the sound of the "ticchettìo della telescrivente" (ticking of the teletype) (*Xenia* I.8, 5).[28] This echoes what happens in Petrarch's *Canzoniere*, where the name of Laura keeps returning phonetically throughout the lines in a sort of "introiezione linguistica e di nominazione dissimulata che rende onnipresente la donna proprio quando è sottratta alla presenza fisica individuata" (a linguistic introjection and a dissimulated nomination that makes the beloved woman omnipresent precisely when she is subtracted from her physical presence).[29] "Che farò senza Euridice?" (What will I do without Euridice?).[30] This is the exclamation by Gluck's Orpheus in the well-known *aria*. Or, before that, "Quid faceret?" as Virgil's Orpheus asked himself in the *Georgics* (IV, 507). This seems to be the same question that haunts the poetic subject throughout the two series of *Xenia* as well. The moment of loss seems to coincide with the eventual possibility of being able to abandon oneself, voluntarily, to the sublime song of Orpheus. In losing Mosca the poetic subject is finally able to acquire a new poetic voice, but in taking possession of Mosca's own voice, the poetic subject makes her silent forever. Her voice echoes throughout those pages only through the pen of her male poet-creator. She is powerless, voiceless, without form. Still poetry "diventa un'invocazione alla presenza che, proprio in quanto parola invocante, istituisce e rinnova l'assenza" (becomes an invocation to presence, that, precisely in its being an invoking word, establishes and renews the absence).[31] Moreover, just as in Gluck's *aria*, one can hear Orpheus lamenting repetition, his invocation of his beloved's name: "Euridice! Euridice!" This similarly functions as the iconic triple invocation of the name of Eurydice in the *Georgics* (IV, 525–27), which stresses the difficulty in recalling the lost beloved back to life. Montale's hammering, obsessive repetition of the pronoun "tu" (you) throughout *Xenia*, as well as the moment in which he highlights the absence of a reply from Mosca, are there as a powerful denouncement of her irrevocable disappearance. In lacking a reply (*Xenia* I.2, 7–9), in the absence of her voice (*Xenia* I.1, 10–11), of her irreverent laughter (*Xenia* I.11, 2), in the absence of her *parola*, of her "parola così stenta e imprudente" (word so weak and reckless) (*Xenia* I.8, 1), we have the ultimate attestation of her absence. Mosca is without "labbra" (lips) (*Xenia* I.2, 10), she is now "non . . . più forma, ma essenza" (no . . . longer form, but essence) (*Xenia* I.14, 4), she now belongs to Montale's "care ombre" (dear shadows) ("Proda di Versilia," *La bufera e altro*, 33). This sustains the view that the female poetic beloved, as is often the case in lyric poetry, becomes a *pretext* for the development and articulation of the male poet-creator's *text* (and self). It is through the monologue (or dialogue *in absentia*) that the poet-creator establishes with the female *other* that a process of elaboration of his own self becomes possible. This is after all an aspect at the core of the Orphic myth as well.

To conclude, by highlighting the chthonic essence of Mosca, it has emerged that the feminine in Montale also belongs to darker and feral spaces not previously considered. From this standpoint, the traditional model of the angelic/salvific/transcendent woman and its counterpart of the monstrous/earthly/erotic woman, as embodied, for instance, in Clizia and Volpe respectively, appears limiting in so far as it does not account for the fundamental feral femininity that plays such a crucial role and that allows us to reach a more complete understanding of Montale's female figures, particularly Mosca, as well as Esterina and Arletta/Annetta. Mosca has allowed us to step into the darker abyss of Montale's poetic (under)world where the much more gloomy essence of the feminine as embodied by some of Montale's chthonic female figures resides, something no longer left unexplored. The Eurydice-

Persephone archetype of the absent, voiceless female beloved appears as the only medium to access that "beyond," that "Niente," (Nothingness) with which the poetic subject seeks to be put in dialogue, and where she is condemned to disappear. From this perspective the female figure is the pretext for the poet(ic subject)'s text. The "text," this *post mortem* narrative, finds its legitimization in the absence of the female beloved. Moreover, the story the reader is told is not so much that of Mosca-Eurydice, but rather of that of the male poet-creator-Orpheus. What we actually hear is the "ticchettìo della telescrivente" (ticking of the teletype) (*Xenia* I.8, 5) and not her voice. Once again, Eurydice is powerless and her fate and the telling of her story are in the hands of someone else. Here lies the fundamental Eurydice-Persephone nature of Mosca in *Xenia*, and *Satura* overall. The long-lasting Orphic tradition to which Cavarero refers and that needs the loved woman to be a dead woman is then the only way for the male poet to engage with the "beyond." Montale finds himself within this poetic tradition and, although he makes Mosca the most earthly female figure of his poetry making it difficult to pin her down to preconceived categories, he is not able to overcome this lyric model that goes back to Petrarch, passes through Leopardi and continues into the twentieth century. Herein lies the significance of the myths of Orpheus and Eurydice and the myth of Persephone in Montale's *Xenia*.

NOTES

1. Giusi Baldissone's classification of Montale's female figures is symptomatic and representative of this tendency toward categorization. In her *Le muse di Montale* she argues that "[l]e donne montaliane sono sostanzialmente raggruppabili in tre tipologie: la donna superiore (angiole stilnoviste), la donna mostruosa (o barbuta), la donna complice e sorella" (Montalean female figures can be categorized in three typologies: the superior woman (stilnovistic angelic figures), the monstrous woman (or bearded), and the companion-like woman or sister). Giusi Baldissone, *Le muse di Montale: Galleria di occasioni femminili nella poesia montaliana* (Novara: Interlinea, 1996), 8.

2. My understanding of the Eurydice-Persephone archetype finds its roots in Emanuela Tandello, "Between Tradition and Transgression: Amelia Rosselli's Petrarch," in *Petrarch in Britain. Interpreters, Imitators, and Translators over 700 years*, ed. Martin McLaughlin and Letizia Panizza, with Peter Hainsworth (Oxford: Oxford University Press for the British Academy, 2007).

3. Virgil, *Georgics*, trans. by Peter Fallon, ed. Elaine Fanthan (Oxford: Oxford University Press, 2009), IV, 458.

4. The most significant reading of Arletta as embodying the Eurydice-Persephone archetype is to be found in Gilberto Lonardi, "Mito e 'Melos' per Arletta: 'Punta del Mesco,'" in *Il fiore dell'addio: Leonora, Manrico e altri fantasmi del melodramma nella poesia di Montale* (Bologna: Il Mulino, 2003).

5. See Francesco Giusti, "Le parole di Orfeo: Dante, Petrarca, Leopardi, e gli archetipi di un genere," *Italian Studies* 64 (2009); Francesco Giusti, "Poesia e performance del lutto," *Mantichora* 1 (2011).

6. Francesco Giusti, "Parlando la Lingua della Mosca: Gli *Xenia* e la Morte tra Dimensione Domestica e Trauma Epistemologico," *MLN* 124 (2009): 240. See also Francesco Giusti, *Canzonieri in morte: Per un'etica poetica del lutto* (L'Aquila: Textus Edizioni, 2015).

7. Maria Antonietta Grignani, *Prologhi ed epiloghi: Sulla poesia di Eugenio Montale. Con una prosa inedita* (Ravenna: Longo Editore, 1987), 31.

8. All quotations from Eugenio Montale's works in Italian are from Montale, *Tutte le poesie*, ed. Giorgio Zampa (Milan: Mondadori, 1984) and they are reproduced here by kind permission of the publisher Mondadori (1984, Arnoldo Mondadori SpA, Milano; 2015 Mondadori Libri SpA, Milano). All translations from English to Italian are mine, except where indicated otherwise. I would like to thank Jennifer Rushworth and Julia Caterina Hartley for their assistance with the translations of Montale's poems, as well as for their attentive reading and valuable feedback on this chapter.

9. Annalisa Cima, "Le reazioni di Montale," in *Eugenio Montale*, ed. Annalisa Cima and Cesare Segre (Milan: Rizzoli, 1977), 193.

10. Echoing Baldissone, Riccardo Castellana wrongly dismisses Mosca based on the fact that her superior vision takes place only in the everyday: "Mosca—grazie al suo 'radar di pipistrello'—sa infatti vedere oltre la superficie delle cose e si conferma come erede della chiarovveggenza di Clizia (ma al tempo stesso il valore di quel dono è diminuito perché ha corso solo nella quotidianità)" (Mosca—thanks to her "bat's radar"—knows how to see beyond the surface of things and confirms herself as heir to Clizia's vision [but at the same time the value of this gift is reduced as it can only occur within the everyday]). As cited in Montale, *Satura*, ed. Riccardo Castellana (Milan: Mondadori, 2009), 60.

11. On how the "ossimoro" emerges in *Xenia* and other poems dedicated to Mosca as a constitutive element of reality, see Francesco Giusti, "Parlando la Lingua della Mosca: Gli *Xenia* e la Morte tra Dimensione Domestica e Trauma Epistemologico," *MLN* 124 (2009): 236–53.

12. Adriana Cavarero, *Tu che mi guardi, tu che mi racconti: Filosofia della narrazione* (Milan: Feltrinelli, 2011), 131. English translation by Paul A. Kottman as reproduced in Adriana Cavarero, *Relating Narratives: Storytelling and Selfhood* (London: Routledge, 2000), 101.

13. Cavarero, *Tu che mi guardi, tu che mi racconti*, 131; Cavarero, *Relating Narratives*, 101.

14. Cavarero, *Tu che mi guardi, tu che mi racconti*, 121; Cavarero, *Relating Narratives*, 94.

15. I borrow the terms "pretext" and "text" from Rebecca West as she employs them in her essay "Wives and Lovers in Dante and Eugenio Montale," in *Metamorphosing Dante: Appropriations, Manipulations, and Rewritings in the Twentieth and Twenty-First Centuries*, ed. Manuele Gragnolati, Fabio Camilletti, and Fabian Lampart (Vienna-Berlin: Verlag Turia + Kant, 2011).

16. Franco Fortini, "*Satura* nel 1971," in *Nuovi saggi italiani* (Milan: Garzanti, 1987), 103.

17. There are no references to Gemma throughout Dante's works, and the few wives in his work are mainly secondary characters with the only exception of the adulterous-wife figure of Francesca. The exclusion of the figure of the wife within modern Italian love poetry persists with only few exceptions, such as Umberto Saba, Edoardo Sanguineti, and a few others who wrote wonderful pages with their wives as their primary subject.

18. Esterina's scopophilic portrayal in "Falsetto" (*Ossi di seppia*) captures her in the moment when she takes the plunge away from the poetic subject. Similarly Mosca stands in front of a crevasse in a precarious balance between life and death (*Xenia* II.4, 8).

19. Francesco Petrarca, *Canzoniere*, ed. Gianfranco Contini (Turin: Einaudi, 1993). See also Marco Santagata, "Il lutto dell'umanista," in *Amate e amanti. Figure della lirica amorosa fra Dante e Petrarca* (Bologna: Il Mulino, 1999).

20. It is possible to identify a third series of *Xenia* spread throughout the second part of *Satura*, to which the poems dedicated to Mosca belong, namely, "La morte di Dio," "Nel fumo," "Lettera," "Piove," "Gli ultimi spari," "Le revenant," "Cielo e terra," "A pianterreno," "Pasqua senza week-end," "Il repertorio," "Nel silenzio," "Luci e colori," and "Il grillo di Strasburgo notturno col suo trapano."

21. See Montale's "note d'autore" in *Poésies IV. Satura (1962–1970)*, trans. Patrice Dyeral Angelini (Paris: Gallimard, 1976), 306.

22. The mysterious G. B. H. leaves the scene set in London "sui gradini automatici che ti slittano in giù . . ." (on the steps of the escalator that slide you down . . .) ("Di un natale metropolitano," *La bufera e altro*, 12), and similarly: "Scenderai | sulle scale automatiche dei

templi di Mercurio tra cadaveri in maschera" (You will descend | on the escalators of Mercury's temples among masked corpses) ("Gli uomini che si voltano," *Satura*, 14–15).

23. See Pierluigi Pellini, "L'ultimo Montale: Donne miracoli treni telefoni sciopero generale," in *Le toppe della poesia. Saggi su Montale, Sereni, Fortini, Orelli* (Manziana, Rome: Vecchiarelli Editore, 2004).

24. Montale, "Sul limite," in *Farfalla di Dinard*, in *Prose e Racconti*, ed. Marco Forti (Milan: Mondadori, 1995), 187–92.

25. Mosca's irreverent laughter recalls the similarly joyful and disruptive laughter of Hélène Cixous' Medusa as portrayed in her "The Laugh of Medusa." Esterina as well is portrayed as laughing, just before she hurls herself into the sea. Arletta too is represented as laughing in "Cigola la carrucola del pozzo, . . .": "Trema un ricordo nel ricolmo secchio, | nel puro cerchio un'immagine ride" (Trembles a memory in the full pail, | in the pure circle an image smiles) (*Ossi di seppia*, 3–4). Hélène Cixous, "The Laugh of Medusa," trans. Keith Cohen and Paula Cohen, *Signs*, 1:4 (1976).

26. See Castellana's comments as already cited in footnote 10.

27. Montale, "Reliquie," in *Farfalla di Dinard*, 144–47 (145).

28. Giusti, *Canzonieri in morte*, 105. See also Stefano Agosti, "Forme trans-comunicative in *Xenia*," in *Il testo poetico: Teoria e pratiche d'analisi* (Milan: Rizzoli, 1972).

29. Giusti, *Canzonieri in morte*, 106. See especially his footnote number 137.

30. *Orfeo ed Euridice* (1762), by Christoph Willibald von Gluck; see Christoph Willibald von Gluck, *Orfeo ed Euridice: Opera in tre atti*, libretto by Ranieri de' Calzabigi (Milan: Ricordi, 1952).

31. Giusti, *Canzonieri in morte*, 40.

WORKS CITED

Agosti, Stefano. "Forme trans-comunicative in *Xenia*." In *Il testo poetico: Teoria e pratiche d'analisi*, 193–207. Milan: Rizzoli, 1972.

Arvigo, Tiziana. *Guida alla lettura di Montale: Ossi di seppia*. Rome: Carrocci, 2001.

Baldissone, Giusi. *Le muse di Montale: Galleria di occasioni femminili nella poesia montaliana*. Novara: Interlinea, 1996.

Bárberi Squarotti, Giorgio. "Su Montale." In *Gli Inferi e il Labirinto: Da Pascoli a Montale*, 193–268. Bologna: Cappelli, 1974.

Cavarero, Adriana. *Tu che mi guardi, tu che mi racconti: Filosofia della narrazione*. Milan: Feltrinelli, 2011; in English as *Relating Narratives: Storytelling and Selfhood*, trans. by Paul A. Kottman. London: Routledge, 1997.

Cima, Annalisa. "Le reazioni di Montale." In *Eugenio Montale*, edited by Annalisa Cima and Cesare Segre, 192–201. Milan: Rizzoli, 1977.

Cixous, Hélène. "The Laugh of Medusa," translated by Keith Cohen and Paula Cohen, *Signs*, 1:4 (1976): 875–93.

Fortini, Franco. "*Satura* nel 1971." In *Nuovi saggi italiani*, 103–24. Milan: Garzanti, 1987.

Giusti, Francesco. *Canzonieri in morte: Per un'etica poetica del lutto*. L'Aquila: Textus Edizioni, 2015.

———. "Parlando la Lingua della Mosca: Gli *Xenia* e la Morte tra Dimensione Domestica e Trauma Epistemologico," *MLN* 124 (2009): 236–53.

———. "Le parole di Orfeo: Dante, Petrarca, Leopardi, e gli archetipi di un genere." *Italian Studies* 64 (2009): 56–76.

———. "Poesia e performance del lutto," *Mantichora* 1 (2011): 350–63.

Gluck, Christoph Willibald. *Orfeo ed Euridice: Opera in tre atti*, libretto by Ranieri de' Calzabigi. Milan: Ricordi, 1952.

Grignani, Maria Antonietta. *Prologhi ed epiloghi: Sulla poesia di Eugenio Montale: Con una prosa inedita*. Ravenna: Longo Editore, 1987.

Lonardi, Gilberto. "Mito e 'Melos' per Arletta: 'Punta del Mesco,'" in *Il fiore dell'addio. Leonora, Manrico e altri fantasmi del melodramma nella poesia di Montale*, 139–59. Bologna: Il Mulino, 2003.

Montale, Eugenio. *La casa di Olgiate e altre poesie*, ed. Renzo Cremante and Gianfranca Lavezzi. Milan: Mondadori, 2006.

―――. *Poésies IV. Satura (1962-1970)*, trans. Patrice Dyeral Angelini. Paris: Gallimard, 1976.

―――. *Prose e Racconti*, ed. Marco Forti. Milan: Mondadori, 1995.

―――. *Satura*, ed. Riccardo Castellana. Milan: Mondadori, 2009.

―――. *Sulla poesia*, ed. Giorgio Zampa. Milan: Mondadori, 1976.

―――. *Tutte le poesie*, ed. Giorgio Zampa. Milan: Mondadori, 1984.

Nascimbeni, Giulio. *Montale, biografia di un poeta*. Milan: Longanesi, 1986.

Pellini, Pierluigi. "L'ultimo Montale: Donne miracoli treni telefoni sciopero generale," in *Le toppe della poesia. Saggi su Montale, Sereni, Fortini, Orelli*, 13–49. Manziana, Rome: Vecchiarelli Editore, 2004.

Petrarca, Francesco. *Canzoniere*, ed. Gianfranco Contini. Turin: Einaudi, 1993.

Santagata, Marco. "Il lutto dell'umanista," in *Amate e amanti: Figure della lirica amorosa fra Dante e Petrarca*, 195–221. Bologna: Il Mulino, 1999.

Tandello, Emanuela, "Between Tradition and Transgression: Amelia Rosselli's Petrarch," in *Petrarch in Britain: Interpreters, Imitators, and Translators over 700 years*, ed. by Martin McLaughlin and Letizia Panizza, with Peter Hainsworth, 301–17. Oxford: Oxford University Press for the British Academy, 2007.

West, Rebecca. *Metamorphosing Dante: Appropriations, Manipulations, and Rewritings in the Twentieth and Twenty-First Centuries*, edited by Manuele Gragnolati, Fabio Camilletti, and Fabian Lampart, 201–11. Vienna-Berlin: Verlag Turia + Kant, 2011.

Chapter Three

Repressed Memory and Traumatic History in Alberto Moravia's *The Woman of Rome*

Charles L. Leavitt IV

Alberto Moravia traced the origin of *The Woman of Rome* (*La Romana*, 1948) to a memory. Although he started to write the novel in late 1946, he located the project's true beginning a decade earlier, in 1936, in a fateful encounter on the streets of Rome. "I found myself in Largo Tritone with Leo Longanesi, after a typically boring evening in Rome, and all of a sudden I saw a woman who seemed to be a streetwalker," he recounted to his biographer, Alain Elkann.

> She didn't appear to be a day over twenty, and she was very beautiful. I said to Leo: "I like that girl, I've got to go." And I approached her: "Where should we go?" "To my house." She brought me to a small and modest apartment in an alley behind the *Messaggero* building. As we entered I realized it was the house where she lived with her family. At a certain point she was nude, she had a splendid body, and she reminded me of a strange short story by Henry James, "The Last of the Valerii," in which a man falls in love with a statue. Then all of a sudden an old woman entered with a pitcher of warm water and a towel, and she said with pride: "Tell me, have you ever seen a body like this, take a look, have you ever seen such a thing . . ." We made love in a sound and simple manner. Afterwards she said to me: "The woman who came with the towel was my mother." That's the story of my encounter with the woman who ten years later would inspire the protagonist of *The Woman of Rome*.[1]

In sharing this memory, it is clear, Moravia sought to draw his biographer's attention not only to the sensual details of his erotic encounter but also to the fecundity of his creative imagination. "At this point I'd like to offer a reflection on how inspiration can shine through," he thus told Elkann:

> As I said, my encounter with the girl lasted an hour, but the phrase "that was my mother" lasted no more than a few seconds. It might be a Romantic touchstone, but so be it: that phrase had the flash and effect of a lightning-bolt in a thunderstorm: it revealed to me an entire human panorama that a sociologist would need a whole book of reflections adequately to explain and to illustrate. More simply, I would say that the phrase "struck me," that is it traumatized me. Then I must have undergone what psychologists call repression. That repression, as I've already said, lasted ten years before collapsing the morning of November 1st, 1946, as soon as I sat down at the typewriter with the idea of dashing off a short story about the relationship between a Roman mother and her daughter. Instead I went ahead for four months working away at the typewriter and on February 28, 1948, I had a novel of 550 pages to which I gave the title *The Woman of Rome*, suggested to me by Elsa [Morante].[2]

Moravia's idea for a short story, this explanation makes evident, was inflected with his memory of the prostitute's laconic reconciliation of the erotic and the domestic, which transformed his initial inspiration into something far more significant. Put simply, the act of writing had inspired his recovery of a repressed memory, and that recovery in turn had inspired his literary invention.

It is the link between Moravia's memory and his inspiration that I wish to explore in this essay. *The Woman of Rome*'s apparent debts to its author's dalliance in an apartment behind the *Messaggero* building are suggestive, and the narrative yields some unexpected insights when it is approached with that encounter in mind. Yet the novel cannot be said straightforwardly or faithfully to rehearse the story that Moravia recounted to Elkann, and the differences, too, are worth contemplating. Ultimately, I am convinced, what distinguishes Moravia's text from his memory is the author's experience of Italian history. The end of the Second Italo-Abyssinian War, as well as World War II, stood between Moravia's rendezvous with the prostitute and his composition of *The Woman of Rome*. Returning to his traumatic memory, therefore, he was also necessarily recalling to mind the historical traumas of Fascism. In turn, I want to argue, in composing his novel he was attempting to redress the twinned traumas of history and memory.

One month after he began work on *The Woman of Rome* Moravia reflected on a different—but I will argue related—memory: his "Ricordi di censura," which offered something more than the "Memories of Censorship" that the essay's title announced.[3] In point of fact, Moravia here shared his experience, and his pointed criticism, not only of the restrictions imposed by

Mussolini's regime but also of the political predispositions and cultural prejudices that had led average Italians to support that regime in its totalitarian rule. Suspected for his Jewish origins, his familial ties to the exiled political dissidents Carlo and Nello Rosselli, and his friendship with noted anti-Fascists in Italy, Moravia had found himself the frequent target of Fascist censors, who suppressed his 1935 novel *Wheel of Fortune* (*Le ambizioni sbagliate*), ousted him from his posts at several prominent cultural journals, and forced him to adopt a series of pseudonyms when he wrote for others.[4] He had ample reason, therefore, to decry the machinations of the Italian Ministry of Popular Culture. Yet he reserved his greatest condemnation for the attitudes of the Italian populace. "Blame for the situation cannot entirely be attributed either to Mussolini or to the Fascists," he maintained, "but rather to the ruling class or the bourgeoisie who conserved (when they conserved) the aesthetics, ideologies, and hierarchies of the previous century, insisting on imposing them with force."[5] Behind the institutions of Fascist censorship, in other words, Moravia identified the predilections of Italian high society. "The bourgeoisie in those years had suppressed any suspicion, any criticism, any skepticism about itself," he argued, "seeking only to enjoy a serene existence inspired by the most vulgar hedonism."[6] Discomfited by modernity—indeed, discomfited by reality itself—the bourgeoisie, Moravia believed, had sought to impose strict limits on Italian culture, denying the spread of information in an attempt to deny truths that it was unprepared to face. He therefore insisted that the censorship imposed by Fascism was intended to facilitate the flight from reality of a social class for whom "the truth, *tout court*, was unhealthy."[7]

Framing the argument in this way, Moravia was able persuasively to draw on his memories of Fascist censorship in order to further his ongoing investigation of the habits and quirks of the Italian ruling classes, which he had been conducting at least since his 1929 debut novel, *The Time of Indifference* (*Gli indifferenti*).[8] Building on that earlier work, the author began after the war effectively to redirect his investigation of bourgeois behavior, devoting his attention to what he now saw as the symptoms of that class's congenital Fascism. Moravia was far from the only critic to condemn Fascism as a bourgeois phenomenon; this was a cultural commonplace, in fact, as well as a central tenet of Marxist doctrine.[9] While drawing on this doctrine, Moravia shaped it to his own ends, conducting a cultural rather than a structural or economic critique of bourgeois society, emphasizing the inclinations toward authoritarianism inherent in bourgeois norms, and positing a causal relationship between the peccadilloes of the Italian ruling classes and the ascension of the Italian Fascist regime.[10] He was thus able largely to maintain the fastidious social investigations that he had begun before the war while claiming for them an increased political significance, since the defects in bourgeois behavior were now understood to have engendered the worst excesses of the totalitarian state.

In his most far-reaching treatment of the connections between (bourgeois) culture and (Fascist) politics, 1947's "La borghesia" (The Bourgeoisie)," Moravia traced what he saw as the dire consequences of the reflexive traditionalism of the Italian ruling classes. As he put it, "Fascism is above all that spirit of small-minded conservatism, ungenerous and opposed to every ideal through which we made known the first cause of all the deficiencies of our bourgeoisie."[11] The attitudes of the ruling classes, Moravia thus forcefully asserted, not only stultified Italian culture but also quickened Mussolini's rise to power. This was an argument Moravia developed with particular acuity in analyzing what he termed "L'impermeabilità degli italiani" (The Impermeability of the Italians): the refusal of the Italian people, and in particular the Italian ruling classes, to countenance even the most salutary social change.[12] Instead of acknowledging that modernity entailed a natural and necessary evolution of the social order, he argued, they sought to shut out reality, deliberately retarding the development of Italian culture by upholding obsolete values and venerating—indeed rigidly enforcing—retrograde tastes, in order to preclude all but the most minimal of transformations. Fascism was the ineluctable result of this reactionary intransigence, since the bourgeoisie was prepared to implement censorship, even dictatorship, to shield its beliefs, customs, and traditions from a confrontation with contemporary reality. It was on these grounds that Moravia asserted a resolutely political imperative to what otherwise might have appeared merely a critical appraisal of bourgeois mores.

There is evidence to suggest that this imperative, in turn, provoked his recovery of the repressed memory that would inspire *The Woman of Rome*. The encounter with a Roman prostitute seems to have been recalled to mind, and more to the point imbued with additional political connotations, in light of Moravia's subsequent analysis of the bourgeoisie's responsibility for Fascism. Signs of the passage from critical reflection to political insight to creative expression can be traced with particular clarity through Moravia's 1947 essay "Dopoguerra bigotto" (Post-war Sanctimony), which explores the persistent censoriousness of Italian society even after the fall of Fascism, and which does so by means of a particularly telling reference. "The Italian bourgeoisie is the most ignorant and inconsequential bourgeoisie in the world," Moravia insisted in that essay.

> They do not read but want books to be confiscated; they do not go to church except on Sundays to make a show of their clothing and their worldliness, but they shout that Christian morality is in danger; they are entirely resistant to cultural influences, but they claim to believe that Sartre's books corrupt the soul. How many souls, then, are lost every day in countless brothels? Without

doubt those brothels, disgusting and barbaric places, have infinitely more regular clients than Sartre has readers. All this uproar regarding two- or three-thousand copies sold and profound silence regarding the twenty- or thirty-thousand visits to the brothels. [13]

Prostitution thus came to exemplify for Moravia the fundamental hypocrisy of the Italian ruling classes, who wanted to banish sex from the culture, forbidding its artistic representation and its mention in polite society, while turning a blind eye to the country's rampant prostitution, which would remain legal until the passage of the Merlin Law in 1958. Moravia's remembered encounter with the prostitute, and in particular his emphasis on the unapologetic candor of the girl's mother in contrast to his own demureness, should be read against his resonant critique of bourgeois hypocrisy.

It should likewise be read against another contemporary invocation of prostitution, this time from his 1946 essay "L'Uomo come fine" (Man as an End)," Moravia's jeremiad against the instrumentalization of human life inherent in modern society. "The world has been broken to pieces, and the brothel-keeper who sells the prostitutes' bodies for profit is every bit as justified in doing so as the head of State who declares war on another State," the author lamented in that essay.

> In the brothel, as in the State, reason reigns supreme inasmuch as the end, that is the preservation and prosperity of the brothel and the State, is attained with adequate means, that is with the means of man—with prostitution in one case and social and military discipline in the other. But in both the brothel and the State there reigns contempt for man, and the air is unbreathable. This is the fundamental characteristic of the modern world. [14]

In this passage, prostitution comes to symbolize something more than the hypocritical moralism of the Italian ruling classes; it now represents the quintessence of human exploitation. In Moravia's account, contemporary society—bourgeois society—strives to maintain the appearance of propriety, all the while ruthlessly disregarding any nontransactional values in the pursuit of profit, power, and expansion. We might interpret the author's self-described trauma at the memory of his encounter with the prostitute and her mother, therefore, as his recognition of the failure of solidarity at the heart of bourgeois culture. Indeed, all of *The Woman of Rome* can be interpreted in these terms, both as a representation of Moravia's indictment of the exploitation inherent in bourgeois social norms and as his emerging recognition of an alternative.

The key is to be found in the confluence of lived memory and literary intertextuality that underwrites *The Woman of Rome*'s penetrating analysis of Italian society under Fascism. [15] Indeed, it was this confluence that allowed

Moravia substantially to transform his furtive conversation with a Roman prostitute and her mother into the symbolic incarnation of—as well as the developing resistance to—bourgeois corruption and Fascist coercion. *The Woman of Rome*, after all, is the story of a Roman prostitute, Adriana, who recounts in the first person her downward trajectory from artist's model to sex worker—a trajectory set in motion, tellingly, by her mother—in a narrative that reveals the inevitable perversion of Italian society between the World Wars, but also Adriana's essential integrity, humility, and tenacity in the face of her systemic exploitation.

If the novel's debts to Moravia's remembered encounter in Largo Tritone are evident, so too are those to Defoe's *Moll Flanders*, with which *The Woman of Rome* shares its narrative conceit, as Moravia repeatedly insisted.[16] In its central moment, however, the turning point of Adriana's life story, *The Woman of Rome* is above all reminiscent of the tale of another literary prostitute: Guy de Maupassant's "Boule de suif." This was a remarkably influential work in postwar Italy, providing a frequent point of reference for artists seeking to dramatize the country's complex politics in the mid-twentieth century. For instance, soon after the liberation Luchino Visconti, Michelangelo Antonioni, Giuseppe De Santis, Antonio Pietrangeli, Gianni Puccini, Vasco Pratolini, and others collaborated on the screenplay for a Resistance film modeled on Maupassant's short story, which was, however, never realized.[17] Several years later, in preparing a treatment for his own Resistance film, to be titled *Viaggio in camion* (Truck Journey), Italo Calvino likewise drew on what he called "that formula which was already adopted by Maupassant in 'Boule de Suif' and by Ford in *Stagecoach*."[18] Beppe Fenoglio, too, appears to have patterned his 1952 Resistance narrative, *The Twenty-Three Days in the City of Alba* (*I ventitre giorni della città*), on Maupassant's work.[19]

It is clear why these authors were drawn to the story. "Boule de Suif," set in the immediate aftermath of France's defeat in the 1870 Franco-Prussian War, recounts the misadventures of several citizens from Rouen who stray into enemy territory during a stagecoach journey and are detained by a Prussian officer, who will only release them if one of their number, the prostitute Elisabeth Rousset, will sleep with him. Driven by her sense of personal and national dignity, Rousset repeatedly refuses his advances, but her purportedly respectable companions—a factory owner and his wife, a Comte and Comtesse, and two nuns—eventually succeed in pressuring her to sleep with the officer so that they can continue on to Le Havre. To its Italian admirers, this story of occupation, coercion, and social corruption presented a number of powerful analogies to the post-war climate that followed Fascism's defeat.

Moravia was among the first to explore these analogies, drawing cogent parallels between the contemporary Italian situation and that which faced Maupassant in the late nineteenth century in two seemingly little noticed but

highly instructive essays: 1944's "Paragone col secondo impero" (Comparison with the Second Empire) and 1945's "La carrozza di Maupassant" (Maupassant's Carriage). Moravia recognized in Maupassant's short story a mode
of implicit social commentary, one in which the interactions between various
classes and factions of a defeated society could be represented figuratively
but not mechanically in a work of fiction. In the various characters of "Boule
de Suif," Moravia identified symbolic embodiments of France's ruling
classes: "the French nobility, so proud and so ostentatious; . . . the haute
bourgeoisie, covetous of honors and positions, respectable and conservative; . . . the mercantile class, cunning, coarse, dishonest," as well as what he
called "the two faiths that divide France: Catholic" and "secular and democratic." Moreover, in the interactions between these representative individuals, Moravia isolated what he called Maupassant's

> moral argument: a reprehensible action . . . often becomes commendable be-
> cause of the thought that inspired it. That is: the ends justify the means. All
> this, without the backdrop of the lost war, would merely offer a general satire.
> But introduced into the broader context of the military disaster, it seems to
> imply a denunciation and an accusation, as if to say: here are those responsible
> for the defeat; here are the people who led France to its present state. The
> accusation and denunciation are not at all explicit, it is true; instead, they are
> suggested by the arrangement of the material and by the insistence on the
> characters' class status.[20]

Moravia thus traced in "Boule de Suif" Maupassant's indictment of the moral bankruptcy of the ruling classes, whose pretense to national loyalty had
been pulled away to reveal their venal expediency. In Moravia's reading, the
story demonstrated that the French leadership, while espousing high-minded
principles and demanding self-sacrificing obedience, was in reality driven by
a disreputable ideology of base consequentialism.

That reading, which chimes with Moravia's critique of the Italian bourgeoisie under Fascism, presents in condensed form the moral and social
analysis, as well as the fundamental narrative structure, of *The Woman of
Rome*. Like Maupassant's Elisabeth, Moravia's Adriana finds herself the
subject of unwanted sexual advances during a journey in the countryside, and
she too is coerced into acceding to her assailant by companions driven by
selfish ambition rather than by concern for her liberation. In *The Woman of
Rome*, this fateful event takes place during a drive from Rome to Viterbo, to
which Adriana—still a model and not yet a sex worker—has been invited by
her friend Gisella, an experienced escort, as well as one of Gisella's lovers,
Riccardo. The invitation is based on an initial deception, however, since
"Riccardo's friend," as the fourth companion on the journey is introduced, is
in fact the same "gentleman"—the same "very nice, decent fellow," Stefano
Astarita, "a big pot in the police"—to whom Gisella has been trying to

introduce Adriana, who has repeatedly refused to meet him.[21] "Come on! . . . What are you waiting for?" shout Gisella and Riccardo as Astarita gropes Adriana, who makes clear that his advances are entirely unwanted.[22] Describing herself as "entirely overcome," stressing her "sharp and lucid sensation of pain," and concluding that, after this assault, her "spirit was entirely changed," Adriana recounts her rape as a decisive moment in her formation, after which she would abandon her "once fresh and ingenuous hopes" and, with "a feeling of complicity and sensual conspiracy," would accept the money that Astarita had offered and begin her life as a prostitute.[23]

As in "Boule de Suif," the behavior of Adriana's companions is suggestive of debased tendencies in Italian society. Not for nothing did Giacomo Debenedetti, one of Moravia's most insightful readers, insist in an early review that "*The Woman of Rome* appears to reproduce a *Sacra Rappresentazione* (liturgical drama) in modern garb."[24] Each character who enters into Adriana's orbit can be seen to embody a particular Italian vice, and to do so precisely in the way that he or she responds to her rape and its aftermath. First, and perhaps most significantly, in light of Moravia's traumatic memory, is Adriana's mother, who has imparted in her daughter a kind of mercenary desire to use her beauty to escape poverty, and who thus accepts the girl's newfound wealth without asking too many questions. No less complicit is Gisella, whose envy of her friend's virtue compels her to debase Adriana, corrupting her so that her righteousness no longer stands as a rebuke. Like Gisella, Gino, Adriana's putative fiancé, who—like a perverted simulacrum of Vittorio De Sica's Bruno in Mario Camerini's 1932 *What Scoundrels Men Are! (Gli uomini, che mascalzoni!)*—has tricked the girl into a relationship by pretending to be a wealthy car owner rather than a lowly chauffeur, is both too dishonest and too jealous to be a reliable confidant.[25] Similarly, the businessman Giacinti, the client to whom Gisella next introduces Adriana after the affair with Astarita, cannot offer anything approaching human companionship, since he is so consumed by money that his every relationship must be purely transactional. Even the priest to whom Adriana first confesses what has happened can offer only spurious counsel, preferring as he does the semblance of propriety to genuine rectitude and thus falsely accusing the girl of giving in to avarice while at the same time advising her, against the entreaties of her conscience, not to return Astarita's money.

Above all, two characters come under particular scrutiny in the course of the novel. The first, for obvious reasons, is Astarita, the Fascist police officer who rapes Adriana, and whose remorse for his crime is offset by his prurient delight at the thought of stealing Adriana's innocence. It is Adriana herself who identifies the social and historical connotations of her tormentor's debauchery, expressing her suspicion that his

strange excitement at imagining me degraded by his own fault had been suggested to him by his profession as a member of the political police; his function, as far as I could understand, was to find the weak point in the accused,
and corrupt and humiliate them in such a way that they would be harmless ever
afterwards. He told me himself, I cannot remember in what connection, that
every time he succeeded in persuading an accused man to confess or break
down, he felt a peculiar kind of satisfaction, like the satisfaction of possession
in love. 'An accused man's like a woman,' he used to say, 'as long as she
resists she can hold her head up. But as soon as she has given way she's a rag
and you can have her again how and when you like.' But more probably his
cruel, complacent character was natural to him and he had chosen his profession simply because that was his character, and not the other way round. [26]

This passage lays bare the structure as well as the substance of the novel's
political critique. By employing rape as the governing allegory for his narrative of national degeneracy, Moravia adapted the central conceit of Maupassant's "Boule de Suif" to the context of Italian Fascism. [27] As this scene makes
clear, however, he also innovated upon this archetype by allowing his protagonist to perform her own allegoresis.

In Moravia's fiction, the prostitute not only embodies but also identifies
and analyzes the narrative's political connotations, recognizing—and forcing
the reader to recognize—how her rape incarnates Fascism's imposition of
authoritarian rule. Adriana thus takes on a kind of power over Moravia's text,
as well as over her assailant, by controlling the meaning of her assault,
making it both literal and metaphorical, and in this way marking Astarita as
both individual Fascist and the personification of Fascism.

She does something similar with Giacomo Diodati, the middle-class student and anti-Fascist activist with whom she has fallen in love, but whose
aromantic asexuality leaves her dissatisfied and alone. [28] Ineffectual both
erotically and politically, Giacomo presents a rather unflattering portrait of
the putative opposition to Fascism; divorced from physical reality, he cannot
offer a substantive solution to Adriana's concrete social struggles. Although
he tries to tutor her politically, he fails entirely to communicate anything of
value, since his abstract principles do nothing to respond to—or even to
acknowledge—her needs and desires. Again, it is Adriana who correctly
identifies the problem. "You want to educate me," she chides Giacomo, "but
the first condition for my education would be to free me of the necessity of
earning my living as I do." [29] A valid politics would aspire to free her from
prostitution. While Adriana wants a material improvement in her situation,
however, Giacomo offers only his empty political ideals. While Adriana
wants to escape from poverty, Giacomo offers only his hollow indictment of
bourgeois luxury. While Adriana wants no longer to sell her body for money,
Giacomo, one of her clients, offers only the disembodied reflections of his
theoretical treatises. Giacomo is helpless, therefore, against Astarita's vio-

lence, both that suffered by Adriana, in the rape at Viterbo, and that with which he believes himself to be threatened, once his meager resistance cell is discovered and he is arrested. More out of indifference than fear, he confesses everything to Astarita before ever being interrogated: his ideas, he tells Adriana in order to explain his lack of opposition, "suddenly didn't seem to matter at all." "Perhaps I only talked because it didn't matter to me whether I did or not—because everything suddenly seemed absurd and unimportant and I didn't understand any of the things I ought to have believed in."[30] Without any deeply felt convictions, without any deep-seated desires, he has no reserves of strength with which to combat his Fascist antagonist. Contrasting the impotent posturing of Giacomo with the sadistic devotion of Astarita, then, the narrative of *The Woman of Rome* offers an unstinting critique of bourgeois anti-Fascism.

It may also be understood to offer a critique of bourgeois culture. It is striking, in this regard, that the suicide letter Giacomo writes to Adriana before taking his own life in penance for his betrayal of the anti-Fascist cause echoes Moravia's critical appraisal of contemporary literary representation. Explaining his acquiescence to Astarita, to cite one resonant instance, Giacomo writes that "*at that moment . . . the character* [*personaggio*] *I ought to have been collapsed, and I was only the man* [*uomo*] *I really am*," reifying a dichotomy that Moravia had developed in his 1941 essay "L'uomo e il personaggio" (The Man and the Character)."[31] Moravia's point was that in the modern novel "the character is in danger of being eliminated in favor of exclusive interest in the writer."[32] Authors no longer sought to produce characters, Moravia was saying, but only to reproduce themselves. "This crisis in the character [personaggio] obviously corresponds to a similar crisis in the concept of man [uomo]," he therefore went on to explain, ascribing the limitations of literary representation to the limitations of contemporary reality, which was no longer conducive to the independent existence of the self-fashioning individual.[33] Giacomo's personal crisis, his failure to maintain his self-fashioned image as anti-Fascist intellectual in the face of social pressure, can thus be understood as a fictionalization of Moravia's critique of contemporary fiction, which lacks the capacity to fashion fully formed, independent individuals, and which thus fails substantially to represent reality. That critique, in turn, can be understood in political terms, since Moravia believed that the failure of fiction resulted from and also reinforced the deficiencies of the modern world, which it was helpless to combat.

Moravia's critique may thus be understood, additionally, as a critical self-assessment of his own literary project, especially given the form in which it is embodied in the narrative of *The Woman of Rome*. It is worth recalling, in this context, that Giacomo Diodati was not only the name of Adriana's lover but also one of the aliases under which Moravia was forced to publish during the Fascist *ventennio*.[34] It is worth recalling, too, that Moravia's visit to the

Roman prostitute, like that of his fictional doppelgänger, took place in 1936, "the year of the Abyssinian war," as Adriana identifies it in the course of the novel.[35] When Giacomo's political posturing is laid bare by Adriana's probing questions, therefore, the novel may also be holding up to scrutiny the self-identified shortcomings of its author. By the time of the encounter in Largo Tritone, after all, Moravia was seven years removed from the publication of *The Time of Indifference*, whose unmasking of the small-mindedness and dishonesty of the Italian bourgeoisie had made the author one of the most prominent social critics of his day. Yet the account of his dalliance with the prostitute suggests real limits to Moravia's bourgeois critique, contrasting his privilege with the girl's privations, his sexual hypocrisy with her unembarrassed sexuality. In short, Moravia's repressed memory suggests that, like Diodati, he remained an "anti-bourgeois bourgeois," wedded to his class even as he criticized it and, more damningly still, unable to envision a social order different from the status quo.[36] If *The Woman of Rome* shows Giacomo Diodati to be a failed anti-Fascist because he is unable to realize his fictional ideal, it may also imply that Moravia was guilty of a similar offense. Appearing to adopt Giacomo as his proxy—and the identification between author and character is precisely the limitation identified in "The Man and the Character"—Moravia may well have crafted his novel in such a way as to critique his fiction as well as his politics.

Yet if *The Woman of Rome*'s narrative can thus be understood to problematize aspects of Moravia's literary practice, it can also be seen to represent his realization of a solution to that same problem. The distance between the author's remembered encounter and the moment of literary composition is in this sense of the utmost significance. In writing *The Woman of Rome* Moravia was no longer the callow young man traumatized by the frankness of the prostitute's mother—he was, in other words, no longer Giacomo Diodati—and he could thus aspire to subject both his past self and his fictional double to critical investigation. More powerfully still, in so doing he could aim to critique the whole of Italian society under Fascism. The success of Moravia's fiction, we might therefore say, is predicated on its ability to demonstrate why Giacomo's fiction fails. Confronting Astarita, Giacomo is no longer able to maintain his fictional ideal, what he has earlier called "the world of 'as if,'" ceasing to believe any longer in his own words.[37] Moravia's fiction, in contrast, sought to represent that failure, and to hold it up for scrutiny. It sought to encompass Giacomo and his bourgeois alienation; Astarita and his Fascist perversion; the priest with his sanctimonious casuistry; Giacinti, with his cynical entitlement; Gino with his craven duplicity; Gisella with her shameless rivalry; Adriana's mother with her consequentialist morality. Above all, Moravia sought to encompass the experience of Adriana herself, making the Roman prostitute, rather than the bourgeois intellectual, the interpreter as well as the narrator of the text's socially symbolic events.

Attempting to transcend his limited viewpoint, in this way, and to embrace all of his representative characters in the manner of Maupassant's "Boule de Suif," Moravia sought to identify the characteristic inclinations of an entire society corrupted by Fascism. More significantly still, he sought to suggest the contours of a possible response.

In 1936, in the apartment of a Roman prostitute, Moravia experienced a moment of social dislocation, one that forced him to perceive the limits of his bourgeois experience: "it revealed to me an entire human panorama," we have seen him recount to his biographer, "that a sociologist would need a whole book of reflections adequately to explain and to illustrate."[38] *The Woman of Rome*, I would suggest, is precisely that "book of reflections," but filtered through a resolutely literary rather than a sociological sensibility. This is a crucial distinction, because it was Moravia's literary approach that allowed him not only to reclaim his repressed memory but also to redeem it, transforming the Roman prostitute into a potent cultural symbol.

Revisiting his repressed memory and reworking it into the narrative of *The Woman of Rome*, Moravia was able to recognize his experience as typical of a historical moment—indeed, as representative of a historical trauma. Not only, but he was also able to reexamine his experience from the prostitute's perspective, and by placing her at the center of an intertextual narrative he was able to discover something more than an apt symbol for Italy's traumatic history. Adriana is deprived, exploited, and assaulted, it is true, and in this way she can be said to stand in for a populace victimized by Italian Fascism.[39] Yet in her resiliency, and most pointedly in her hopeful resolution—that is, in the child she is expecting at the novel's conclusion—she suggests the persistence of an implicit popular sovereignty whose ingrained opposition to Fascism is far more potent than is Giacomo's idealized resistance. If the characters who betray and violate her can be said to represent incarnations of the ideologies that upheld Mussolini's Fascist regime, therefore, Adriana herself should not be taken merely as a representation of society's oppression by that regime. She also embodies an undertaking intrinsically opposed to the inescapable authoritarianism of the bourgeoisie.

Moravia imbued his Adriana with a host of figurative associations that lent her narrative—and her narrating voice—a profoundly transformative significance. That significance structures *The Woman of Rome*: as Adriana recounts her descent into prostitution she becomes Defoe's Moll Flanders; as she resists the descent into the depravity that perverts the surrounding society she becomes Maupassant's Elisabeth Rousset. This symbolic structure, moreover, is reinforced within Moravia's fiction, as each character imposes additional symbolic resonances onto the protagonist: in the eyes of the artist who first paints her Adriana recalls Danae, mother of Perseus; to her own mother she evokes Mary, mother of Jesus; to Giacomo she figures first as

Venus and then, most significantly, as Italy, that "loveliest of ladies [formo-sissima donna]" of Leopardi's poem.[40] The surfeit of literary symbolism the prostitute thus assumes in Moravia's novel stands in significant contrast to the repression she had formerly undergone in his memory. If in her apartment behind the *Messaggero* building she had suggested the existence of a reality the author was unprepared to face, in other words, in her representation in *The Woman of Rome* she symbolizes the superabundance of reality that had come to supplant the fiction of his bourgeois moralism.

Moravia hinted at this passage from repression to expression when, as we have seen, he recounted that the Roman prostitute he frequented had recalled "a strange short story by Henry James, 'The Last of the Valerii,'" the tale of a man who prefers the love of a statue—a creation, a fiction—to that of a real woman. Moravia was suggesting that he had been such a man, that like James's protagonist—a modern Pygmalion, who in Ovid's telling is moti-vated by disgust at prostitution to create a fictional woman, a statue, with which he then falls in love—he too had created a fiction in order to escape reality. In *The Woman of Rome*, in contrast, Moravia created a work of fiction that attempts to confront reality, to acknowledge sexuality, to recog-nize the prostitution that Italy's bourgeoisie would rather ignore. Through the figure of Adriana, we might therefore say, Moravia was not only reclaiming his repressed memory but also revealing the structures of bourgeois social domination, which had governed his encounter with the prostitute, and of bourgeois morality, which had caused him to repress that encounter for a decade. More to the point, he was exploring the power of literary symbolism to transcend those structures, and to dismantle them. Put differently, if for the bourgeoisie "the truth, *tout court*, was unhealthy," as we have seen Moravia argue, Adriana can be said to embody the truths that bourgeois society sought to deny, the reality it had sought to restrict.[41]

She can be said, as well, to represent the author's rejection of those bourgeois restrictions, his determination to pursue truths formerly denied, and his developing ability to represent them in his fiction. Indeed, as the subjective center of his fiction, and as the symbolic embodiment of the confluence between his remembered encounter and his intertextual explora-tion, the prostitute Adriana can be said to signify Moravia's renewed com-mitment to unseating the established order through the unfettered representa-tion of uncensored reality.

NOTES

1. Alberto Moravia and Alain Elkann, *Vita di Moravia* (Milan: Bompiani, 2007), 161. All translations from the Italian are my own unless otherwise indicated.

2. Moravia and Elkann, *Vita di Moravia*, 161.

3. Alberto Moravia, "Ricordi di censura," *La Rassegna d'Italia*, December 1946, 95–106.

4. On Moravia and Fascist censorship, see esp. Giorgio Fabre, *L'elenco: Censura fascista, editoria e autori ebrei* (Turin: Silvio Zamorani editore, 1998), 34–38, 396–402; Guido Bonsaver, *Censorship and Literature in Fascist Italy* (Toronto, Buffalo, and London: University of Toronto Press, 2007), 156–58, 238–41.

5. Moravia, "Ricordi di censura," 104.

6. Moravia, "Ricordi di censura," 101.

7. Moravia, "Ricordi di censura," 97.

8. On Moravia's critique of the bourgeoisie, see Pasquale Voza, *Moravia* (Palermo: Palumbo, 1997), 28; Roberto Tessari, *Alberto Moravia: Introduzione e guida allo studio dell'opera moraviana* (Florence: Le Monnier, 1977), 36–37.

9. La Rovere has attributed Italians' desire to blame Fascism on the bourgeoisie to the widespread desire to reject attributions of collective guilt and to impose more limited blame. See Luca La Rovere, "L''esame di coscienza' della nazione," *Mondo contemporaneo* 3 (2006): 23.

10. For the author's acknowledgment of the validity of the Marxist indictment of bourgeois Fascism, see Alberto Moravia, "Situazione della psicoanalisi: Opinioni di due narratori," *La Fiera letteraria* 1:16 (July 25, 1946), 3. On Moravia's own postwar Marxism, see Alberto Sebastiani, "Moravia, il comunismo e l'anticomunismo nel dopoguerra," *Poetiche* 1-2 (2008): 272.

11. Alberto Moravia, "La borghesia," in *Dopo il diluvio. Sommario dell'Italia contemporanea*, ed. Dino Terra (Milan: Garzanti, 1947), 213–14.

12. Alberto Moravia, "Impermeabilità degli italiani," *Mercurio* 2:15 (November 1945), 23–26.

13. Alberto Moravia, "Dopoguerra bigotto," *La Fiera letteraria* 2:20 (May 1947): 1.

14. Alberto Moravia "Man as an End," in *Man as an End: A Defense of Humanism: Literary, Social and Political Essays*, trans. Bernard Wall (Westport, CT: Greenwood Press, 1965), 32.

15. Links between Moravia's encounter in Largo Tritone and his composition of *La romana* can be found in Maria Grazia Di Mario, *La Roma di Moravia tra narrativa e cinema* (Rome: Aracne Editrice, 2013), 32; Renzo Paris, *Moravia. Una vita controvoglia* (Florence: Giunti, 1996), 203. An analysis of the novel's literary models can be found in Alberto Limentani, *Alberto Moravia tra esistenza e realtà* (Venice: Neri Pozza Editore, 1962), 73–74.

16. For the author's recognition of Defoe's influence, see Alberto Moravia, "Scrittori allo specchio," *La Fiera letteraria* 1:24 (September 19, 1946): 2. Nevertheless, the resemblance between the two novels is at best imperfect, as Moravia himself noted. See Alberto Moravia, "Perché ho scritto 'La Romana,'" *La Fiera letteraria* 2:27 (July 3, 1947): 3.

17. Gianni Rondolino, *Luchino Visconti* (Turin: UTET, 1981), 154.

18. Italo Calvino, "Viaggio in camion," in *Romanzi e racconti*, eds. Mario Barenghi and Bruno Falcetto (Milan: Mondadori, 1994), 499 [originally published in *Cinema Nuovo* 4:57 (April 25 1955)].

19. On this line of influence, see Luca Bufano, *Beppe Fenoglio e il racconto breve* (Ravenna: Longo, 1999), 71–84.

20. Alberto Moravia, "La carrozza di Maupassant," *Domenica*, February 18, 1945, 1, 6.

21. Alberto Moravia, *The Woman of Rome*, trans. Lydia Holland (Harmondsworth: Penguin, 1952), 63, 66.

22. Moravia, *The Woman of Rome*, 76.

23. Moravia, *The Woman of Rome*, 77–78, 83.

24. Giacomo Debenedetti, "Moravia e i sette peccati," *L'Unità*, September 14, 1947: 3. On the characters of *The Woman of Rome*, see too Vittorio Spinazzola, "Moravia, la vitalità della Romana," in *L'egemonia del romanzo: La narrativa italiana nel secondo Novecento* (Milan: Il Saggiatore, 2007), 158; Sharon Wood, *Woman as Object: Language and Gender in the Work of Alberto Moravia* (London: Pluto Press, 1990), 13.

25. That the echo of Camerini's film is intentional is suggested by Gisella's warning to Adriana, after learning of Gino's designs: "Men are all scoundrels ['gli uomini sono tutti dei mascalzoni']." Moravia, *The Woman of Rome*, 116.

26. Moravia, *The Woman of Rome*, 159.

27. Representing Fascism as a manifestation of Astarita's aberrant sexuality, Moravia offered one of many psycho-sexual interpretations of Fascism, borrowing from a tendency that had gained notable cultural prominence in the decade before he published his novel. For the historiography on Fascism as sexual dysfunction, see A. James Gregor, *Interpretations of Fascism* (Morristown, NJ: General Learning Press, 1974), 49–77. For an analysis of the Italian contributions to this tendency, see Barbara Spackman, *Rhetoric, Ideology, and Social Fantasy in Italy* (Minneapolis and London: University of Minnesota Press, 1996), 24–33.

28. The terms aromantic asexuality are used here in their generic meaning to indicate Giacomo's lack of interest in sex and romance. On the textual and ideological implications of Giacomo's troubled relationship with Adriana, see Valentina Mascaretti, *La speranza violenta: Alberto Moravia e il romanzo di formazione* (Modena: Gedit Edizioni, 2006), 348; Guido Baldi, "La Romana: Alienazione e naturalità innocente," in *Eroi intellettuali e classi popolari nella letteratura italiana del Novecento* (Naples: Liguori Editore, 2005), 193; Tommaso Soldini, "Alberto Moravia e la figura dell'intellettuale: Da *Gli indifferenti* a *La ciociara*," *Versants* 49 (2005): 93–94.

29. Moravia, *The Woman of Rome*, 302.

30. Moravia, *The Woman of Rome*, 338–39.

31. Moravia, *The Woman of Rome*, 376 (emphasis in the original).

32. Alberto Moravia, "The Man and the Character," in *Man as an End*, 70.

33. Moravia, "The Man and the Character," 70.

34. This point is noted but only briefly explored in René De Ceccatty, *Alberto Moravia*, trans. Sergio Arecco (Milan: Bompiani, 2010), 312, 364 n. 13.

35. Moravia, *The Woman of Rome*, 191.

36. I have borrowed this description from Vittorio Spinazzola, "Un borghese antiborghese," in *Per Moravia: Press Book della sua morte*, ed. Jader Jacobelli (Rome: Salerno Editrice, 1990), 174–77. On the novel's critique of Mino as a reflection on Moravia, see Edoardo Sanguinetti, *Alberto Moravia* (Milan: Mursia, 1962), 101–4.

37. Moravia, *The Woman of Rome*, 306.

38. Moravia and Elkann, *Vita di Moravia*, 161.

39. Prostitution was a frequent cultural symbol for Italy's postwar struggles. See Millicent Marcus, "The Italian Body Politic Is a Woman: Feminized National Identity in Postwar Italian Film," in *Sparks and Seeds: Medieval Literature and Its Afterlife: Essays in Honor of John Freccero*, eds. Dana E. Stewart and Alison Cornish (Turnhout, Belgium: Brepols Publishers, 2000), 329–47.

40. Moravia, *The Woman of Rome*, 1, 9, 250, 276. There may be another allegory implied in Giacomo's suicide letter, when he instructs Adriana to contact his lawyer: *Francesco Lauro, Via Cola di Rienzo, 3*" (377). Is this perhaps an invocation of Petrarch's "Spirito gentil," which tradition holds was dedicated to Cola di Rienzo, and which in its 3rd stanza offers what might be read as a hopeful message for Moravia's protagonist: "My Rome shall be beautiful again! [Roma mia sarà ancora bella!]"?

41. Moravia, "Ricordi di censura," 97.

WORKS CITED

Baldi, Guido. "La Romana: Alienazione e naturalità innocente." In *Eroi intellettuali e classi popolari nella letteratura italiana del Novecento*, 193–208. Naples: Liguori Editore, 2005.

Bonsaver, Guido. *Censorship and Literature in Fascist Italy*. Toronto, Buffalo, and London: University of Toronto Press, 2007.

Bufano, Luca. *Beppe Fenoglio e il racconto breve*. Ravenna: Longo, 1999.

Calvino, Italo. "Viaggio in camion." In *Romanzi e racconti*, edited by Mario Barenghi and Bruno Falcetto, 499–508. Milan: Mondadori, 1994.

Debenedetti, Giacomo. "Moravia e i sette peccati," *L'Unità*, September 14, 1947.

De Ceccatty, René. *Alberto Moravia*. Translated by Sergio Arecco. Milan: Bompiani, 2010.

Fabre, Giorgio. *L'elenco. Censura fascista, editoria e autori ebrei*. Turin: Silvio Zamorani editore, 1998.

Di Mario, Maria Grazia. *La Roma di Moravia tra narrativa e cinema*. Rome: Aracne Editrice, 2013.

Gregor, A. James. *Interpretations of Fascism*. Morristown, NJ: General Learning Press, 1974.

La Rovere, Luca. "L'esame di coscienza' della nazione," *Mondo contemporaneo* 3 (2006): 5–61.

Limentani, Alberto. *Alberto Moravia tra esistenza e realtà*. Venice: Neri Pozza Editore, 1962.

Marcus, Millicent. "The Italian Body Politic Is a Woman: Feminized National Identity in Postwar Italian Film." In *Sparks and Seeds: Medieval Literature and Its Afterlife. Essays in Honor of John Freccero*. Edited by Dana E. Stewart and Alison Cornish, 329–47. Turnhout, Belgium: Brepols Publishers, 2000.

Mascaretti, Valentina. *La speranza violenta: Alberto Moravia e il romanzo di formazione*. Modena: Gedit Edizioni, 2006.

Moravia, Alberto. "La borghesia." In *Dopo il diluvio: Sommario dell'Italia contemporanea*. Edited by Dino Terra, 199–215. Milan: Garzanti, 1947.

———. "La carrozza di Maupassant." *Domenica*, February 18 1945.

———. "Dopoguerra bigotto." *La Fiera letteraria* 2:20 (May 1947): 1.

———. "Impermeabilità degli italiani." *Mercurio* 2:15 (November 1945): 23–26.

———. "Man as an End." In *Man as an End: A Defense of Humanism: Literary, Social and Political Essays*. Translated by Bernard Wall, 13–63. Westport, CT: Greenwood Press, 1965.

———. "Perché ho scritto 'La Romana.'" *La Fiera letteraria* 2:27 (July 3, 1947): 3.

———. "Ricordi di censura." *La Rassegna d'Italia*, December 1946, 95–106.

———. "Scrittori allo specchio." *La Fiera letteraria* 1:24 (September 19, 1946): 2.

———. "Situazione della psicoanalisi. Opinioni di due narratori." *La Fiera letteraria* 1:16 (July 25, 1946), 3.

———. *The Woman of Rome*. Translated by Lydia Holland (Harmondsworth: Penguin, 1952).

Moravia, Alberto, and Alain Elkann. *Vita di Moravia*. Milan: Bompiani, 2007.

Paris, Renzo. *Moravia. Una vita controvoglia*. Florence: Giunti, 1996.

Rondolino, Gianni. *Luchino Visconti*. Turin: UTET, 1981.

Sanguinetti, Edoardo. *Alberto Moravia*. Milan: Mursia, 1962.

Sebastiani, Alberto. "Moravia, il comunismo e l'anticomunismo nel dopoguerra." *Poetiche* 1-2 (2008): 265–85.

Soldini, Tommaso. "Alberto Moravia e la figura dell'intellettuale. Da *Gli indifferenti* a *La ciociara*." *Versants* 49 (2005): 75–116.

Spackman, Barbara. *Rhetoric, Ideology, and Social Fantasy in Italy*. Minneapolis and London: University of Minnesota Press, 1996.

Spinazzola, Vittorio. "Un borghese antiborghese." In *Per Moravia: Press Book della sua morte*. Edited by Jader Jacobelli, 174–77. Rome: Salerno Editrice, 1990.

———. "Moravia, la vitalità della Romana." In *L'egemonia del romanzo. La narrativa italiana nel secondo Novecento*, 148–75. Milan: Il Saggiatore, 2007.

Tessari, Roberto. *Alberto Moravia: Introduzione e guida allo studio dell'opera moraviana*. Florence: Le Monnier, 1977.

Voza, Pasquale. *Moravia*. Palermo: Palumbo, 1997.

Wood, Sharon. *Woman as Object: Language and Gender in the Work of Alberto Moravia*. London: Pluto Press, 1990.

Chapter Four

Reconstructing the Maternal

Transmission of Memory, Cultural Translation and Transnational Identity in Igiaba Scego's La mia casa è dove sono

Maria Cristina Seccia

In this chapter, I will analyze the reconstruction of the maternal transmission of memory in Igiaba Scego's *La mia casa è dove sono* from a postcolonial translation studies perspective. Starting from the narrator's association between the maternal figure and culture of origin, I will read Somali-Italian narrator's representation of her Somali mother and the reconstruction of her memories as a form of cultural translation, namely as a transfer of a cultural reality in a different language.[1] By reconstructing her mother's memories, in fact, the narrator represents Somali culture, which is "other" to her Italian readers. Talal Asad pointed out a potential imbalance of power relations implied by cultural translation when this involves languages of dominated and dominant societies.[2] However, as stressed by Loredana Polezzi, cultural translation is also useful to readers to gain an understanding of the culture represented.[3] As noticed by Polezzi and Kate Sturge, the transfer of a cultural reality in a different language is premised on a notion of culture as a text,[4] which brings "translation of culture" closer to notions of interlingual translation.[5] In light of these observations, I will present the memories of the narrator's mother and Somali culture as the narrator's source text that she translates through processes of selection, analysis, and interpretation. I will discuss firstly whether our Somali-Italian narrator assumes authority to interpret the Somali culture that she "translates" to her Italian readers and, secondly, what understanding of Somali culture she offers to her readership. In order to do this, I will draw on Bella Brodzki's association between transmission of memory and translation, but at the same time I will take a step further from her theorization.[6] While the gender and translation studies scholar focuses on the transition from oblivion to "survival" of a memory/text enabled by inter-generational transmission and translation respectively, I argue that "survival" inevitably implies a recreation of a new entity—be it a memory or a text (and I would add a culture, following my engagement with "culture as a text"). The association between intergenerational *trans*mission and *trans*lation is to be found in the prefix *trans*, which suggests a *trans*it: while the former implies the *trans*fer of a memory from one temporal (and cultural) context to another, the latter implies the *trans*position of a text from one cultural (and temporal) context to another, from one language and literary system to another. In both cases, the memory/text undergoes a *trans*formation depending on the translator's interpretation and agency. As noted by Polezzi, translation dynamics, in fact, imply mechanisms of selection, analysis, appropriation, and at times even distortion.[7]

Before starting my analysis, I will contextualize it through a brief introduction to the memoir *La mia casa è dove sono* (first published by Rizzoli in 2010 and republished by Loescher Editore in 2012),[8] which was awarded the *Premio Mondello* (2012), the first Italian international literary prize.[9] As suggested by the title, the book reflects Scego's transnational identity, which moves across national borders: between Rome, where she was born and raised, and Mogadishu, from where her parents fled following Siad Barre's coup d'état in 1969. From the very first chapter the narrator challenges the idea of national identity as a fixed essence conceived in binary terms: in a vain attempt to label it, she continually reformulates it, thus showing the impossibility of finding one single and exhaustive definition. The narrator started reflecting on her own national identity when she was drawing a map of Mogadishu with her family (in an attempt to remember pre–civil war Mogadishu) and her little nephew unexpectedly asked her whether it is the map of *her* city. She feels uncomfortable in answering: she is not sure whether she can define Mogadishu, where she only lived for a year and a half, as "her" city or not. Her mother Kadija suggests that she complete the map (the "maabka,"[10] to put it in her Somali words) of Mogadishu by surrounding it with sticky notes representing areas and monuments of her other city, Rome.

Although Igiaba feels hurt by her mother's observation, which seems to question her belonging to Somali culture, she accepts her suggestion. The complementary maps of Mogadishu and Rome, the two "gemelle siamesi separate alla nascita"[11] (Siamese twins separated at birth), and more specifically the sticky notes, something "provvisorio e scomponibile"[12] (temporary and take-apart-able), evoke a transitory state as well the fragmentariness and yet plurality of the narrator's national identity, which undergoes continuous transformations. Moreover they represent how Italian and Somali histories are made tightly imbricated by the colonial past and the continuing contemporary migration.

The narrator associates six of the emblems of Rome with a member of her family or a specific period of her life, and reconstruct their history in six different chapters named after the specific places and monuments drawn on the map: *Teatro Sistina*; *Piazza Santa Maria sopra Minerva*; *La stele di Axum*; *Stazione Termini*; *Trastevere*; and *Stadio Olimpico*. In such a way, the narrator shows how the map "can become connectable to emotional spaces in migrant imaginaries," as noted by Jennifer Burns.[13] *La mia casa è dove sono* therefore foregrounds how the family is crucial in memory transmission, and how it is important not only for personal but also collective memory.[14] In fact, recounting her family's story does not only help the narrator to construct her transnational identity but also enables episodes of the Somali collective memory (like colonialism, the civil war, and the consequent diaspora) to cross national borders and to be transferred to the Italian context, thus reshaping Italians' collective memory of colonialism, often erased or distorted.[15]

Within this context, my analysis focuses on the narrator's reconstruction of her Somali mother's memories of two of the most significant episodes in her life: her infibulation as a child and her delivery as a refugee in Italy, included in the chapter *Piazza Santa Maria sopra Minerva*. The association between this square and the narrator's mother is to be traced back to Gian Lorenzo Bernini's statue of the Elephant (adjacent to the church of Santa Maria sopra Minerva), which reminded little Igiaba of Somalia and which is associated by the adult narrator with Mamma Kadija.

The narrator, in fact, compares her mother's gaze, which reflects perturbing events of her life, like infibulation and migration, with the sad gaze of Bernini's Elephant, which in turn she sees as similar to exiled Somali people's gaze and as reflecting the dramatic events of Somali history, like colonialism, Siad Barre's dictatorship, the civil war, and the resulting diaspora. The presence of the Elephant (which she saw as a typical African animal) in Piazza della Minerva confuses little Igiaba, who asks her mother whether Rome is in Somalia or vice versa. Her question is representative of Scego's postcolonial narrative of Italy as a former colonizer and the host country of Somali refugees, thus reminding Italian readers of the double relationship between the two countries and cultures. The narrator's association between her mother and Bernini's Elephant, which in turn comes to symbolize Somalia, sheds light on how the maternal figure comes to represent one's own culture of origin in the transnational narrator-daughter's imaginary, which is at the core of my engagement with the theory of cultural translation.[16]

Significantly, before reconstructing two episodes of her mother's story, the narrator explains that she wants to pay homage to all those women who are still fighting to use their voice, and to save their stories from oblivion.

From this perspective, Brodzki's focus on "survival" proves to be particularly relevant. The gender and translation studies scholar presents the transmission of memory as an act of translation because it inscribes memories in a culture in a similar way to what happens to texts when translated from one language into another: "Here I direct my attention to processes of intergenerational and intercultural transmission, conceived as acts of translation, to how the value of memory or remembrance as an instrument of historical consciousness is inscribed in a culture."[17]

At the same time Brodzki sees translation as implying acts of memory transmission: "Translation's intersecting temporal and spatial processes underwrite acts of intergenerational transmission, operating as the crucial means by which imperiled narratives are passed down, received, and survive in memory."[18] Her observation is therefore based on transmission's and translation's shared act of transition of memories/texts from potential oblivion to survival: from potential death to "afterlife." In both cases the aim is to grant a future to a memory/text. Walter Benjamin's notion of "afterlife," which suggests that a translation "marks th[e] stage of continued life of a text,"[19] is precisely the starting point for Brodzki's theorization. More specifically, Brodzki draws on Jacques Derrida's translation of Benjamin's term *"Fortleben"* as *"survivre"*—survival.[20] In light of this, I would argue that Scego seems to feel "duty-bound" to reconstruct her mother's story in order to give voice to her experience—shared by several other women—thus granting its survival, just as a translator "is duty-bound to do something for the original."[21]

Interestingly, the narrator specifies that she is reconstructing her mother's memories also for her own writing, "che molto deve a quelle voci di coraggio"[22] (which owes much to those brave voices), which reveals how this helps her to construct her transnational identity. Moreover, she identifies with all women who, like her mother, were silenced: "Nonostante gli orrori commessi sulla nostra pelle noi donne abbiamo avuto la forza di superare l'infame tradizione del silenzio"[23] (Despite the atrocities we experienced first-hand, we women have been strong enough to break the infamous silence imposed by our tradition). I would like to point out, however, that the ambiguity of "noi donne" (we women) can be problematic: while the narrator might refer to Somali women who experienced traumatic experiences like her mother, with whom she identifies, it can be interpreted as "Italian women" by her (female) readers.

By using "donne" (women) as a category without specifying a cultural context, the narrator risks essentializing the very concept of "woman" and disregarding how women encounter different levels and kinds of difficulties in speaking up depending on the sociocultural context in which they live. Moreover, whether the narrator might be referring to Somali or Italian women—including herself as a Somali *and* Italian woman in "noi donne" (we women)—is equally problematic because she seems to ignore the intersection between transnational and gender identity and how living across national borders might affect the way in which women perceive and express their gender identity.

As mentioned earlier on, the narrator's reconstruction of her mother's story is focused on two experiences that marked her life: being infibulated as a child and giving birth as a refugee in Italy. The selection of infibulation as an object of cultural translation for Italian readers is particularly interesting from a postcolonial and transnational perspective. As noticed by Egyptian writer and scholar Nawal El Saadawi, this practice, together with other forms of genital mutilation, has attracted great—in fact excessive—critical attention within the Western audience to the extent that it has become the main focus when representing African Muslim women.[24] More specifically, the Italian literary system includes different works representing infibulation, like Scego's third novel *Oltre Babilonia* (2008), Garane Garane's *Il latte è buono* (2005), Sirad Salan Hassan's *Sette gocce di sangue* (1996), Hirsi Ali's *Infedele* (2006), and Alice Walker's *Possedere il segreto della gioia* (1993).[25] If we consider how well Italian readers know this cultural practice through literature, Scego's decision to translate her mother's infibulation can be seen as a way of conforming to her readership's expectations, which shows how the process of selection of a text is regulated by the receiving cultural system and is influenced by elements such as the target-text readers' beliefs.[26] Lawrence Venuti sees this tendency to select source texts that can be more easily assimilated in the target culture as a domesticating—namely, familiarizing—approach to translation.[27] Through the analysis of the following two passages I will show that Scego's selection of her mother's memories is only one of the several domesticating strategies she uses when reconstructing her story and therefore translating Somali culture:

> Aveva circa otto anni, la mia mamma. Come vuole la tradizione le fecero fare un bagno e le donne si misero a cantare per lei. Quel giorno sarebbe diventata donna. Sapeva benissimo che sarebbe stato doloroso, sua madre le aveva spiegato tutto. Arrivò dalla mammana, addetta all'orazione, con una tremarella da fare tenerezza. Ogni volta sogno che qualcuno porti via mia madre da lì. La salvi. Invece non è stato così. Allargò le gambe. Fu ubbidiente come si erano raccomandate le donne della famiglia. «In quel momento ho cercato Dio. Chiedevo: 'O Allah Clemente e Misericordioso, . . . ti prego fammi essere coraggiosa. . . . Pregai tanto il nome di Dio. . . . Due donne le tenevano le gambe, per impedirle di muoversi durante l'operazione. Tutto avvenne senza anestesia; mamma non dimenticherà mai quel dolore fortissimo. Fu brava.[28]

> (She was about eight years old, my mum. As tradition requires, they gave her a bath and the women started singing for her. On that day she was going to become a woman. She knew very well that it was going to be painful; her mother had explained everything to her. She came before the *mammana*, the

woman in charge of the prayer, with an endearing shivering. Each time I dream that somebody takes my mother away, rescues her from there. But it didn't happen. She spread her legs. She was obedient, as advised by the women of her family. "At that moment I called on God. I kept asking him: 'Oh Allah, Most Gracious, Most Merciful, Allah, Lord of the Worlds, I beg you, let me be brave. Let me feel less pain.' I prayed so much in the Lord's name. I didn't want to think about the blood which was spurting down below." Two women were holding her legs to prevent her moving during the operation. It was all done without anesthesia; Mum will never forget that extremely sharp pain. She did well.)

Brodzki's observation that intergenerational memory can be conceived as acts of translation is useful in seeing how the value of Kadija's memories as an instrument of cultural consciousness is inscribed in Italian and Somali cultures. In reconstructing her mother's memories of her experience of infibulation, the narrator explains that her mother was shaking so much that it was very affecting to see her, thus emphasizing her position as a victim of a cruel practice. The narrator's comments on her mother's attitude seem to suggest that the experience has been transmitted to her so deeply and affectively that she has internalized her mother's memories to such an extent that she describes her reaction as though she had actually witnessed it.

The third-person narrative that suddenly slips into an autobiographical authorial perspective in the present is eloquent of how the narrator-translator feels involved in her mother's pain. The repetitiveness with which she dreams of her mother being spared that cruel practice reminds us of the traumatic flashbacks distressing people who experienced this trauma firsthand and shows that the daughter-narrator "assumes the burden of memory and the burden of intergenerational transmission as they were implicitly passed on to her."[29] Kadija is represented not only as a victim but also as a good girl: she did well, she stayed still and didn't cry. Particularly significant is the narrator's use of direct speech through which she presents the experience of infibulation from her mother's point of view and suggests how these memories are still engraved on her mind. Direct speech is also used to report Kadija's prayer to Allah: in that case it seems to be an attempt to convince Italian readers that this cruel practice is not related to Islam. The voice of the narrator's mother is made audible through words that, however, were probably not spoken by her.

Kadija's use of *maabka* reported earlier in this chapter, in fact, reveals that she mixes her native Somali language with Italian. If we consider that Kadija's reported words were probably not spoken entirely in Italian and underwent an interlingual translation, the use of direct speech can be seen as an example of the intervention of the narrator, who appropriates her mother's experience just as a translator transforms a source text into an independent target text by inscribing her own interpretation. In fact, as Brodzki points out, "although the translation owes its existence to the original, [the original] also gains something, becomes more than itself by virtue of its being translated: both need each other to fill in spaces that would otherwise remain in the realm of images, unarticulated and unsignified."[30]

The narrator's use of direct speech emphasizes Kadija's pain: it is as though she not only wants to inform her readers of the dynamics of the practice, but also what it is like to experience it by explaining that the pain canceled out any other feeling. The narrator's empathy toward her mother results in an equally empathetic bond between the Italian readership and the Somali mother, which seems to create a dialogue between the two cultures.

However, while the narrator emphasizes her mother's pain, she does not offer any insight to the reason for infibulation. On the one hand, as a cultural translator, she explains that it is not a religious practice; on the other, however, Italian readers might not be aware that in reality it is often perceived as such by Muslim Somali women because of the oral traditions through which most of them learn the Qu'ran.[31] Moreover, the narrator explains to Italian readers that infibulation is a rite of passage that initiates young girls into womanhood, but they are not informed how womanhood is conceived of from a Somali Muslim gender perspective. As shown by Janice Boddy in another African Muslim context, Sudanese Muslim women, in fact, see motherhood as a means of asserting their importance in their society and infibulation represents an act of purification and protection, which they perceive as necessary not only to be eligible as wives but also to become mothers.[32]

The narrator's translation of infibulation is made problematic in the introduction to her mother's story, where the narrator pays homage to women's history, thus inevitably associating Mamma Kadija's experience with all other women's experiences. While the narrator might implicitly refer exclusively to those women who experienced infibulation as a trauma, she inevitably also includes those women who, instead, underwent infibulation later in their life, consciously, and firmly believing in its cultural value.

Although the narrator mentions the *mammana*'s role and other women's presence, and explains that Mamma Kadija had been informed by her own mother about the practice, she seems to undervalue the fact that this practice is actually carried out by women. This raises questions about the notion of Muslim Somali women's agency. While Scego might give voice to Somali women to make her own voice as a writer with Somali origins audible and therefore to construct her own transnational identity, at the same time she seems to use her position of a writer to make the "subaltern speak," to put it in Gayatri Spivak's terms.[33] However, as noted by the postcolonial gender theorist, the idea of subalternity becomes imbricated with the idea of non-recognition of agency.[34] In the analysis of the representation of infibulation in other postcolonial literary works, Sandra Ponzanesi points out that we should wonder where Muslim Somali women's oppression stops and self-determination begins.[35]

The passages analyzed show how the interaction between the narrator and the translated Somali culture is complex: while she identifies with Somali women, as revealed by "noi donne," she represents them as unequivocally victims of a traumatizing experience, thus showing paradoxically a Western gender perspective. She seems to essentialize the concept of a universal Somali woman who needs to be liberated from cultural traditions, thus inevitably excluding those for whom being infibulated means embracing their own culture. While from a Western gender perspective the narrator's condemnation of infibulation can certainly be read as an act of resistance and denunciation of what, understandably, can be seen as an inhuman patriarchal practice, a postcolonial approach suggests that Scego applies a notion of universal human rights. In this respect, I entirely agree with Ponzanesi that resistance needs to be placed within the sociocultural context in which it is awakened instead of being measured according to international standards.[36] Scego, instead, does not seem to distance herself from Western universalistic assumptions objectifying African women, which have been criticized by Black feminists like El Saadawi.[37]

In light of the cultural meaning of infibulation within Somali Muslim women's communities, the strategies used by the narrator to reconstruct her mother's memory of this episode of her life can be seen as domesticating translation strategies, namely strategies that present the translated text to Italian readers in such a way that it conforms to their expectations. More specifically, to summarize, the narrator's comments on her mother's attitude, which present her as a victim and yet as a good and obedient girl, the use of direct speech to report her mother's voice and make her voice audible, and the narrator's intervention in the first-person showing her involvement in her mother's suffering, put emphasis on Kadija's pain. This not only shows the narrator's empathy with her mother and the continuing process of identification with her but also creates empathy in Italian readers toward the translated Somali mother, which confirms Polezzi's observation that processes of appropriation set in motion by translation affect the relationship between the source culture and the target-text readers. In this way, the narrator has domesticated infibulation as a cruel practice and might have involuntarily confirmed the image of Somali culture as barbaric and patriarchal.

The relevance of the maternal figure as a site of gender and cultural identification is clear when the narrator refers to herself as her mother's "map," which confirms how her mother represents her cultural origins but might also reveal that she feels as though she is tracking her mother's itinerary, as though she is the personified result of her mother's experiences. Kadija's courage in breaking the silence and preventing her daughter from undergoing this cultural practice herself turned her, in fact, into Igiaba's role model.

The narrator's expression that she feels like a "map of her mother" sheds light on the process of identification with the maternal figure. Her mother's courage in rebelling against her society's rules allowed the narrator to be "una donna completa"[38] (a complete woman). Scego's explanation of "complete woman," namely with all organs in the right place—and more implicitly with no danger for her sexual life—confirms her Western gender perspective; this clashes with how wholeness is conceived in the Somali cultural context, where women often see infibulation—and more specifically suture—as a means of guaranteeing the integrity of their genital internal organs.[39] From a postcolonial and cultural translation perspective, the narrator intervenes in Somali culture by reducing infibulation to a question of sexuality without taking into account the complex cultural layers of the practice.

The second event of Kadija's life that I will analyze, reconstructed by the narrator, is giving birth as a refugee in Rome. As revealed in the following passage, the narrator reconstructs her own birth:

> Mia madre del travaglio, quello che le ho procurato io, non mi ha mai raccontato molto. . . . Mamma di quel travaglio in terra straniera si ricorda la freddezza degli infermieri, la solitudine e l'inesperienza di chi l'ha assistita. . . . La vedo . . . , lei disorientata, lei che non parlava ancora bene l'italiano, una donna che aveva bisogno di un volto amico e che invece era stata costretta dalle circostanze a cavarsela da sola. Ogni volta penso come sia stato difficile per mia madre mettermi al mondo a Roma. Con gli altri figli stava a casa sua, in Somalia, attorniata da persone che le volevano bene. . . . Tutte le donne intorno a lei sorridevano, per renderle il travaglio meno pesante e per accompagnarla dolcemente nel suo nuovo ruolo.[40]

> (My mother has never told me much about her labor—the one that *I* caused. She told me that the hospital staff were on strike that day. Mum remembers the nurses' coldness, the loneliness and the inexperience of those who attended her during that labor in a foreign land. . . . Every time this story takes my breath away. I can see her with her very long hair tied up in a bun, she was disoriented, she couldn't speak Italian well yet, she was a woman who needed a friendly face and who, instead, was being forced by circumstances to manage on her own. Every time I think how hard it was for my mother to bring me into the world in Rome. With her other children, she was at home, in Somalia, surrounded by people who loved her. All the women around her were smiling, to make her labor less hard and to accompany her gently into her new role.)

As in the first example analyzed, the narrator makes herself visible as a translator when she intervenes in the first person during the third-person narration to clarify that she is referring to the labor that *she* caused to her mother. This suggests that she identifies with her mother's experience, that she "assumes the burden of memory and the burden of intergenerational transmission as they were implicitly passed on to her."[41]

The use of the first-person pronoun also reveals the narrator's sense of guilt, which is reiterated when she confesses that every time she thinks about that event it takes her breath away. She tries to imagine how difficult it might have been for her mother to give birth as a refugee in Italy, where she was not only experiencing linguistic difficulties and loneliness but also encountered unfriendly nurses who provided no comfort, unlike Somali women who gave her such love and attention when she gave birth to her older children.

Interestingly, the stress in the narrator's reconstruction is on her mother's loneliness, although she migrated to Rome with her husband and her older children. The completely traumatizing nature of the experience of childbirth can therefore be seen as the result of the narrator's manipulation of her mother's memories. By emphasizing her feelings at the start of the passage, the narrator–cultural translator faces her Italian readers with the difficult situations experienced by women refugees. At the same time, by crossing national boundaries, she explains how in Somalia childbirth is seen as an important occasion when women are initiated into the difficult task of motherhood thanks to other women's help, thus shedding light on the crucial role played by solidarity in Black women's communities.[42]

As in the previous passage, the narrator reports her mother's memories as if she had witnessed her own birth, as revealed by her statement that she can picture her mother. As suggested by Brodzki, "this mode of secondary witnessing compels an exploration of the intricate and intimate process of re-memoration" and shows how imagination is also involved.[43] It is particularly interesting that the narrator selects her own birth as an object of translation, confirming her attempt to construct her transnational identity through the reconstruction of her mother's memories.

In conclusion, by reconstructing both episodes the narrator allows her mother's story "to be verbalized and communicated, to be integrated into one's own, and others' knowledge of the past."[44] Her narration seems to confirm Brodzki's observation that "each generation rewrites its relations with the past in the hopes of inscribing a future, that to translate and to be translated is to be saved from oblivion."[45] However, as shown in my analysis above, both transmission of memory and translation imply processes of appropriation, manipulation, and intervention, which result in the transformation of the memory and text.[46]

As a consequence, while the narrator's reconstruction of her mother's story and its implicit association with women's history can be seen as a way of realizing Somali collective memory, this has inevitably involved its manipulation. By using direct speech, for example, the narrator has appropriated her mother's voice and, since she comes to embody Somali culture, the appropriation could be extended to all women's voices, which implies a distortion of Somali culture.

By crossing temporal and national boundaries, therefore, images of Somali culture have been appropriated by Italian discourses following the narrator's Western feminist agency. This narrative confirms Polezzi's observation that agency proves to be crucial in processes of cultural translation,[47] and that this might imply asymmetrical relationships of power. While Scego's postcolonial perspective, from which she represents Somalia's past as a former Italian colony and Somalis' migration to Italy, is usually very clear in her works, I have argued that in this specific case her representation of Somali culture reveals her indirect experience with it. From a cultural translation perspective, she encourages cultural awareness of Italian society and intercultural dialogue by addressing otherness within the Italian multicultural context and presenting a specific aspect of Somali culture to Italian readers.

In the case of otherness, giving voice to her mother's loneliness as a new mother recently migrated to Italy shows not only how the potential trauma of giving birth can be exacerbated in women refugees but also confronts Italian readers, more generally, with the inhospitality of their society. By representing her two cultures in conflict in the way they welcome the newly arrived, the author attempts to create a dialogue between them. Similarly, the narrator seems to try to bridge a gap when she makes her readers empathetic toward her mother—and by extension Somali women—who underwent infibulation; in such a way she brings Somali culture toward Italian readers just as a translator brings a text toward her readership to make it as readable as possible in linguistic and cultural terms.

While Scego usually takes her readers toward Somali culture by confronting them with Italy's colonial history in an attempt to reshape their collective memory, in this specific case she did not seem to oppose resistance to established images of Somali culture in the Western discourse and therefore she does not help her Italian readers to gain a new understanding of it. Like readers of a translated text, her audience experiences a "reading of a reading": it interprets a text produced by the narrator's interpretation of Somali culture.[48] Interestingly, while she claims the source culture as her culture of origin, she seems to share cultural values with her target-text readers. Her Somali cultural origins might be what makes her feel somehow justified in assuming authority to interpret Somali culture. Her intermediate position in translating Somali culture confirms her transnational identity that she constructs through the reconstruction of her mother's memories: by identifying with her mother and the other Somali women and by reconstructing her own birth.

NOTES

I would like to thank Katia Pizzi for inviting me to the *Centre for the Study of Cultural Memory* seminar *Transcultural Memory and the Intersection of Migration and Colonialism* (held on May 14, 2016 at the Institute of Modern Languages Research, University of London), where I presented a shorter version of this chapter. I am very grateful also to Simone Brioni for his insightful comments on a previous version of this chapter.

1. For a translation studies perspective on the notion of "cultural translation" see Kate Sturge, "Translation Strategies in Ethnography," *The Translator* 3, no. 1 (1997): 21–38; Ovidio Carbonell, "The Exotic Space of Cultural Translation," in *Translation, Power, Subversion*, ed. Roman Alvarez and M. Carmen-Africa Vidal (Clevedon and Philadelphia: Multilingual Matters, 1996), 79–98; Kate Sturge, *Translation, Ethnography and the Museum* (Manchester: St Jerome Publishing, 2007); Kate Sturge, "Cultural Translation," in *Routledge Encyclopedia of Translation Studies*, ed. Mona Baker and Gabriela Saldanha, second edition (London and New York: Routledge, 2009), 67–70; Loredana Polezzi, *Translating Travel: Contemporary Italian Travel Writing in English Translation* (Aldershot and Brookfield: Ashgate Publishing, 2001). Talal Asad's essay "The Concept of Cultural Translation in British Cultural Anthropology" is one of the core studies on cultural translation, first theorized in ethnography and anthropology. A detailed discussion of the importance of Asad's concept of cultural translation for the development of Translation Studies can be found in Douglas Robinson, *Translation and Empire: Postcolonial Theories Explained* (Manchester: St. Jerome, 1997).

2. Talal Asad, "The Concept of Cultural Translation in British Social Anthropology," in *Writing Culture: The Poetics and Politics of Ethnography*, ed. James Clifford and George E. Marcus (Berkeley and Los Angeles: University of California Press, 1986), 164.

3. Polezzi, *Translating Travel*, 97.

4. Polezzi, *Translating Travel*, 97.

5. Sturge, *Representing Others*, 7.

6. Bella, Brodzki, *Can These Bones Live? Translation, Survival, and Cultural Memory* (Stanford: Stanford University Press, 2007).

7. Loredana Polezzi, "Reflections of Things Past: Building Italy through the Mirror of Translation," *New Comparison* 29 (2000), 29.

8. The passages under analysis are taken from the second edition of the book.

9. Igiaba Scego was also winner of the literary prize *Ex&Tra* (2003) with her first short story "Salsicce" (published in the same year), and she was shortlisted for the *Segafredo Zanetti Prize* (2016) with her latest novel *Adua* (published in the previous year). These two works have also been translated into English and published under the titles "Sausages" (2005) and *Adua* (2017) respectively. A further literary text available in English is the short story "Dismatria," translated as "Exmatriates" and published in 2011.

10. Scego, *Casa*, 58.

11. Scego, *Casa*, 14.

12. Scego, *Casa*, 36.

13. Burns, *Migrant Imaginaries*, 202.

14. For an analysis of the representation of family memory transmission in transnational fictional literary works, see Emma Bond, "'Let me go back and recreate what I don't know': Locating Trans-national Memory Work in Contemporary Narrative," *Modern Languages Open* (2016): 1–21. Accessed December 3, 2016. https://www.modernlanguagesopen.org/articles/10.3828/mlo.v0i0.134/.

15. On the erasure of Italian colonial memory, see for instance Nicola Labanca, *Oltremare: Storia dell'espansione coloniale italiana* (Bologne: Il Multino, 2002) and Sandra Ponzanesi, "The Postcolonial Turn in Italian Studies," in *Postcolonial Italy: Challenging National Homogeneity*, ed. Cristina Lombardi-Diop and Caterina Romeo (Basingstoke: Palgrave Macmillan, 2012), 51–70.

16. The relationship between the maternal figure and the daughter-narrator cultural origins in transnational women's writing has been pointed out by several scholars, like Adalgisa Giorgio, "Writing the Mother-Daughter Relationship," in *Writing Mothers and Daughters*, ed. Adalgisa Giorgio (Oxford: Berghahn Books, 2002), 11–46.

17. Brodzki, *Translation, Survival*, 111–12.

18. Brodzki, *Translation, Survival*, 145.

19. Benjamin, *Illuminations*, 71.

20. Jacques Derrida, *The Ear of the Other: Otobiography, Transference, Translation* (Lincoln: University of Nebraska Press), 1988.

21. Derrida, *Transference, Translation*, 122.

22. Scego, *Casa*, 58.

23. Scego, *Casa*, 58.

24. Nawa El Saadawi, *The Hidden Face of Eve: Women in the Arab Worlds* (London: Zed Press, 1980).

25. Ali's *Infedele* and Walker's *Possedere il segreto della gioia*, originally written in Dutch and English respectively, have entered the Italian literary system through translation. For an analysis of the literary representation of infibulation in Ali's, Walker's and Hassan's texts, see Sandra Ponzanesi, "Writing against the Grain: African Women's Texts on Female Infibulations as Literature of Resistance," *Indian Journal of Gender Studies* 7 (2000): 304–18. The representation of infibulation in Hassan's *Sette gocce di sangue* is also analyzed in Sandra Ponzanesi, *Paradoxes of Postcolonial Culture: Contemporary Women Writers of the Indian and Afro-Italian Diaspora* (Albany: State University of New York Press, 2004), 185–206. Some brief considerations on infibulation as object of representation in Italian postcolonial literary texts are also included in Piera Carroli, "Oltre Babilonia? Postcolonial Female Trajectories towards Nomadic Subjectivity," *Italian Studies* 65, no. 2 (2013): 204–18 and Simone Brioni, "Memory, Belonging and the Right for Representation: Questions of 'Home' in Kaha Mohamed Aden's Fra-intendimenti," in *Shifting and Shaping a National Identity*, ed. Grace Russo Bullaro and Elena Benelli (Leicester: Trobadour, 2014), 23–42.

26. The norms that regulate the selection and translation of literary texts were first identified in Gideon Toury, "Translated Literature: System, Norm, Performance—Toward a TT-Oriented Approach to Literary Translation," *Poetics Today* 2, no. 4 (1981): 9–27. See also José Lambert, "Translation, Systems and Research: The Contribution of Polysystem Studies to Translation Studies." *TTR* 8, no. 1 (1995): 105–52 and André Lefevere, *Translation, Rewriting, and the Manipulation of Literary Frame* (London and New York: Routledge, 1992).

27. Venuti, Lawrence, *The Translator's Invisibility: A History of Translation*, London and New York: Routledge, 1995.

28. Scego, *Casa*, 68.

29. Brodzki, *Translation, Survival*, 120.

30. Brodzki, *Translation, Survival*, 124.

31. On the meaning of infibulation in Somali women's communities see, for example, Rima Berns McGown, *Muslims in the Diaspora: The Somali Communities of London and Toronto* (Toronto: University of Toronto Press, 1999), 149.

32. Janice Boddy, *Wombs and Alien Spirits: Women, Men, and the Zar Cult in Northern Sudan* (Madison: University of Wisconsin Press, 1989), 55. On the meaning of motherhood in Black women's communities, see also Patricia Hill Collins, "The Meaning of Motherhood in Black Culture and Black Mother-Daughter Relationships," *Sage* 4, no. 2 (1987): 3–10 and Patricia Hill Collins, *Black Feminist Thought: Knowledge, Consciousness, and the Politics of Empowerment* (New York and London: Routledge, 1990).

33. Gayatri Spivak, "Can the Subaltern Speak?" in *Marxism and the Interpretation of Culture*, ed. Cary Nelson and Lawrence Grossberg (Urbana: University of Illinois Press, 1988), 271–313.

34. Gayatri Spivak, *Outside in the Teaching Machine* (New York and London: Routledge, 1993), 476.

35. Ponzanesi "African Women's," 304.

36. Ponzanesi "African Women's" 307.

37. El Saadawi, *Hidden Face*, xvi.

38. Scego, *Casa*, 70.
39. On reproduction and motherhood in Somali women's communities from a cross-cultural perspective, see for example Paula Hernandez, "Sensing Vulnerability, Seeking Strength: Somali Women and Their Experiences during Pregnancy and Birth in Melbourne," in *Reproduction, Childbearing and Motherhood: A Cross-Cultural Perspective*, ed. Pranee Liamputtong (New York: Nova Publishers, 2007), 195–208.
40. Scego, *Casa*, 61–62.
41. Brodzki, *Translation, Survival*, 120.
42. On the solidarity among Black mothers and surrogate motherhood in Black women's communities, see Collins, "The Meaning," 3–10, and Collins, *Black Feminist*.
43. Brodzki, *Translation, Survival*, 115.
44. Brodzki, *Translation, Survival*, 122.
45. Brodzki, *Translation, Survival*, 145.
46. On translation as an act of manipulating and rewriting the source text, see Lefevere, "Translation."
47. "Translation and Migration," *Translation Studies* 5, no. 3 (2012): 348.
48. Polezzi, *Translating Travel*, 176.

WORKS CITED

Asad, Talal. "The Concept of Cultural Translation in British Social Anthropology." In *Writing Culture: The Poetics and Politics of Ethnography,* edited by James Clifford and George E. Marcus, 141–64. Berkeley and Los Angeles: University of California Press, 1986.
Benini, Stefania. "Tra Mogadiscio e Roma: Le mappe emotive di Igiaba Scego." *Forum Italicum: A Journal of Italian Studies* 48, no. 3 (2014): 477–94.
Benjamin, Walter. *Illuminations*. Translated by Harry Zohn. New York: Schocken Books, 1999.
Boddy, Janice. *Wombs and Alien Spirits: Women, Men, and the Zar Cult in Northern Sudan.* Madison: University of Wisconsin Press, 1989.
Bond, Emma. "'Let Me Go Back and Recreate What I Don't Know': Locating Trans-national Memory Work in Contemporary Narrative," *Modern Languages Open* (2016): 1–21. Accessed December 3, 2016. https://www.modernlanguagesopen.org/articles/10.3828/mlo.v0i0.134/.
Brioni, Simone. "Memory, Belonging and the Right for Representation: Questions of 'Home' in Kaha Mohamed Aden's Fra-intendimenti." In *Shifting and Shaping a National Identity*, edited by Grace Russo Bullaro and Elena Benelli, 23–42. Leicester: Trobadour, 2014.
Brodzki, Bella. *Can These Bones Live? Translation, Survival, and Cultural Memory.* Stanford: Stanford University Press, 2007.
Burns, Jennifer. *Migrant Imaginaries: Figures and Themes in Italian Immigration Literature* Oxford: Peter Lang, 2013.
Carbonell, Ovidio. "The Exotic Space of Cultural Translation." In *Translation, Power, Subversion*, edited by Roman Alvarez and M. Carmen-Africa Vidal, 79–98. Clevedon and Philadelphia: Multilingual Matters, 1996.
Carroli, Piera. "Oltre Babilonia? Postcolonial Female Trajectories towards Nomadic Subjectivity." *Italian Studies* 65, no. 2 (2013): 204–18.
Collins, Patricia Hill. *Black Feminist Thought: Knowledge, Consciousness, and the Politics of Empowerment.* New York and London: Routledge, 1990.
———. "The Meaning of Motherhood in Black Culture and Black Mother-Daughter Relationships." *Sage* 4, no. 2 (1987): 3–10.
Derrida, Jacques. *The Ear of the Other: Otobiography, Transference, Translation.* Lincoln: University of Nebraska Press, 1988.
El Saadawi, Nawal. *The Hidden Face of Eve: Women in the Arab Worlds*, London: Zed Press, 1980.
Garane Garane. *Il latte è buono*. Isernia: Cosmo Iannone, 2005.

Giorgio, Adalgisa. "Writing the Mother-Daughter Relationship." In *Writing Mothers and Daughters*, edited by Adalgisa Giorgio, 11–46. Oxford: Berghahn Books, 2002.

Hassan, Sirad Salad. *Sette gocce di sangue: Due donne somale*. Palermo: Arcidonna, 1996.

Hernandez, Paula. "Sensing Vulnerability, Seeking Strength: Somali Women and Their Experiences during Pregnancy and Birth in Melbourne." In *Reproduction, Childbearing and Motherhood: A Cross-Cultural Perspective*, edited by Pranee Liamputtong, 195–208. New York: Nova Publishers, 2007.

Hirsi, Ali. *Infedele*. Translated by Irene Annoni and Giovanni Giri. Milan: Rizzoli, 2006.

Labanca, Nicola. *Oltremare: Storia dell'espansione coloniale italiana*, Bologne: Il Multino, 2002.

Lambert, José. "Translation, Systems and Research: The Contribution of Polysystem Studies to Translation Studies." *TTR* 8, no. 1 (1995): 105–52.

Lefevere, André. *Translation, Rewriting, and the Manipulation of Literary Frame*. London and New York: Routledge, 1992.

McGown, Rima Berns. *Muslims in the Diaspora: The Somali Communities of London and Toronto*. Toronto: University of Toronto Press, 1999.

Polezzi, Loredana. "Reflections of Things Past: Building Italy through the Mirror of Translation," *New Comparison* 29 (2000): 27–47.

———. *Translating Travel: Contemporary Italian Travel Writing in English Translation*. Aldershot and Brookfield: Ashgate Publishing, 2001.

———. "Translation and Migration," *Translation Studies* 5, no. 3 (2012): 345–56.

Ponzanesi, Sandra. *Paradoxes of Postcolonial Culture: Contemporary Women Writers of the Indian and Afro-Italian Diaspora*. Albany: State University of New York Press, 2004.

———. "The Postcolonial Turn in Italian Studies." In *Postcolonial Italy: Challenging National Homogeneity*, edited by Cristina Lombardi-Diop and Caterina Romeo, 51–70. Basingstoke: Palgrave Macmillan, 2012.

———. "Writing against the Grain: African Women's Texts on Female Infibulations as Literature of Resistance." *Indian Journal of Gender Studies* 7 (2000): 304–18.

Robinson, Douglas. *Translation and Empire: Postcolonial Theories Explained*. Manchester: St. Jerome, 1997.

Scego, Igiaba. *Adua*. Milan: Giunti Editore, 2015.

———. *Adua*. Translated by Jamie Richards. New York: New Vessel Press, 2017.

———. "Dismatria." in *Pecore nere: Racconti*, edited by Flavia Capitani ed Emanuele Coen, 5–21. Rome: Laterza, 2005.

———. "Exmatriates." Translated by Hugh Shankland. in *Rome Tales*, edited by Helen Constantine. Oxford: Oxford University Press, 2011. Kindle edition.

———. *La mia casa è dove sono*. Turin: Loescher Editore, 2012.

———. "Salsicce." In *Impronte: Scritture dal mondo*. Nardò: Besa, 2003.

———. "Sausages." Translated by Giovanna Bellesia-Contuzzi and Vittoria Offredi Poletto. *Metamorphoses* 13, no. 2 (2005): 214–25.

Spivak, Gayatri. "Can the Subaltern Speak?" In *Marxism and the Interpretation of Culture*, edited by Cary Nelson and Lawrence Grossberg, 271–313. Urbana: University of Illinois Press, 1988.

———. *Outside in the Teaching Machine*. New York and London: Routledge, 1993.

Sturge, Kate. "Cultural Translation." *Routledge Encyclopedia of Translation Studies*, edited by Mona Baker and Gabriela Saldanha, 67–70. Second edition. London and New York: Routledge, 2009.

———. *Representing Others: Translation, Ethnography and the Museum*. Manchester: St Jerome Publishing, 2007.

———. "Translation Strategies in Ethnography." *The Translator* 3, no. 1 (1997): 21–38.

Toury, Gideon. "Translated Literature: System, Norm, Performance—Toward a TT-Oriented Approach to Literary Translation." *Poetics Today* 2, no. 4 (1981): 9–27.

Venuti, Lawrence. *The Translator's Invisibility: A History of Translation*. London and New York: Routledge, 1995.

Walker, Alice. *Possedere il segreto della gioia*. Translated by Laura Noulian. Milan: Rizzoli, 1993.

Section II

Trauma and Divided Memory

Chapter Five

At the Edge. Divided Memory on Italy's Borders

The Case of Trieste and the Foibe di Basovizza

John Foot

Italy's borderlands were places where divided memories were played out in the landscape, in the political world, and on the battlefield. These were and are disputed regions, for which hundreds of thousands of people died in both world wars, and the legacy of those conflicts is still with us today. Here, mental boundaries, prejudices, and divisions have proved—for many years— more durable than the shifting boundaries between states.

Every community—political, "ethnic," territorial—created its own narratives of victimhood, which went into battle with those of the other communities.[1] Competing pasts clashed in the streets, on the pages of newspapers, and in the history books. Here, more than anywhere else in Italy, political activism was understood as a battle of memory. Politics was often practiced through the defense of one set of memories, and the destruction of another. History and memory were very different on Italy's borders, in a whole series of ways. Historical interpretations of this area differed widely—and wildly— from the idea of a melting pot of cultures to an exceptional zone of ethnically inspired conflict—the opposite of a melting pot. This chapter will take one case study of a contested site—the so-called *Foibe di Basovizza*—to try and map and understand the relationship in this place between history, memory, and political mobilization. To do this, we need to start with the Fascist regime.

BASOVIZZA, 1930; OPICINA, 1941

Basovizza is a small town, outside and above Trieste, criss-crossed by a number of important and contrasting places of memory. The name itself of the place is contested—it is a place with two names, like many places in this area—Basovizza and Basovica. On September 6, 1930, four Slovene anti-Fascists, aged between twenty-two and thirty-four, were executed at dawn by a Fascist firing squad in the military firing range. According to the rigors of Fascist law, they were shot in the back. Ferdo Bidovec, Franjo Marušiè, Zvonimir Miloš, and Lojze Valenèiè had all been given death sentences by the *Tribunale speciale per la sicurezza dello Stato*, a special legal body set up in 1926 by the regime to judge "crimes against the state." The four men (who became known as the "Martyrs of Basovizza") were all part of an illegal anti-Fascist organization that had carried out a number of bomb attacks in Trieste. One of their targets had been a Fascist monument—the so-called Lighthouse of Victory. For the *Tribunale* judges this sentence was a "provvedimento di legittima difesa della civiltà contro la barbarie"[2] (an action of self-defense of civilization against barbarity). Five other men were given long prison sentences. The *Tribunale* had made its first "trip" outside of Rome to condemn the four men in 1930.

Commemorations were organized throughout the 1930s in defiance of the regime, and on September 9, 1945 a monument was erected on the spot where the men were killed, which is the site of annual commemorations, as well as of a sports tournament. For the ex- or post-Fascists, the 1930 Basovizza monument remains a bridge too far, an unacceptable part of any "shared memory." When Walter Veltroni visited the *foiba di Basovizza*, the Risiera but also the monument to the *fucilati* of 1930 (accompanied by the mayor), the vice mayor of the city, Paris Lippi, was unhappy. Veltroni, he said "non avrebbe dovuto andare a rendere omaggio ai fucilati di Basovizza: erano terroristi, avevano dato vita a una banda armata che voleva separare Trieste dall'Italia"[3] (he should not have paid tribute to the ones shot in Basovizza: they were terrorists and had organized an armed gang to separate Trieste from Italy). Over the years, there have been a number of disputes, for example, over the signs indicating the monument and the wording of these directions.

In February 1941, an even more spectacular trial was held in Trieste under the auspices of the *Tribunale*. The fate of the accused from this particular trial tells us a lot about the ways in which the postwar period has been simplified by politicians and others since 1945. Twelve death sentences were handed down this time, and on December 15, 1941, five of these were carried out at the shooting range at Opicina, on the hills above Trieste. Today, a small plaque remembers these "martyrs," alongside other plaques relating to later shootings there, but the shooting range is still in use. An annual commemoration is held for these victims.

THE FOIBE[4]: BLACK HOLES OF HISTORY, AND MEMORY

The word *foibe* is used in Friuli and in Istria to indicate deep natural cavities in the limestone terrain of the Carso. There are hundreds of such profound holes in the ground in that zone. These "cavernous pits [are] characterized by a narrow and often hidden opening on the surface."[5] They "descend for various hundreds of meters in the bowels of the earth."[6] However, this word also indicates something even more sinister—the deaths of thousands of people, the vast majority of whom were Italian, in September 1943 in Istria and May 1945 in Trieste, Gorizia, and the surrounding provinces.

The first wave of *infoibamenti* exploded in 1943, in Istria, after September 8. The collapse of the Italian state left a power vacuum. It was a time of local revolution, an overturning of the past. A number of Italians—as representatives of that state, but also for social and ethnic reasons—were arrested. Some six hundred to seven hundred were shot, normally—but not always—after summary trials. Some of these were thrown into *foibe* across the region. Then the Nazis arrived and *these* killings stopped. During their occupation of the area, the Nazis carried out their own series of massacres, round-ups, and executions.

After two years of a ferocious war—which was also a series of civil wars—the area was liberated from the Nazis, thanks largely to the Tito's Yugoslav army. Tito's partisans won the race for Trieste in May 1945 and quickly began to arrest and take away thousands of people in the city, and in Gorizia. Most of the arrested were Italians—policemen, soldiers, tax officers, administrators, teachers—but there were also Croats and Slovenes among those picked up. Tito's plan was to install a new state—a Communist state. All potential opposition was to be eliminated, and thus also those anti-Fascists who did not identify with the communist project. This "preventative purge," as it has been called, was accompanied by moments of class and ethnic hatred, and some personal settling of accounts. Twenty years of "denationalisation" had left its mark. More than ten thousand people were arrested in this way, and "thousands" of these disappeared, never to return.[7] Most historians have settled on a figure of four thousand to five thousand dead.

Not all of those who were arrested were killed immediately, and only a relatively small number were murdered and thrown in the *foibe*, with an even smaller number being killed by being thrown into *foibe*. Many ended up in camps in Yugoslavia—where some were killed, while others died on long forced marches. Not all these people were killed merely because they were

Italian, but it often seemed that way. The killings were rarely random. The Italians felt that they were being wiped out—and many waited years before they were able to know what had happened to their fathers and sons who had been arrested. Often it was impossible to even hold a funeral for these victims. Many lived for years in uncertainty. It was easy for politicians to exploit this climate of fear and doubt for their own ends, both in 1945 and in subsequent years. When the dust had settled, it seems that some four thousand to five thousand people had been killed in the wave of violence in May 1945, with around ten thousand arrests. Those who returned, in any case, had lived through a trauma that they would carry with them for the rest of their lives.

Thus, beyond all the symbolic use of the *foibe*, and the political struggles over memory since 1943, the events that gave birth to this term took place at two precise historical moments, in two specific places: in Istria after September 8, 1943, for a period of more or less one month, and then a much larger zone—taking in Trieste and Gorizia—in the spring of 1945, again for a month or so. Both periods had some similar features—a power vacuum, with disputes over who was in charge and over the law itself, and a sense of "comeback time" after twenty years of Italian Fascism.

We can only understand the importance of the *foibe*, and the ways in which they created radically divided memories, if we see them from both points of view. It is clear, for example, looking back, that the violence of September 1943 in Istria had complicated roots and outcomes, but as Pupo has written, "the perception of these events by the Italian population was far more simple and one sided."[8] The *foibe* were powerful symbols of elimination. They were traditionally places where things were disposed of, thrown away, made to disappear—but also sites of murder, suicide, threats, and fear. They were places of nightmares.

But there was something of a gap between the events of 1943 and 1945 and the way they were understood by the local population. After the first wave of violence subsided, the explorations of the *foibe* began, in Istria. Thirty-one *foibe* were examined in 1943, with 217 bodies recovered, of whom 16 were identified as soldiers. This was a time of confusion, of dual or sometimes triple power, of panic and anger, of spies and counterspies, of misinformation, propaganda, of collapse and attempts to recreate new forms of state power, of invasion and occupation and liberation.

On May 1, 1945, Tito's partisan troops took over the institutions of the state as they marched into Trieste. In other parts of Italy, the Committees of National Liberation were seen as the center of the new democratic state-system. Trieste was different. There, the Italians in the CLN were thrown out of the prefect's palace and their Italian flags were taken down by force. In their place there was often a new version, with a red star in the middle, or the Yugoslav flag, or red flags. Clocks were set to Yugoslav time. The "45 days" had begun. But Tito's troops left the city—forever—on June 12, 1945. At that point, the period of the *foibe* was over.

Ever since, the debates over what happened, why and to whom—and thus over how to remember those events—has occupied the hearts and minds of the local population, causing endless debates, arguments, and occasionally further violence. The events on the northeast border of Italy during and after World War II have created the most celebrated and debated case of divided memory in Italy. It remains difficult—even today—on the left, to discuss the *foibe* without sweating a bit, without looking over your shoulder, without endless justifications, without changing the subject.

There have been a series of attempts in recent years to overcome this taboo, above all by local politicians and historians, but there remains a tendency to exploit this issue for propaganda and short-term gain—on the right and the left—and this has made the history and memory of the *foibe* a story crammed with and patterned by politics, a classic case of the "public use of history."[9] When discussing the *foibe*, there is a need for clarity, and great caution. And this isn't easy, because this area of Europe has been marked by civil wars, ethnic conflict, and opposing historiographies that have often created confusion, reciprocal negationisms, and strong tendencies toward exaggeration or minimalization. History fought its own wars here. One side's victims went into battle against those of the other side, well after the war itself was over. The dead were never simply dead, they were "martyrs" and/or "Fascists," "terrorists," and/or "freedom-fighters."

To understand the *foibe*, we need to look back in time—to the history of Austria, to the histories of Croatia, Slovenia, and Serbia, to Fascism and the violent occupation of Yugoslavia by the Italian army after 1941. We need to understand and unpack a series of historical myths—the myth of the "good Italian," the myth of the resistance, the idea that Fascism was essentially benign, at least in comparison with the Nazis. We need to see all points of view, that of the Slovenes, that of the exiles and refugees from Istria, that of the Italians in Trieste and Gorizia. After Mussolini, the Nazi occupation and a war that was also a series of civil wars, class war, and a war of national liberation, the *foibe* events took place. This in turn was one of the key contributing factors behind the mass and permanent exodus—the *esodo*—of around three hundred thousand Italians from Istria to Italy in the 1940s and 1950s. The *foibe* thus became the terrifying and powerful symbol—for some—of a season of violence. So the term *foibe* has this catch-all connotation, indicating the "mass violence against soldiers and civilians, who were mostly Italians, which took place in the autumn of 1943 and the spring of 1945 in different areas of Venezia Giulia and led to thousands of victims."[10] In terms of the popular imaginary, the *infoibati* are all those killed in these two moments, at the hands of the Yugoslav authorities, Slovene and Croat

partisans as well as by or with the help of pro-Yugoslavian Italian communists.

THE NUMBERS GAME

Debates over the numbers who died are still ongoing—and seem endless. But
they are also more or less irrelevant for this study. *They tell us very little
about postwar history or memory.* In fact, these debates themselves are part
of the history of divided memory over these issues. What did the actual
numbers of dead matter to those who saw Tito's troops arrive, watched them
shoot on those demonstrating behind the Italian flag, and witnessed them
making house-to-house arrests, lists in hand? What did the actual numbers of
dead matter to those who saw their fathers and sons taken away in the night
or marched through town? Myth, fear, and reality have always played a part
in the history of the *foibe*. Historians and history played little role here.

By talking *only* about numbers and explorations of *foibe*, and by concen-
trating on a "dismantling" of obviously propagandistic accounts by the right,
there was no need to talk about the *foibe* at all. A number of straw men were
constructed—and then knocked down. Basovizza wasn't a "real" *foibe*, the
bodies found there were probably not Italians, and so on. What this failed
miserably to deal with was the reality of two crucial moments: the purging of
Italians—and not just "fascists" after 1943 (in a revolutionary moment in
Istria itself) and in Trieste and Gorizia in 1945—and the connection between
these moments and the *grande esodo* (mass exodus) of Italians from Istria to
Italy, when more than a quarter of a million people left their homes forever.

On the other side of the fence, the tendency to ignore the historical context that led to the *foibe* and deportations leads naturally to an ethnic explanation for what happened—Italians were killed *just because they were Italian*,
because the Slavs were animals. No thanks to more than twenty years of
oppression—savage even by Fascist standards, to numerous show trials, to
humiliation on a daily basis, and in the wake of a vicious civil war and an
occupation that left thousands dead. It is this context that is missing from the
celebratory and commemorative industry that has been built up over the *foibe*
and the *esodo* in recent years. Without a clear acknowledgement of the context of the *foibe*, then the *foibe* commemorations are themselves incomplete—and inevitably divisive.

One problem with the numbers debate is a confusion about *how* people
died. The tendency to include all those killed in 1943 and 1945 as *infoibati*
has not helped the debate, inflaming opinions on either side and leading to an
obssession with body counts. People died in many different ways, and usually not through the act of being thrown physically into *foibe*. Bodies were
found in various *foibe*—but they were not always Italian bodies, or even

identifiable. Many people were shot after summary trials—or even without such "justice"—as during the *resa dei conti* (settling of accounts) in Italy. People who had escaped this fate arrived back in dribs and drabs, as with those from Dalmazia and the Quarnero in 1944 and in March 1945 from Pola.[11] We will never have a final, undisputed figure for the *infoibati*, just as we are condemned to work with rounded-up or rounded-down figures with the *resa dei conti*. There has never been an official, complete public investigation into those events.

But the numbers game was crucial for the debates over memory and commemoration. Various lists of the *infoibati* did the rounds in the 1940s, 1950s, and 1960s. The most important of these was the book published by Gianni Bartoli, mayor of Trieste from 1949 to 1957 and a leading Christian Democrat (as well as being born in Rovigno), a copy of which was buried near to the *Foibe di Basovizza* (and is now on show in the new documentation/exhibition center). Some of these names later ended up on monuments, graves, or plaques—665 in Gorizia in 1985. Trieste's library collected names from the 1950s onward and finished doing so in 1983. This archive was updated continually over the years. Bartoli's book was produced in various editions. Four thousand one hundred and twenty-two names were listed in the most well-known edition from 1961. From the right Luigi Papo, one of the most active propagandists on *foibe* issues, published another *albo d'oro* (hall of fame)—with numbers at the top end of the scale.[12]

INTERPRETATIONS: THE FOIBE AS REVENGE, AS A POLITICAL PROJECT, AS "BARBARITY"

No extended comparison has been carried out between the *resa dei conti* in Italy and the *foibe* killings and deportations in the northeast and Istria. There are obviously comparisons to be made—the anger, the public humiliation, the targeting of leading Fascists. But we also need to be aware of the differences—the ethnic and national nature of the northeast *resa dei conti*, Tito's political project for that zone, the divisions in the resistance here. For Pupo, Trieste was closer to Lubiana in 1945 than to Reggio Emilia. But Guido Crainz was reminded of his own work on the *resa dei conti* when he began to look at the *foibe* and the *esodo*.[13] Giampaolo Valdevit has called the events of May 1945 a system of "preventative purging" as part of the attempt to "overturn" everything—the state, the nation, the past.[14]

Were Italians killed just *because they were Italians*? Sometimes, this clearly happened. Being Italian was a reason to be killed or deported. But it was rarely enough *on its own*. Italians were targeted because they were Fascists, largely, or as part of the Fascist state. This was not ethnic hatred but a political question. The oft-used phrase "they were killed just because they were Italian" thus gives us only a part of the story and, if used in isolation, tends to paint an ahistorical picture of what happened. The *foibe* were certainly not random—there were lists of people to arrest, especially in 1945. If being Italian was all that mattered, why bother to have lists? Tito's oppression was anything but random. Istria in 1943 was a somewhat different story, with its revolutionary and class characteristics that bring it much closer to Reggio Emilia in 1945 than Trieste in 1945. The ethnic nature of Istria 1943 was strong and often spontaneous. By 1945, things were very different.

Tito was more interested in those who were part of the state machine, rather than the big names at the top. Participants in potentially alternative projects to that of a Yugoslav communist state were often the first to be removed from the scene, as with the autonomists in Fiume. After May 1 there was a "diluvio di sequestri, di arresti, di uccisioni" (a flood of kidnappings, arrests, killings) in a heady mix of "vendetta, odio e progetto" (revenge, hatred and project).[15] The arrests of Slovenes and Croats—especially around Gorizia—creates further problems for any interpretation based around "ethnic cleansing."[16] But the subjective experience of violence was often interpreted in ethnic terms, especially after twenty years of anti-Slav propaganda and a bitter and partly civil war. Without an understanding of the power of this subjective experience, we cannot grasp the importance of the *foibe* issue in postwar Trieste and Istria. Given these radical divisions over what had happened, and why, it was hardly surprising that the memory of these contested events should produce deep contrasts and long-lasting debates.

FOIBE, MEMORY, AND MONUMENTS: BASOVIZZA SINCE 1945[17]

The so-called *foibe of Basovizza* is just outside of the city of Trieste, a short bus ride or car journey away. But Basovizza is not a natural *foibe* but a deep hole in the ground, created to look for coal in the early twentieth century and then abandoned. It originally reached down 256 meters into the ground, but in the 1930s there were signs that material had been dumped into the shaft.

In 1980 the Basovizza shaft became a "monument of national interest" (along with another *foibe* nearby) and in 1992 its status was elevated to that of a *national monument*, like the Risiera di San Sabba (a Nazi ex-detention and transport camp) in Trieste itself.[18] In recent years there has been a proliferation of plaques, monuments, and other commemorative signs around the site of the hole in the ground, which is now marked out by a surrounding wall. In 2005 Basovizza was at the center of the commemorations for the first "day of remembrance" of the *foibe* and the *esodo*. It is the most famous and most visited of all the sites that go under the name of the *foibe*, and the number of visitors is increasing every year, including many school groups.

In 2007 a new monument was inauguarated at the site, with a metallic cover over the shaft entrance and a sculpture that represents the crane used by the Allies to try and recover bodies after the war. When I visited Basovizza in 2008, a sparkling new visitor center had just been opened, with a small exhibition on the history of the *foibe* and Basovizza, plus a bookshop, a new guide in four languages and some exhibits, like the original—and once buried—copy of Gianni Bartoli's list of *infoibati*. Eight thousand five hundred people visited the site in the two months after the new visitor center was opened.

For many years, the memory of the *foibe* was a local memory, making it extremely difficult to have an impact beyond Italy's northeast borders. At a national level, the *foibe* was an issue for the neo-Fascist right who looked to create a different set of memories of the war, an alternative to the fragile anti-Fascist consensus that still held sway in Italy. For the neo-Fascists, the *foibe* were an ideal vehicle with which they could attempt to "de-nationalise the Resistence" and create their own memories.[19] While neo-Fascists celebrated *foibe* victims as Italian heroes, they also saw many of them as specifically *Fascist* victims—as with the *resa dei conti* in the rest of Italy. This apparent contradiction was rarely underlined in the *foibe* debates. The association of the neo-Fascists—who were excluded from the national political system until the 1990s—with the exile community and the memory of the *foibe* was a key factor in the silence over these issues at a national level and amongst mainstream historians.

The *foibe* contained a number of elements that combined to bring this memory to the fore in the 1990s—at a national level. As we have seen, the *foibe* were a potent political memory in a local sense from 1943 onward, even if official monuments did not become the norm until the 1980s, in Gorizia, and the 1990s, in Trieste. For one thing, the *foibe* allowed for an alternative view of World War II to emerge and be given recognition. This was a version that problematized the whole idea of "liberation." In some parts of Italy, the country was not "liberated" by the Allies, and even where this liberation did take place, it was neither linear nor pain-free—bombings, rapes, violence against the local population were also carried out by the Allies, as David W. Ellwood's chapter in this volume discusses. The *foibe* allowed this kind of experience, which had largely been ignored by historians, to be given form. The postwar consensus around anti-Fascism had started to break down in the 1980s, if not before. Other memories, uncomfortable memories, began to make inroads. Other narratives came into play. The good guys—or the victims—were no longer exclusively the partisans and/or the Allies.

Moreover, this was designed to be a *national* memory—Italians were killed, in some ways, because they were Italians. The story of the *foibe* took charge just as two political forces were looking for further legitimacy at a national political level—the post-communists and the post-Fascists. *Alleanza Nazionale* (AN) were adept at pushing alternative memories from World War II. Meanwhile, for the ex-communists anxious to distance themselves from their own past, the *foibe* offered an ideal point of rupture.

The context of the break-up of Yugoslavia and the overturning of previously dominant memories in Croatia and Serbia was also central. In the early 1990s, Yugoslavia broke up through a horrific civil war, a war where history and memory played a key role before, during, and after the conflict, above all with reference to World War II. With the end of that war, the formerly dominant myth of the communist partisan as national hero has collapsed. Today's national heroes from the past—in Serbia—are the anti-communist chetniks. In Croatia, a similar about turn has taken place. As Gobetti has written, "in both Serbia and Croatia, in the 1990s, the partisans became associated with enemies of the nation."[20] This was not the case in Italy, where things certainly shifted, but there was still opposition to any wholesale overturning of classic accounts of the resistance.

In Italy, references to the *foibe* often used the racial stereotype of the brutality of the Slavs, and the "instability" of the Balkans. The images of the Yugoslav civil war in the 1990s, which was read as a repetition of a violent past, inherent to the region, affected the terminology linked to the *foibe*, especially through the use of the term "ethnic cleansing."[21]

In the 1990s, the neo-Fascist right was brought back into the national fold, in part through a renunciation (in 1994) of its own past. *Alleanza Nazionale* politicians have since governed at both national and local levels, including in the cities of Trieste and Gorizia. Once in power, these politicians have opened up the issue of the *foibe*, and have created public memory around the *foibe* and the *esodo*. There are now hundreds of roads and square across the country named after the "martyrs of the *foibe*," as well as thousands of plaques and monuments. In 2004, this process was institutionalized with a bipartisan vote (the far left voted neither in favor nor against) on a day of remembrance for the victims of the *foibe* and the *esodo*. This was the text of the law: "The Republic recognizes February 10 as Day of Remembrance to preserve and renew the memory of the tragedy of the Italians and of all the victims of the *foibe*, of the exodus of the inhabitants of Istria, Fiume and Dalmatia from their lands after the Second World War and of the more complex events of the Eastern Border."[22]

Since then, this memory creation has proceeded apace. Three Italian presidents have visited Basovizza—Cossiga in 1991 (where he famously knelt in front of the monument), Scalfaro in 1993, and Ciampi in 2000. Myriad ceremonies, plaques, and monuments dedicated to the *foibe* are also being extended to Slovenia, where the opening of the frontier has led to a rich historical debate.

It would thus appear that divided memories have come together around the *foibe*. But things are more complicated than they seem. One problem was the choice of the date for the day of remembrance. February 10, the anniversary of the 1947 Peace Treaty, is so close to January 27, the day of memory for the Shoah, that it risks weakening the impact of both annual events. It seemed to reflect a desire to divide the Italians into those who commemorate one event, or the other—but not both. The presence at either day has become a sign of belonging for some, an element of political, ethnic, or religious identity. Memory and propaganda are often closely linked.

Historians often expressed their anger about the proximity of the two most important days of memory.[23] There was—and is—considerable resistance to any kind of comparison between the *foibe,* as represented by Basovizza, and the Holocaust, as symbolized in Risiera di San Sabba—also in Trieste. For Collotti, the only thing that these two "events" had in common was "l'appartenere tutte all'esplosione, sino allora inedita, di violenze e sopraffazioni che hanno fatto del secondo conflitto mondiale un vero e proprio mattatoio della storia"[24] (their being part of the explosion, unknown up until then, of violence and abuses that have made of the Second World War a real abattoir of history). By leaving just two weeks between the days of memory, the Italian state seemed to acknowledge that memories would remain divided, but also recognized the importance of both sets of memory. This was a form of pacification through division. Each side could celebrate its own memory in peace—at least in theory. For Franzinetti, "with the two days of memory in place, the 'Holocaustisation' of the *foibe* was complete. The symmetry between the *Giorno della Memoria* (for the extermination of the Jews) and the *Giorno del ricordo* (for the *foibe*) was intentional and perfect. Just as Italian schools have to commemorate the first date, so they have to commemorate the second date."[25]

Divisions about the past continue to reemerge at regular intervals, including those about the form and content of the various complicated commemorative ceremonies that are now in place, and which undergo subtle changes every year. Despite significant moves toward consensus amongst historians about the events in question, the memory of those years still divides Italians, Croats, Slovenes, and Serbs. This tension was seen dramatically during the third "day of remembrance" in 2007, when Giorgio Napolitano, a lifelong but now ex-communist, and president of Italy, made a short but explosive speech. One phrase was particularly controversial:

> Vi fu dunque un moto di odio e di furia sanguinaria, e un disegno
> annessionistico slavo, che prevalse innanzitutto nel Trattato di pace del 1947, e
> che assunse i sinistri contorni di una "pulizia etnica."[26]

(There was then a wave of hatred and bloody rage, and a Slav annexation
project that prevailed first of all in the 1947 Peace Treaty, and that acquired the
sinister form of "ethnic cleansing").

Two days later, there was a furious response from the president of Croatia, Stipe Mesic, "Queste affermazioni, nelle quali uno non può non vedere
elementi di aperto razzismo, revisionismo storico e ricerca di vendetta politica, sono difficili da mettere accanto al dichiarato desiderio per la promozione
di relazioni bilaterali."[27] (These statements, in which it is not possible not to
see elements of open racism, historic revisionism and a desire for political
revenge, are hard to be placed together with the declared desire for the
promotion of bilateral relations).

The spat was soon closed, but it was revealing. Napolitano's version of
events could have been taken right out of a right-wing speech on the *foibe*
from the 1950s and 1960s. The desire to break with the past had led to
adoption of phrases from what had once been the opposite side of the political spectrum, and terms—such as ethnic cleansing—that were not part of the
historical consensus about the *foibe*. Memories had not been reconciled, it
seems, as some had claimed in the 1990s. It is difficult to imagine the *foiba
of Basovizza* becoming a site of shared memory, without recognition of other
sites in the area, including those in Basovizza itself.

BASOVIZZA: THE DEVELOPMENT OF A MEMORY SITE

Basovizza's postwar history has been marked by constant conflicts over the
use, memory, and access to the *foibe*. Basovizza is a largely Slovenian town,
extremely close to the frontier, and it was also the site for a large refugee
center. Some argue that these refugee centers were placed close to the fron-
tiers as "barriers" against the East.[28] Today, this refugee center has become a
museum, which can be visited at the same time as the *foiba*.

Basovizza has not always been a memorial site of this importance. Controversy was created by the abandonment of the site at various times. In 1950
the mine was used as a rubbish dump for the Allies, and in November 1953
official permission was given for a company to collect iron deposits from the
bottom of the pit, a strange decision given the supposed importance of this
site as a *foiba*. At this time some workers descended as far as 226 meters
under the surface, without coming across bodies or explosives. In 1954 the
pit became a rubbish dump again. It was finally covered over in 1959 and
made into a monument, under the auspices of the war memorial committee of
the Ministry of Defence.

A simple but large gray stone cover was placed over the mine entrance,
with a cross, and a plaque containing the "prayer for the *infoibati*" was added
(and composed by Bishop Antonio Santin). To the left, a plaque showing

various measurements inside the shaft was accompanied by a religious lamp. The plaque carried the controversial and unproven claim—first aired by a journalist in 1945—that there were five hundred square meters of "dead bodies" (or *salme infoibate*—which identified the bodies as a certain kind of victim) inside the shaft. The idea that there were so many bodies inside the *foiba* that they had to be measured in this way has been a powerful feature of the propaganda around this site since 1945, and this particular plaque has been subject to a number of defacings, including adjustments (later "corrected") to the five hundred meters "figure."[29] Numerous commemorations have taken place at Basovizza since 1945, many of which are recorded in the local press or in the work of Spazzali. The Santin prayer was usually pronounced during ceremonies at Basovizza. In fact, the history of the commemorations here constitutes a "history within a history."

One of the features of the debates over Basovizza has been precisely around the question of the numbers of bodies found here, and their identity.[30] Claim has followed counterclaim, with entire books being produced on this subject. Basovizza is a controversial site for this key reason. The evidence of deaths here is problematic, and the site was subsequently used in so many different ways—and then closed—that it has become almost impossible to establish what actually happened here, when, and why. This uncertainty has led many historians from the left and the Slovenian side of the divide to argue that the Basovizza site is a "lie," a *falso storico*. It is not difficult for these historians to counter some of the more absurd claims around numbers made by others—in particular those on the right. Some of the numbers used were clearly exaggerated, as with Luigi Papo's claim that 2,500 Italians had died at Basovizza alone.

However, this "debate" really misses the point of what Basovizza has become. The site is a now a symbol for the whole series of deportations, killings, and intimidations that took place in 1943 and then in 1945. It has become a collective place of memory for that whole range of activities that now go under the collective title of *foibe*. As such, there is no need to prove that thousands or even hundreds of people were killed here. And in fact the site itself makes no such claims—apart from the highly controversial plaque. This is clear from the official booklet produced for the new documentation center in 2008. This symbolic nature was true for both "sides" of the memory divide, as protests about the *foibe* and its linked commemorative activities often focus on Basovizza.

Evidence relating to Basovizza ranges from eyewitness statements collected by the Allies, an exploration of the mine shaft—again by the Allies—in 1945 using a winch and various other documents collected by politicians, journalists, Yugoslavia representatives, and other Italian organizations.[31] So, despite the doubts over the bodies found here, and their numbers, Basovizza remains the best documented of all the *foibe* sites, thanks to the variety of material available from various sources. Basovizza also became the symbol of all the *foibe* thanks to its proximity to the city. Those in Istria were off-limits for many years, and the other *foibe* around the city were more difficult to use for commemorations and "pilgrimages." The symbolic centrality of Basovizza thus came at a price. Basovizza "divenne il memoriale per tutte le vittime degli eccidi del 1943 e 1945, ma anche il fulcro di polemiche per il prolungato silenzio e il mancato omaggio delle più alte cariche dello stato" (became the memorial for all the victims of the 1943 and 1945 massacres, but also the cornerstone of controversy for the prolonged silence and the missed tribute of the highest offices of State). [32]

This site had a long and complicated history. With the first covering over in 1959, Basovizza started to play a dominant role. A committee was formed to organize commemorations, with gatherings on June 12 (the anniversary of when Tito's troops left Trieste) and in November (on the double anniversary of the victory in World War I and the return of Trieste to Italy in 1954), but also at other points throughout the year. Annually, the same kinds of arguments were trotted out, in what Spazzali has called "un rito della polemica" [33] (a ritual of controversy). This rite included frequent complaints about the presence of elected officials. When Trieste's mayor was absent from Basovizza in 1972, the Lega Nazionale argued that the *foibe* had been "ufficialmente dimenticate" (officially forgotten). [34] In 1980, as we have seen, the Pozzo di Basovizza was made into a monument of national interest (a slightly lesser category than the Risiera, and there were many complaints about this comparison). Debates raged on in the press. Local communist (and Slovene) administrators occasionally complained about work at the *foibe* site.

On August 6, 1989, three Italian Communist Party politicians visited the site—in a gesture that confirmed the symbolic importance of Basovizza, and not just for the right and the exiles. The communists also went to the Arbe camp on what is now the island on Rab (Croatia) and the Risiera in Trieste. The three were Trieste-born Gianni Cuperlo, the national secretary of the young communists (now a leading figure in the Democratic Party); Stojan Spetic, a Senator; and Nico Costa, the secretary provincial of the PCI at the time. Journalist Claudio Erne understood the importance of this small gesture, as he wrote in *Il Piccolo*, "per salire i due gradini della foiba di Basovizza ci sono voluti 44 anni" [35] (it took 44 years to go up the two steps of the foiba di Basovizza). Cuperlo said that "siamo qui per ricordare, per capire quello che è accaduto, per segnare linee dalle quali non tornare più indietro" [36] (we are here to remember, to understand what has happened, to draw the lines from where never to go back).

Many conflicts were intensely ritualized; during every election campaign, the MSI would hold a meeting in Basovizza, which would invariably be accompanied by incidents. In 1991 the Comune of Trieste took over the organization of the ceremony from the Lega Nazionale, a move that significantly increased the importance of Basovizza in terms of commemorations and the number of politicians attending them. From a simple site, with the covered *foiba* itself with a solitary (if controversial) plaque beside it, the Basovizza area has seen a proliferation of symbols, signs, and memory objects in recent years. Plaques have appeared dedicated to the *Finanzieri*, and to many others, including the alpine troops.

The ongoing story of Basovizza and the divided memories linked to the *foibe* and the day of remembrance (which have continued in recent years) shows how history and memory are still open wounds in Italy—and on its edges. Attempts to close or pacify these divisions through monuments, museums and commemorations have created new forms of shared-divided memories that are both institutionalized and overtly political and politicized. Each side can now commemorate its "own" memories without accepting the validity of those of its opponents. A consensus has been reached over a lack of consensus. It remains to be seen if, as with other fragmentations from the past, time and generational change will lead to a softening of debate and the end of Italy's period of divided memories.

NOTES

1. Pamela Ballinger, *History in Exile: Memory and Identity at the Borders of the Balkans* (Princeton: Princeton University Press), 5.

2. Tristano Matta, "I fucilati di Basovizza," in *Un percorso tra le violenze del novecento nella Provincia di Trieste*, ed. IRSML (Trieste: IRSML, 2006), 37–46.

3. Cited in John Foot, *Fratture d'Italia: Da Caporetto ak G8 di Genova: La memoria divisa del paese* (Milan: Rizzoli, 2009), 124.

4. In this chapter, the terms "foibe," "foiba," and "infoibati" will be used largely in their symbolic sense—to indicate those people (the vast majority of whom were Italians) arrested and killed in two separate moments, September 1943 (Istria) and May 1945 (Trieste and Gorizia and their provinces). Generally, this does not mean that I am claiming that all these people were killed *by* being thrown into "foibe," or that their bodies were disposed of in foibe.

5. Katia Pizzi, *A City in Search of an Author: The Literary Identity of Trieste* (London: Sheffield Academic Press, 2001), 90.

6. Ballinger cited in Pizzi, *A City in Search of an Author*, 90.

7. Raoul Pupo, "La foiba di Basovizza" in IRSML, *Un percorso*, 61.

8. Raoul Pupo, *Il lungo esodo: Istria: le persecuzioni, le foibe, l'esilio* (Milan: Rizzoli, 2005), 75.

9. Nicola Gallerano, ed., *L'uso pubblico della storia* (Milan: Franco Angeli, 1995); Jürgen Habermas and Jeremy Leaman, "Concerning the Public Use of History," *New German Critique*, 44 (1988) 40–50.

10. Raoul Pupo and Roberto Spazzali, *Foibe* (Milan: Mondadori, 2003), 2.

11. Roberto Spazzali, "Contabilità degli infoibati: Vecchi elenchi e nuove fonti," in *Foibe: Il peso del passato: Venezia-Giulia 1943*–1945, Giampaolo Valdevit, ed. (Venice: Marsilio 1997), 97–127.

12. Luigi Papo, *Albo d'oro, la Venezia Giulia e la Dalmazia nell'ultimo conflitto mondiale* (Trieste: Unione degli Istriani, 1995).

13. Guido Crainz, *Il dolore e l'esilio: L'Istria e le memorie divise d'Europa* (Rome: Donzelli, 2005), 53–56.

14. Giampaolo Valdevit, "Foibe: L'eredità della sconfitta," in *Foibe*, Valdevit, ed., 15–32.

15. Annamaria Vinci, "Storia e storie di confine," *Qualestoria*, 2 (December 2007): 112.

16. Raoul Pupo, "Violenza politica tra guerra e dopoguerra: Il caso delle foibe giuliane 1943–1945," in *Foibe*, Valdevit, 50.

17. For the history of Basovizza (and the foibe in general) as memory and anthropology, see Ballinger, *History in Exile*, 129–67.

18. See John Foot, *Fratture d'Italia: Da Caporetto al G8 di Genova: La memoria divisa del paese* (Milan: Rizzoli, 2009), 149–60.

19. Francesco Germinario, *L'altra memoria: L'estrema destra, Salò e la Resistenza* (Turin: Bollati Boringhieri, 1999), see chapter 4 and in particular 91–97.

20. Eric Gobetti, *L'occupazione allegra: Gli italiani in Jugoslavia (1941–1943)* (Rome: Carocci, 2007),18. See also, for these processes, Pamela Ballinger, *History in Exile*, 106–12.

21. See Ballinger, *History in Exile*, 145–46.

22. Law March 30, 2004, n. 92, "Istituzione del 'Giorno del Ricordo' in memoria delle vittime delle foibe, dell'esodo giuliano-dalmata, delle vicende del confine orientale e concessione di un riconoscimento ai congiunti degli infoibati," *Gazzetta Ufficiale*, n. 86, April 16, 2004. For the *esodo* see John Foot, "Memories of an Exodus: Istria, Fiume, Dalmatia, Trieste, Italy, 1943–2010" in *Totalitarian Dictatorships: New Histories*, Daniele Baratieri et al., eds. (London: Routledge, 2014), 232–50.

23. Enzo Collotti, "Prefazione," in Giacomo Scotti, *Dossier Foibe* (Lecce: Manni, 2005), 7.

24. Ibid.

25. Guido Franzinetti, "The Rediscovery of the Istrian Foibe," *Jahrbücher für Geschichte und Kultur Südosteuropas*, 8 (2006), 90.

26. Giorgio Napolitano, President of the Italian Republic, February 10, 2007.

27. For an acute analysis of the content of Napolitano's controversial, if short, speech, see Franzinetti, "The Rediscovery of the Istrian Foibe," 90–92.

28. Sandi Volk, *Esuli a Trieste: Bonifica nazionale e rafforzamento dell'italianità sul confine Orientale* (Udine: Kappa Vu, 2004).

29. For the symbolic importance of Basovizza to the right and to exile groups, see Ballinger, *History in Exile*, 144.

30. Claudia Cernigol, *Operazione foibe a Trieste: Tra storia e mito* (Udine: Kappa Vu, 2005), Giorgio Rustia, *Contro operazione foibe a Trieste*, 2000, also available online via the site of the Lega Nazionale. For Basovizza, see also the material available at http://www.nuovaalabarda.org.

31. See Pupo and Spazzali, *Foibe*, pp. 71–82 and 225–35 for a selection of documents and a commentary.

32. *Foibe*, 235.

33. *Foibe*, 261.

34. Roberto Spazzali, *Foibe: Un dibattito ancora aperto: Tesi politica e storiografica giuliana tra scontro e confronto* (Trieste: Editrice Lega nazionale, 1990) 262.

35. Cited in Spazzali, *Foibe*, pp. 399–400.

36. Ibid.

WORKS CITED

Ballinger, Pamela. *History in Exile: Memory and Identity at the Borders of the Balkans.* Princeton: Princeton University Press, 2003.

Cernigol, Claudia. *Operazione foibe a Trieste: Tra storia e mito.* Udine: Kappa Vu, 2005.

Collotti, Enzo. "Prefazione." In Giacomo Scotti, *Dossier Foibe.* Lecce: Manni, 2005.

Guido, Crainz. *Il dolore e l'esilio: L'Istria e le memorie divise d'Europa* (Rome: Donzelli, 2005).

Foot, John. *Fratture d'Italia: Da Caporetto ak G8 di Genova: La memoria divisa del paese.* Milan: Rizzoli, 2009.

———. "Memories of an Exodus: Istria, Fiume, Dalmatia, Trieste, Italy, 1943–2010." In *Totalitarian Dictatorships: New Histories* edited by Daniele Baratieri et al., 232–50. London: Routledge, 2014.

Franzinetti, Guido. "The Rediscovery of the Istrian Foibe," *Jahrbücher für Geschichte und Kultur Südosteuropas*, 8 (2006): 85–98.

Gallerano, Nicola, ed. *L'uso pubblico della storia*. Milan: Franco Angeli, 1995.

Germinario, Francesco. *L'altra memoria: L'estrema destra, Salò e la Resistenza*. Turin: Bollati Boringhieri, 1999.

Gobetti, Eric. *L'occupazione allegra: Gli italiani in Jugoslavia (1941–1943)*. Rome: Carocci, 2007.

Habermas, Jürgen, and Jeremy Leaman. "Concerning the Public Use of History." *New German Critique*, 44 (1988): 40–50.

Matta, Tristano. "I fucilati di Basovizza" in IRSML, *Un percorso tra le violenze del novecento nella Provincia di Trieste*. Trieste: IRSML, 2006.

Papo, Luigi. *Albo d'oro, la Venezia Giulia e la Dalmazia nell'ultimo conflitto mondiale*. Trieste: Unione degli Istriani, 1995.

Pizzi, Katia. *A City in Search of an Author: The Literary Identity of Trieste*. London: Sheffield Academic Press, 2001.

Pupo, Raoul, and Roberto Spazzali. *Foibe*. Milan: Mondadori, 2003.

———. "La foiba di Basovizza." In *Un percorso, tra le violenze del novecento nella Provincia di Trieste*, edited by IRSML, 81–90. Trieste: IRSML, 2006.

———. *Il lungo esodo: Istria: le persecuzioni, le foibe, l'esilio*. Milan: Rizzoli, 2005.

Spazzali, Roberto. "Contabilità degli infoibati: Vecchi elenchi e nuove fonti." In *Foibe: Il peso del passato: Venezia-Giulia 1943–1945* edited by Giampaolo Valdevit, 97–127. Venice: Marsilio 1997.

———. *Foibe: Un dibattito ancora aperto: Tesi politica e storiografica giuliana tra scontro e confront*. Trieste: Editrice Lega nazionale, 1990.

Volk, Sandi. *Esuli a Trieste: Bonifica nazionale e rafforzamento dell'italianità sul confine Orientale*. Udine: Kappa Vu, 2004.

Valdevit, Giampaolo. "Foibe: L'eredità della sconfitta." In *Foibe: Il peso del passato: Venezia-Giulia 1943–1945* edited by Giampaolo Valdevit, 15–32. Venice: Marsilio 1997.

Vinci, Annamaria. "Storia e storie di confine," *Qualestoria*, 2 (December 2007): 107–14.

Chapter Six

Remembering War

Memory and History in Claudio Magris's Blameless

Sandra Parmegiani

In a 1974 interview, Michel Foucault spoke of "a battle for and around history going on at this very moment. . . . The intention is to reprogramme, to stifle what I've called 'popular memory,' and also to propose and impose on people a framework in which to interpret the present."[1] His concept of popular memory refers to those memories articulated by individuals whom society has increasingly prevented from producing their own history. Among the tools used in this battle Foucault points to the manipulation of memory: "[I]f one controls people's memory . . . one also controls their experience, their knowledge of previous struggles."[2]

In May 1974, Diego de Henriquez died in Trieste in a mysterious fire in the warehouse where he lived, surrounded by a vast and bizarre collection of war memorabilia, which also included a personal archive. In it, among piles of recorded notes and historical documents on his collection, were de Henriquez's notebooks that allegedly contained sensitive information about the only German concentration camp on Italian soil: the Risiera of San Sabba. This early twentieth-century rice-husking facility on the outskirts of Trieste was turned, after the September 1943 German occupation of the city, into a camp where Jews, political dissidents, and partisans were imprisoned, tortured, and either killed, or sent to other camps in Central and Eastern Europe. From April 1944 to the liberation of the city at the end of April 1945, the Risiera had an operational oven that the Germans blew up before their final capitulation. De Henriquez's death has never been fully explained and it probably never will, but his decades-long plans to build a museum of war that would contribute to an everlasting peace, and his connection to the Risiera and to the trial that in the 1970s put an end to a thirty-year forgotten chapter of Trieste's history, captured Claudio Magris's imagination and free-ly inspired *Blameless*, his latest novel.[3] The struggle for the eradication of an established collective memory that—as Foucault points out—"develops in a kind of conscious moving forward of history"[4] is the overarching subject of the novel.

Magris's post-millennial narrative has been increasingly characterized by a consistent inquiry into individual and collective memory, its fragmentary nature and compelling relation to history, and by an ongoing interrogation into the very possibility of cultural transmission. In the last two decades his work has also formally taken a turn toward stylistic fragmentation and poly-phonic narrative, emphasizing his exploration of the past from a marginal and subaltern perspective. *Blameless* tells the intersecting stories of the anon-ymous deceased collector and of Luisa, the woman in charge of preparing a first plan of the future museum that will host the collector's material. In the background, his mysterious death and the disappearance of the notebooks that contained lists of compromising names, raise questions about the conni-vance of local Triestine personalities as supporter or informers of the Ger-mans, people instrumental to the efficient daily running of the concentration camp and of its load of human suffering.

The fifty-three chapters of the novel are organized as a virtual itinerary along the museum's rooms that host an array of machines and instruments of war (tanks and rifles as well as bows and arrows, specimens of cactuses, an anti-aircraft siren and much more), notes, posters, uniforms, and pages of his surviving notebooks from where the collector's voice speaks with persuasive force and eloquence. Eight additional sections distributed at irregular inter-vals tell the story of Luisa Brooks, the daughter of Sara, a Triestine-Jewish woman whose mother Deborah died in the Risiera, and of Sergeant Brooks, an Afro-American soldier who came to Trieste with the Allied army to liber-ate the city. He did not leave after the end of the Allied military government and in 1954 joined the United States Air Force in Europe at the NATO base of Aviano, not far from Trieste. Luisa embodies the encounter of a lineage of persecution, her genealogy is defined by two century-old exiles of the pre-modern and modern world on both the maternal and paternal side. Her story and the story of her family, interwoven and scattered amid other narrative lines, surfaces through progressive revisitations, in a circular manner that at each reiteration provides incremental knowledge. The reader comes to know that Luisa's grandmother Deborah, arrested in the street and taken to the Risiera, had probably revealed to her jailers the names of the relatives with whom she was hiding in the house of a well-known Fascist sympathizer, an individual above suspicion:

> attorney Radich, later Radice, an old friend of the family since the early beginnings of Fascism when they had found themselves in sympathetic accord

with the regime, like many of Trieste's Jews, Freemasons and Irredentists in love with an anticlerical *Italietta* and a quintessentially Italian Trieste. [5]

Deborah's cousins, the Simeoni, died in the Risiera and also the Aryan attorney Radice in the end "paid for it." [6] This knowledge shatters Sara's life; she retreats into a muted existence from which she emerges only through her short-lived marriage to Sergeant Brooks, who dies when Luisa is still a child in a plane crash at the Aviano base. The cultural accumulation of the generational transmission of knowledge from both the maternal and paternal sides finds in Luisa a subject able to look at her heritage with a new, unique attitude. [7] Through her, the past is "concretely incorporated in the present" [8] and as such it acquires new relevance. It is from this vantage point that she can engage with the collector's material and explore its omnivorous accumulation of traces of remembrance—as well as the eloquent absence of the missing diaries—that in his plans should have constituted a museum of war for the promotion of perpetual peace.

There is also a third narrative line in *Blameless*, comprised of four independently titled sections that form a series of mini-narratives, at first sight only loosely connected to the rest of the novel. These four sections, chronologically and narratively removed from the main plot lines, appear as digressions, but in fact constitute the foundation of the novel's engagement with history and memory. They function as commentaries and, at the same time, as a scaffolding of this composite edifice built on a web of intersecting memories and narratives, which in their uncanny combination flash a blinding light on a dark chapter of failed de-Nazification in postwar Trieste. What ties together the story of the collector and his museum; the account of the Chamacoco Cherwuish, brought from Paraguay to Prague during Kafka's time by the botanist and traveler Vojtec Frič; the story of Schimek, the Austrian soldier who perhaps died refusing to shoot innocent Polish civilians during World War II; the description of Lucia de Navarrete (the Black Pearl of the Caribbean); the retelling of the chaotic days of the liberation of Trieste and of the role then played by Bishop Santin; and the chronicle of the celebrations of Hitler's birthday in Miramare castle on April 20, 1945, a few days before the final capitulation of the Reich? If, as Birgit Neumann states, "[F]ictions of memory . . . turn out to be an imaginative (re)construction of the past in response to current needs," [9] in *Blameless* Magris responds with unprecedented sophistication to the need to provide a counter-memory that "presents its own claim for a more accurate representation of history." [10] This relentless offering of alternative ways of reading and representing the past is not limited to one specific event, but reverberates in every narrative aspect, making the novel an echo chamber of subversion.

Blameless incorporates references to Magris's previous narratives, from *Inferences on a Sabre*, *Danube*, *The Exhibit*, and *Blindly*. This indicates not only an overt and acknowledged continuity with his past works, but the revisitation of themes, subjects, and narrative voices that maintain an enduring relevance and epistemological value. On the other hand, from a narratological perspective, while in Magris's literary works the erratic and splintered nature of the text acquires progressive prominence, the reiteration of a set of foundational concepts provides an endless series of variations on the themes of memory, history, and identity.

The collector's museum becomes in Magris's pages the virtual place of memory where Luisa attempts to order a heterogeneous accumulation of unconnected fragments of life. The museum is both a place of what Lévi-Strauss designates as "radical contingence" and of physical historicity.[11] The collecting mania started when he was eight years old and never faded. Luisa asks herself, "How to organize that insane Museum, excessive even after the funeral pyre had destroyed a large part of the collection, in addition to its even more excessive creator?"[12] In his cataloguing delirium, the collector wanted to trace the genealogy of each piece, from the manufacturing facility in which it was built to the story of its inventor, the people who used it and those it killed. His approach to the collection is the very opposite of the museum that Adorno defines as a mausoleum in which any "vital relationship" to the objects exhibited and "in the process of dying"[13] has ceased. Ironically though, it is Adorno's very critique of the exhibition as a "mockery of what it pretends to conserve"[14] that best describes the ultimate goal of the collector, who wanted to call his museum "Ares for Irene or Arcana Belli: A Comprehensive Museum of War for the Advent of Peace and the Deactivation of History."[15] His intention was to mock war itself: "If everyone gave me their weapons, if all the world's weapons were in the Museum, the world would be disarmed, there would finally be peace. But it would take a huge Museum, as vast as the world."[16]

History, whose impaired vision Magris had explored in his novel *Blindly*, is here described as a "garbage dump,"[17] "an electroshock,"[18] "a crust of blood,"[19] a glioblastoma on an MRI scan; it resembles the hollow center of a geode that

> works behind the frontal lobes, it carves out cavities, fills them, causes them to collapse by filling them with increasingly numerous, ever larger proliferating cells, little snakes that multiply merge split, countless small polyps, the mass of an octopus which expands and destroys its own home. Destroys to expand, to survive, to capture more *Lebensraum*. More space, that is more emptiness. Once the world is empty—a desert, uninhabited, leveled, free.[20]

How to deactivate the mechanism of history gone astray? The museum is the ultimate answer:

All you can do is transport everything into a Museum, where there is no more war because there is no more life. Already a scientist at age five and an inventor at nine, at sixteen I conceived and actually designed fantastic, terrible weapons, but I decided that I would make those models known when there were no more wars in the world and those weapons would be harmless and useless. We must make life—all life, all things—useless, unusable. The price of usage is always, in some way, the price of killing. Blunt the spears, rust the rifles, dull the blade edge, until life, always so razor sharp, no longer cuts. [21]

The museum then is the place where life must be acknowledged in the traces of its destruction and, even more eloquently, in their absence. The collector's frenzied activity to accumulate more and more traces is a never-ending battle against forgetting, in an act of "historical remembrance." Jay Winter in *Remembering War* identifies it as the "symbolic exchange between those who remain and those who suffered and died . . . the recognition, the rethinking, and the restating aloud of claims—moral, political, material— which other human beings have on us." [22]

The museum's material that Luisa painstakingly combs through and orga-nizes is however in the end defined more by absence then by presence. The burning core of the novel (and the implied reason for the final *Auto da fé*–like pyre) is constituted by the missing notebooks with the names of the Triestine informers and the visitors that the prisoners of the Risiera scribbled on the walls of their cells and that were conveniently painted over and removed from the city's memory and its history. Of the collector's transcriptions only a half-portrait survives, anonymous and generic, copied in the dim light during his three-days' feverish activity in the empty shell of the Risiera.

The names of the victims are well known and were for the most part not removed, as are well known the names of those in charge of the camp: among them High Commissioner Reiner and Höherer SS und Polizeiführer Globočnik, who met their death soon after the end of the war; Colonel Ernst Lerch, "the president of the Tradesmen Association of Klagenfurt, where he also has a nice café." [23] He kept a villa on the hills on the Karst for a few years after the war and socialized with the Allied government representatives "because Trieste has lingered in his heart and he feels a sincere brotherhood-in-arms for those officers who are now allies." [24] There is also "Joseph Gas-par Oberhauser, an SS lieutenant who ended up as a contented brewpub keeper in Monaco." [25] By transcribing the names and the drawings etched on the cells' walls, the collector preserved the agency of the vanquished, while the disappearance of those documents "mutilates" the dead. As the collector states after the walls were painted over:

The memory of what happened doesn't exist, it never existed, you don't know that it existed and that it was excised, because it took away with it everything that had happened and that therefore never happened. The smoke from the Risiera's chimney drifts out, recycled and blameless.[26]

The witnesses' absence and their reinflicted muteness can be inscribed in the "legal muteness"[27] identified in the nonverbal by Marianne Hirsch and Leo Spitzer. Magris here fully embraces the eloquent stance of the silent witness and in *Blameless* "silence and muteness" are at times "more telling and forceful than verbal narratives."[28] Like Levi, the collector wants to speak by proxy, as a "mouthpiece" for the dead to whom he bore witness:

> Here they are, the names of those who came to visit, maybe some who were spies. Not many, of course. Still, it's fortunate enough that prisoners were able to leave us those graffiti, those sketches, those names. The Book of Judgment was written by them, with their fingernails and their teeth. I am merely the copyist, the registrar of Judgment Day.[29]

It is difficult not to interpret the unrestrained verbosity of scattered thoughts, digressive narratives, personal confessions, here as in *Blindly*—another novel that invokes the witness as a "continuing presence of the past" and as an "embodiment of memory (*un homme-mémoire*)"[30] —as a device to offset the outrage of the victim's absence.

Trieste emerges from these pages as a laboratory of how to maximize and practice oblivion:

> He was right. Neurosurgery has made astonishing progress. In Trieste it was on the cutting edge. A huge brain, the city; brilliant, troubled, torpid, resilient. They managed to remove a nice piece of this brain's hippocampus, the part that contained the Risiera. Excellent scalpel job, meticulous work, which did not cause any harm or negative consequences. The seahorse extracted with such skill is sitting in a glass case at the Museum of Natural History. The memory of the atrocities is well-guarded and isolated inside the armor of osseous cutaneous shields. . . . Now it's all dried up, but in the mating season the seahorse is very lively; like the city, for that matter, a little withered but libertine and somewhat depraved.[31]

The collector's task was to bring back what must have been part (albeit briefly) of the city's memory and to reimplant that memory of atrocities in its living fabric. Trieste in the immediate postwar period was a divided and scarred city, which opted for a convenient and "therapeutic" forgetfulness. It had inscribed in its political and cultural identity a number of unresolved conflicts and historical clashes between its Italian and Slavic roots, its Jewish and Fascist identity, its German occupation—which was not without support—and a divided allegiance to a multiplicity of liberators (Tito's partisans, CLN partisans, Catholic partisans, the Allied army)[32] with whom at any given time a portion of the population could neither sympathize nor identify.

And then there was the gaping whole of the Risiera, a whole that after thirty years—when all the other conflicts were finally more or less resolved in stable compromises or authentic new solidarities—was still conveying its vexing indictment. In this cacophony of identities and political allegiances it was maybe difficult to keep a straight record and to know one's lasting place in the world, but, Magris suggests, it is always a good idea to set the record straight, first and foremost with oneself. This is why he can have Santin, Trieste's bishop during the crucial hours of the liberation, ask himself, "But have I always protected the flock . . . the Slovenes in the Karst and the Croats of Istria from the Black Shirts, the Triestines who ended up in the Risiera?"[33] To which the narrator notes,

> When they'd sent him to prohibit the *s'ciaveto*, the ancient Glagolitic ritual of the Mass, in some villages in Istria, he certainly hadn't wanted to humiliate those Slavs, he was simply obeying his superiors—but is it right to obey? Is a Christian obedient or rebellious? The Germans who load Jews into the trucks are also obeying.[34]

The answer is in the end-sum of the bishop's deeds, and the provocative question deflates, but Magris suggests that it is good and right to ask it. Those who never ask similar questions—to themselves or to others—have a much heavier and compromised conscience, and after the liberation (for some a new occupation) have instead conveniently reentered the ranks of Trieste's public life, often in prominent positions. The collector's disquieting diaries bring back an absence that had to remain unquestioned and they must therefore be eliminated together with their author: "[A] vacuum is tenacious, it doesn't let you wipe it clean like a stain. But it can be done, yes, absolutely. All of human history is a wiping away of consciousness, above all the consciousness of what disappears, of what has disappeared."[35]

In his account of the creation and persistence of collective memories and their "manufacturing of continuity," Halbwachs notes that it is often sufficient to rekindle a flame and to recover a memory through its preservation among a small portion of a community.[36] Luisa, the female narrator, is well aware of her task—to bring to completion, as best as she can and with the material that the fire left behind, the project that the collector had started. The two communicated extensively, and it is her voice that often complements and completes the collector's scattered thoughts recorded on his notes, and also provides the reader with biographical information that reveals his emotional blocks, his compensatory compulsions, and his grandiose impossible obsessions. Among them there was the creation of a Definitive Universal Dictionary and his belief that death was just a defect of perception and that instead of the disappearance of every trace of our existence, its machine-like device (called the "inverter") would allow us to regain the past up to the point of origin. Fascinating ideas, but quite bizarre—to say the least—that she faithfully acknowledges.

Luisa's family history positions her at a vantage point, a crossroads of culture and history from where she can see farther than other sons or daughters of the city. Luisa's mother had been a belated victim of the Risiera, collateral damage after the fact. After the short interlude of her marriage, her life had returned to the muteness that had characterized her youth, marked by the tragic discovery that placed her on the margins of victimhood and in the impossibility of mourning within the collective memory of her own community.

Once the accident had taken her father away, Luisa had to live with that silent, emotionally withdrawn mother. She treasured the memory of her father's vitality, the stories of his life in Martinique, Puerto Rico, and Memphis, the creole songs that he sang to her at night, the image of her aunt Kasika and of her great-grandmother Tati. These became for the little child, and then for the young woman, a magic world of exotic and all-embracing affections. They too, though, held dark secrets and unspeakable suffering, of which the little girl was, of course, unaware. The city that mastered the oblivion of its own past—in which the Allies willfully played their role—is the same place where Luisa's mother and father could start a new life and where Sara could set aside her inner demons. It was a fresh slate for two human beings who recognized each other and embraced the confluence of their respective exiles:

> Deep river, the River Jordan is wide and deep, yet another river to cross, always yet another river to cross, the promised land always on the other side. The same songs, songs of lost tribes, ten for Israel, countless for Africa; there is no place to hide on this side or on the other side of the river and the sea, under a fierce sun that leaves prey exposed to the hunter. Run nigga' run, I'm burnin' too, crossing the desert, the armored train rushes to Treblinka, the stench of piled-up bodies and the stagnant pall of their breath is the fetid reek that they will soon smell though they will cease smelling it forever the next moment.
> The train of History has bad breath.[37]

Their love is real, profound, a sentiment in which Magris indulges as one of the few (only?) respites in this whirlwind narrative. Sara forgets her pain and her life is renewed, her psychological and emotional makeup radically altered. Her husband too finds closure and sets aside the memories of discrimination and the emotional disruption caused by the death of his sister, Luisa's aunt Kasika, an Army Nurse Corps member who had been beaten to death in a London pub in a random racist episode toward the end of the war. Love regenerates them and the brief romance of this novel acquires a salvific prominence. For Joseph Brooks, postwar Europe seems to hold more promises than America, at least when it comes to his memories of Memphis. Luisa intuitively knows that racism was for him a daily occurrence there, and since her mother too knew very little of those years, she guesses that he "must have been embarrassed to talk about racial insults to someone who had endured the Holocaust."[38]

In retracing her own ancestral roots Luisa tries to imagine an encounter between Mama Tati (her paternal grandmother who had raised her father and his sister in Martinique) and her bourgeois Triestine grandmother Rachel:

> Luisa tried to imagine that face of black clay—there were no photographs of her great-grandmother Tati, unlike her great-grandmother Rachel—mud-caked by the sun despite the wide-brimmed hat, the ancient face of a Mother Earth who can offer her child only two weary breasts, generous and inexhaustible, and the *morne*, the hill over which to escape and become free. A Black Madonna pierced by seven swords, who had too many times survived the torment of having her flesh ripped from her breast, and ready to offer that breast, blessed with milk, to her oppressor's child, because every child is only a child and not the child of an oppressor or future oppressor.[39]

Mama Tati's face fades away in a silent multitude. One has the sense that Magris would love to narratively "rescue" her, if he could. He is partial to those realms of memory that are "estranged from and discontinuous with the present,"[40] modes of life that can't be accessed anymore and have receded, together with the human beings that inhabited them, into an irretrievable past. In a fitting analogy with Magris's approach to history, David Gross states that "in Hegelian terms, this cast off 'stuff' of history represents merely the refuse of the dialectic, the wreckage left over after the 'Worldspirit' (*Weltgeist*) has departed from the scene."[41]

The four independent sections of the novel follow this very path of inquiry and ground the narrative in a return to the non-contemporaneous, through which, Gross states, "one not only pays respect to what has failed or been silenced but also acquires a standpoint from which to criticize the contemporary age—an age that does not seem much inclined to encourage criticism of any kind, above all criticism of itself."[42]

The first of these "historical debris"[43] is the story of Cherwuish Piošad Mendoza, a Paraguayan Chamacoco—"an Indian tribe living (had lived, extinct?)"[44] in the Gran Chaco"—and of Albert Vojtěch Frič, the "explorer, ethnologist, anthropologist and botanist"[45] who brought him to Prague in 1908 to cure him of an intestinal disease. In Kafka's Prague Cherwuish is for everyone an exotic attraction, except for the children who don't mind him and soon ignore his inability to abide by the incomprehensible code of a foreign world.

Frič takes him to his talks around the city and showcases the true materialization of otherness. His "exploitation" of Cherwuish is ambiguous, however, because Albert Vojtěch Frič is himself an embodiment of otherness and also a secular narrative prefiguration of the Triestine collector. The enormous amount of heterogeneous material (trophies, plants, roots, axes, tents, etc.) that he brings to Prague defies every cataloguing effort and he is forced to set up quarters not in a house but in a "sort of eccentric warehouse, a jungle of the Chaco moved into a Prague's lodging."[46] Cherwuish and Frič sleep in two hammocks mounted across a room full of boxes and the scattered items of his collection. His obsessions are cactuses (of which he was probably the greatest European expert)—he names one "Hitler," a hideous one that belongs to an invasive species—and the South American population of the Mato Grosso, with whom he in the end felt more at home than with his peers in Prague.

The problem of identity emerges with force in these Mitteleuropean pages, where Magris promotes a cultural heritage that questions its own responsibilities toward the "other," reflects on its modes of historical and cultural production and on the self-image it conveys—often marked by a treacherous self-glorification. He has Karel Krejčí, a nonconformist writer of false exotic travels in Prague, mock the concept of a "clash of civilizations" that an eminent professor had articulated:

> Dramatic encounter-clash between different cultures, the man—who? Červíček? or any Praguer who sees him on the street?—loses his identity and his place in life because elements and values which are foreign to him are introduced into his worldview." Who is foreign to whom?[47]

There is then the story of the young creole Luisa de Navarrete who had been kidnapped in Puerto Rico by Caribs and brought to Dominica in 1576. The homonymic Luisa decides to rewrite this story (one of those that her father used to tell her), "filling the gaps"[48] and to include it in the museum. Luisa's testimony to the Inquisition is a masterpiece of self-preservation, with the manipulation of her interrogators and her extreme ability to protect from any indiscreet gaze the four years that she spent with the Kalinagos in the forest. There she was the woman of their chief and gave him four children whose names were never inscribed in the pages of official history: "With her return, her story ends . . . sinks back into the domestic shadows, into the obscurity of the feminine condition, less fearful, but more opaque than the obscurity of the forest."[49]

In the continuous mirroring and foreshadowing of the narrative, Luisa de Navarrete (but also Cherwuish) prefigures Pearl, the black slave that the collector's great-great-grandfather (who made a living in that line of trade) had brought to Trieste in the late eighteenth century, spellbound by her beauty. Pearl was more at ease in the slightly more cosmopolitan Trieste than Cherwuish in Prague; she nonetheless caused uproar with a butchered theater performance of a Carlo Gozzi play that was recorded in the local press. Pearl disappeared together with Carl Philipp, and two hundred years later his great-great-nephew searched for years for the treasure that his ancestor supposedly left in the underground tunnels that traverse the belly of the city. The hypocrisy of Carl-Philipp, who "had bothered to maintain good relations with the Société des Amis des Noirs at the time when, in Delagoa Bay, he was still trafficking in slaves on behalf of Bolts and also in his own interest,"[50] foreshadows the hypocrisy of other Triestine citizens who found it convenient to maintain good relations with the Allies while keeping quiet about their previous collusions with the powers in control of the Adriatisches Küstenland. In another, more subtle prefiguration, the language of the Chamacoco, whose negative form is expressed as a future tense, echoes the collector's linguistic innovations:

> He will love . . . that is, he does not love. The future is a great not prefixed to every word, to every thing; it is what is not, nothing. The future of Cherwuish's people, Frič knows, is also not-being, negation. The Old World discovered the New World to destroy it. Sixty years after the Europeans' arrival in the Americas, of the 80 million Indians only ten remained. And the Indians continue to die off even now, like the Chamacoco."[51]

What does this signify for the grammar of our own history, of the history of the Risiera? What is the future? The stubborn persistence of a negation, a void.

By interweaving these multiple strands of individual and collective histories and memories, Magris reveals that each strand is always contaminated and indebted to other memories; it is spurious, "a palimpsest, a page wiped clean so it can be written on again, always the same story but superimposed on a previous one, writing that covers other writings with corrections difficult to read but not erased, it too destined to be retouched and rewritten but not completely obliterated, passing from mouth to mouth and from page to page."[52]

While in *Blindly* Magris had already adopted such interweaving of Western and Postcolonial history and memory, the radical novelty of *Blameless* is marked by Magris's daring and yet controlled inclusion of the Holocaust in an expanded dimension of what Levy and Szneider address as "cosmopolitan memory" and Michael Rothberg identifies as "multidirectional memory."

Cosmopolitan memory is a concept developed to attune collective memory to the reality of Second (or Global) Modernity, and to allow it to transcend the limits of ethno-national boundaries. Levy and Szneider speak of the difficulty to define collective memory in the age of globalization outside of the binary positions of the proponents of nation-oriented memory and their critics, who consider it outdated and as such to be discarded: "Instead of rejecting collective memory because of its alleged murkiness or questionable ideology, the challenge is to redefine its sociological conditions of possibility and specify its relevance to the question of memory in the global age."[53]

Hirsch and Spitzer adopt this concept and state that such cosmopolitan memory of the Holocaust would incorporate "the responsibility of perpetrators, the complicity of bystanders and the willingness of their descendants to claim the legacy of a traumatic past," thus avoiding the hyperbole of national-specific discourses in favor of "nation-transcending commonalities."[54] They also point out that cosmopolitan memory "does not in any sense aim to diminish or relativize the experiences and suffering of European Holocaust survivors," but rather Holocaust memory can become a catalyst and a mode of interpretation and formation of "local, regional, national and trans-national, testimonies about slavery, colonialism, genocide and subordination."[55]

Rothberg, on the other hand, asks, "What happens when different histories confront each other in the public sphere? Does the remembrance of one history erase others from view?"[56] He compares two models of memory: competitive and multidirectional, and proposes the latter as a productive and creative way to look at the process of memory in a dialogic fashion. He sees Levy and Szneider's "cosmopolitan memory" as a positions still too limited, based on the inclusion or universalization of the Holocaust in relation to other discourses of slavery and oppression, and on the founding of a universal moral code. In his view this position fails to pay attention to the "multidirectional currents of history and layers of unevenly worked through historical time."[57] He thus specifically addresses the possible coexistence of Holocaust and postcolonial memories in a noncompetitive fashion, but rather as "subject to ongoing negotiation, cross-referencing, and borrowing; as productive and not privative . . . [that] has the potential to create new forms of solidarity and new visions of justice."[58]

While in *Blindly* Magris addresses political ideologies, classical myth, the suffering in Stalinist gulags and in the penal colonies of Tasmania, broadening the field of memory beyond national boundaries and ethic specificity, in *Blameless* he connects the Holocaust to a larger tapestry of suffering that transcends time and space. It is a courageous choice, and Magris is able to maintain a remarkable balance, avoiding both the risks of relativizing the paradigmatic meaning of the Shoah as a benchmark of humanity's horrors, and of subordinating events remote in time and space through a pale comparison to the mute lost humanity of the concentration camp.

Levi and Szneider maintain that half a century after the Holocaust the focus has shifted from the atrocities to "how the heirs of the victims, the perpetrators and bystanders are coping with these stories and the evolving memories."[59] This is precisely the subject matter that Magris engages with and that Trieste and its history made possible through a fictional revisitation of its past. By broadening the scope of the Holocaust narrative and the human absence that characterizes its core, *Blameless* "acknowledges how remembrance both cuts across and binds together diverse spatial, temporal, and cultural sites."[60]

In this sense the novel not only provides a new negotiation of cultural memory, but also creates a specific new model of multidirectional memory. The multi-temporal levels of Magris's post-millennial fictions of memory that have become increasingly complex, reach in *Blameless* the highest degree of sophistication and dynamism in terms of how "each event is related to others in both a forward and backward direction."[61] Luisa as the "official" narrator ensures that the museum and its heterogeneous content support the temporal tension of the disjointed memories that the collector's notes, scattered information, and verbal memories accumulate on the page. The intersecting of the two narrative voices is further complicated by the unstable and tenuous identity of the collector's "I," whose narrative function he willfully abdicates:

> Dr. Brooks, when you write about me, please write "I" or "he," it makes no difference, write what you want, however you want, even when copying my words, because the hand that writes is the real author. Master Sun said . . . No one dares ask how he knows what he says.[62]

Luisa follows his wish and in several occasions blurs the lines of the homodiegetic narrative voice. Neumann speaks in such instances of a "biographical break," a "dissolution into disparate fragments of memory which indicate the instability of the meaning-making process" and of "the identity-creating appropriation of the past."[63] *Blameless* is one of those "fictions of meta-memory" in which the functioning of memory itself is problematized, "'thus rendering the question of how we remember the central content of remembering."[64]

Despite investing Luisa with the task of bringing the various narrative (and temporal) streams of memory to coalesce into a complex and necessarily loose narrative structure, Magris makes the present the most unstable temporal level of the novel. Unlike Luisa's constant use of the past tense to create a coherent unfolding of memory—especially in relation to her own family history—the dead collector's experiencing "I" and narrating "I" repeatedly blend and merge on the page, not allowing the reader to secure a stable homodiegetic place for the retrieval of his memory. Even in those instances when Luisa acknowledges her appropriation of the collector's life-story (as in the final hallucinatory chapter in which the fire spreads to the warehouse and kills him), the position from which the fictionalized memory is articulated is barely mentioned and therefore goes easily undetected: "When you write about me, write what you want, however you want . . . well then, maybe just to keep my word to him."[65]

The temporal and authorial tension is always present and the enduring ambiguity between internal and external focalizer keeps the reader engaged and, in Brechtian terms, alienated. It is in fact not a coincidence that Luisa decides to include Brecht's ballad of Mackie Messer in the museum. By the end of the book the plan of the museum is still just sketched and far from its final implementation. A cursory overview of its contents and of its missing pieces has made clear only that through its "spatial disorder . . . the access to the past is difficult, intricate or even impossible."[66]

Magris does not bring his long and meandering process of institutional remembrance (through the museum) to a conclusion/closure. This would mark, according to Ann Rigney, the beginning of amnesia, unless institutional remembrance "is continuously invested with new meaning."[67] This unfinished revisitation of meaning that leaves a series of counter-memory practices open to further questioning is one of the strengths of *Blameless*, a novel in line with what Rigney describes as the shift from sites (full-fledged interpretations of the present-past relation and closed systems of value) to processes of memory.

Light and tragic at the same time, the narrative leads the reader to the last room of the museum, envisioned as a dead end, after which point the visitor has to turn and face a daunting accumulation of historical debris. Placed in the position of Benjamin's angel of history, unlike the "Angelus Novus" the visitor is not pushed into the future by the storm of progress, but ironically retraces his steps to the point of origin (the first room), which is a figurative representation of the collector's inverter. Peace is achieved and death is defeated, at least symbolically.

Magris's narrative has reached with *Blameless* a new level of engagement with the "turn to memory" that characterizes our time. Poised between the impossibility to remember and the need to do so, this novel captures and reflects what Andreas Huyssen defines as a resistance "against obsolescence and disappearance to counter our deep anxiety about the speed of change and the ever shrinking horizons of time and space."[68]

NOTES

1. Michel Foucault, "Film in Popular Memory: An Interview with Michel Foucault," in *The Collective Memory Reader*, ed. Jeffrey K. Olick et al. (Oxford: Oxford University Press, 2011), 253.

2. Ibid.

3. The original title is *Non luogo a procedere* (Milan: Garzanti, 2015). Its literal translation is "No cause to indict."

4. Foucault, "Film," 253.

5. Claudio Magris, *Blameless*, trans. Anne Milano Appel (New Haven and London: Yale University Press, 2017), 87.

6. Ibid.

7. The concepts of "cultural creation and cultural accumulation not accomplished by the same individuals" are found in Karl Mannheim, *Essays on the Sociology of Knowledge*, ed. Paul Kecskemeti (London: Routledge and Kegan Paul, 1952), 293.

8. Ibid., 295.

9. Birgit Neumann, "The Literary Representation of Memory," in *A Companion to Cultural Memory Studies*, ed. Astrid Erll and Ansgar Nünning (Berlin and New York: De Gruyter, 2010), 334.

10. Yael Zerubavel, "Recovered Roots: Collective Memory and the Making of Israeli National Tradition," in *The Collective Memory Reader*, 240–41. Foucault's view of counter-memory is fragmentary, while Zerubavel considers the challenging of a single event as highly dynamic, with a "cascade effect" that has an impact beyond the event opposed in the counter-memory practice. Magris bridges in his narrative these two approaches to counter-memory, adopting extreme formal fragmentation and amplifying its historical and cultural impact beyond a set of chronological or spatial limits.

11. Claude Lévi-Strauss, from "The Savage Mind," in *The Collective Memory Reader*, 175.

12. Magris, *Blameless*, 9.

13. Adorno, Valéry Proust Museum, in *The Collective Memory Reader*, 110.

14. Ibid.

15. Magris, *Blameless*, 9.

16. Ibid., 194–95.

17. Ibid., 190.

18. Ibid., 227.

19. Ibid., 122.

20. Ibid., 237.

21. Ibid., 27.

22. Jay Winter, *Remembering War: The Great War between Memory and History in the 20th Century* (New Haven and London: Yale University Press, 2006), 275.

23. Magris, *Blameless*, 84.

24. Ibid.

25. Ibid., 301.

26. Ibid., 302.

27. Marianne Hirsch and Leo Spitzer, "The Witness in the Archive: Holocaust Studies/ Memory Studies," *Memory Studies* 2(2) (2009): 154.

28. Ibid., 158.

29. Magris, *Blameless*, 315.

30. Hirsch and Spitzer, "Witness," 155. Hirsch and Spitzer quote here from Annette Wieviorka's *The Era of the Witness*, trans. Jared Stark (Ithaca, NY: Cornell University Press, 2006), 88.

31. Magris, *Blameless*, 301–2.

32. "History is an electroshock; that's why we've all become crazed, even the insurgents. Everyone against everyone, the Slavic KMT, Kommando Mesta Trst, against the Nazis but also against the Italian democratic brigades of the Freedom Volunteer Corps, the Pisoni and Foschiatti Brigades, which fought against the Nazis. Foschiatti died in Dachau, 'Death to Foschiatti,' the Fascists shouted, 'Death to the partisans of the Foschiatti Brigade,' cried the Titoists. Death to death that bestows death, thinks Don Marzari; this is why he gives the order for the siren to sound the insurgency." Magris, *Blameless*, 227.

33. Magris, *Blameless*, 234.

34. Ibid.

35. Ibid., 300.

36. Maurice Halbwach, from "The Collective Memory," in *The Collective Memory Reader*, ed. Jeffrey K. Olick et al. (Oxford: Oxford University Press, 2011), 144.

37. Magris, *Blameless*, 137.

38. Ibid., 219.

39. Ibid., 215–16.

40. David Gross, *Lost Time: On Remembering and Forgetting in Late Modern Culture* (Amherst: University of Massachusetts Press, 2000), 149.

41. Gross notes that "[v]ery much like Hegel two hundred years ago, we today also appear to be more interested in the forward-looking side of the dialectic. For the most part, we warm to those aspects of the past that anticipate the present or point in the direction of a future yet to come, and we lose interest in those that have become passé." Ibid.

42. Ibid., 149–50.

43. Ibid., 149.

44. Magris, *Blameless*, 54.

45. Ibid, 55.

46. Claudio Magris, "Dalla Mitteleuropa alla giungla: Avventure e follie di un botanico," *Corriere della Sera*, August 7, 2010, 46. Magris introduced the historical figures of Cherwuish and Frič in one of his many editorials for the Italian daily *Corriere della Sera.* Almost all the details outlined in the article found their way into the novel.

47. Magris, *Blameless*, 70.

48. Ibid., 267.

49. Ibid., 277.

50. Ibid., 147.

51. Ibid., 59.

52. Ibid., 267.

53. Daniel Levy and Natan Sznaider, *The Holocaust and Memory in the Global Age* (Philadelphia: Temple University Press, 2006), 25.

54. Hirsch and Spitzer, "Witness," 165.

55. Ibid.

56. Michael Rothberg, *Multidirectional Memory: Remembering the Holocaust in the Age of Decolonization* (Stanford: Stanford University Press, 2009), 2.

57. Ibid., 266.

58. Ibid. 3, 5.

59. Daniel Levy and Natan Sznaider, "Memory Unbound: The Holocaust and the Formation of Cosmopolitan Memory," *European Journal of Social Theory* 5(1) (2002): 103.

60. Rothberg, *Multidirectional Memory*, 11.

61. Neumann, "Literary Representation," 336.

62. Magris, *Blameless*, 324.

63. Neumann, "Literary Representation," 337.

64. Ibid.

65. Magris, *Blameless*, 325.

66. Neumann, "Literary Representation," 340.

67. Ann Rigney, "The Dynamics of Remembrance: Texts Between Monumentallity and Morphing," in *A Companion to Cultural Memory Studies*, ed. Astrid Erll, and Ansgar Nünning (Berlin and New York: De Gruyter, 2010), 345.

68. Andreas Huyssen, from "Present Past: Media, Politics, Amnesia," in *The Collective Memory Reader*, ed. Jeffrey K. Olick et al. (Oxford: Oxford University Press, 2011), 433.

WORKS CITED

Foucault, Michel. "Film in Popular Memory: An Interview with Michel Foucault." In *The Collective Memory Reader*, edited by Jeffrey K. Olick et al., 252. Oxford: Oxford University Press, 2011.

Gross, David. *Lost Time: On Remembering and Forgetting in Late Modern Culture*. Amherst: University of Massachusetts Press, 2000.

Halbwach, Maurice. "The Collective Memory." In *The Collective Memory Reader*, edited by Jeffrey K. Olick et al., 139–49. Oxford: Oxford University Press, 2011.

Hirsch, Marianne, and Leo Spitzer. "The Witness in the Archive: Holocaust Studies/Memory Studies." *Memory Studies* 2 (2009): 151–70.

Huyssen, Andreas. "Present Past: Media, Politics, Amnesia." In *The Collective Memory Reader*, edited by Jeffrey K. Olick et al., 430–36. Oxford: Oxford University Press, 2011.

Lévi-Strauss, Claude. "The Savage Mind." In *The Collective Memory Reader*, edited by Jeffrey K. Olick et al. Oxford: Oxford University Press, 2011

Levy, Daniel, and Natan Sznaider. *The Holocaust and Memory in the Global Age*. Philadelphia: Temple University Press, 2006.

———. "Memory Unbound: The Holocaust and the Formation of Cosmopolitan Memory." *European Journal of Social Theory* 5 (2002): 87–106.

Magris, Claudio. *Blameless*. Translated by Anne Milano Appel. New Haven and London: Yale University Press, 2017.

———. "Dalla Mitteleuropa alla giungla: Avventure e follie di un botanico." *Corriere della Sera*, August 7, 2010, 46.

———. *Non luogo a procedure*. Milan: Garzanti, 2015.

Mannheim, Karl. *Essays on the Sociology of Knowledge*. Edited by Paul Kecskemeti. London: Routledge and Kegan Paul, 1952.

Neumann, Birgit. "The Literary Representation of Memory." In *A Companion to Cultural Memory Studies*, edited by Astrid Erll and Ansgar Nünning, 333–45. Berlin and New York: De Gruyter, 2010.

Rigney, Ann. "The Dynamics of Remembrance: Texts Between Monumentallity and Morphing." In *A Companion to Cultural Memory Studies*, edited by Astrid Erll, and Ansgar Nünning, 345–53. Berlin and New York: De Gruyter, 2010.

Rothberg, Michael. *Multidirectional Memory: Remembering the Holocaust in the Age of Decolonization*. Stanford: Stanford University Press, 2009.

Winter, Jay. *Remembering War: The Great War between Memory and History in the 20th Century*. New Haven and London: Yale University Press, 2006.

Zerubavel, Yael. "Recovered Roots: Collective Memory and the Making of Israeli National Tradition." In *The Collective Memory Reader*, edited by Jeffrey K. Olick et al., 240–41. Oxford: Oxford University Press, 2011.

Chapter Seven

Blood, Sand, and Stone

Trieste's Transcultural Memories

Katia Pizzi

"Cities," affirms Andreas Huyssen in his celebrated *Present Pasts* (2003), "are palimpsests of history, incarnations of time in stone, sites of memory extending both in time and space."[1] Prior to Huyssen, it has long been acknowledged that the city is a *locus* of production and consumption of shared and, frequently, contested memories, from Maurice Halbawchs's "collective memories" through Walter Benjamin's *flâneries*, to Pierre Nora's *lieux de mémoire*. Frameworks of urban memory are discussed here with reference to the case study of Trieste, perched perilously at the Pillars of Hercules in the upper Mediterranean basin.

Trieste is well known for its geographical eccentricity, its coarse-grained and fraught history, its plural and contested identity, at once insularly entrenched and also radiating out to a wider region at the confluence (and collision) of Roman, Slav, and Germanic civilizations. A "memoryscape" typified by unreconcilable cultures and memories—a set of mnemonic short-circuits John Foot pertinently referred to as "fractured memories."[2] Huyssen's historical and memorial urban layering is tailored to Trieste's incompatible, contradictory, and ambiguous memories, a hive of cosmopolitan commercial activity and yet a culturally peripheral backwater; a crucible of cultures and, at once, a "crucible manqué;"[3] an open door for the European avant-gardes, championing and disseminating their concerns, from psychoanalysis to constructivism and, at the same time, a fanatic supporter of patriotic *fascismo*, laboratory and testing ground of Mussolini's cult; a cacophony of heterogeneous languages and an archaeology of incompatible cultures mired in chronic ethnic and national strife.

Following multiple geopolitical refigurations after World War I, national memories have become paramount in Trieste. Financially wiped off by the collapse of the Austro-Hungarian Empire, the affluent mercantile middle class continued to uphold overwhelmingly its national loyalty to Italy, in collision course with the rising national consciousness of autochthon Slovenian and Croatian communities. Following shortly, the fascist nationalist emphasis further divided and entrenched the diverse national and ethnic groups. The national and ethnic underpinnings of these rifts invite critical reappraisals best encapsulated by Pierre Nora's notion of *lieux de mémoire*. Nora's terminology has been deployed extensively to denote urban features tasked with social remembrance, such as museums, cemeteries, monuments, memorials and ruins, a range of sites through which the city embodies and indexes its social memory. In this framework, the city is perceived as a palimpsest, a fabric where memories and pasts are folded and layered in. If the urban landscape is central to the spatial and social production of memory, Trieste's "fractured" history and memory are eminently legible through the lens of those sites whose ubiquitous presence acts as a memorial device itself, and whose architecture consists of exclusive, partisan, and tensive forms of memory.[4]

A wider critical debate needs to take into account the incisive contributions of Mario Isnenghi, who explored the real and imaginary character of memory sites advocating for an extension of the reach of memory to the "realm of social history."[5] Furthermore, in *Sites of Memory, Sites of Mourning* (1998), Jay Winter cogently revisited sites of memory and monuments to fallen soldiers in a comparative and transnational key belying Nora's *lieux de mémoire*, and with special attention for the language and the protocols of mourning and commemoration.[6] Along the lines of Benjamin's *angelus novus*, Winter's sites of memory are past-facing rather than future oriented. Finally, mindful of the seminal lesson of Aby Warburg, Alon Confino scoped out the national and ideological horizon underpinning memory sites, inviting scholars to remain mindful of the wider social and cultural contexts that feed the interpretation and transmission of collective memories. The power to make memories significant is, in other words, embroiled in relations that bring different mnemonic communities in conflict over their respective understanding of the past.[7]

The rich and diverse scholarship on trauma of the past two decades further attests to the reciprocity between memory and trauma and the impossibility to continue pinning down traumatic events in univocal national and cultural frameworks.[8] This past decade has witnessed a transcultural turn in memory studies predicated on the ruptures, passages, and translations that account for the internal heterogeneity of memory: Astrid Erll and Ann Rigney's "remediations" of memory brought to the fore a complexity that calls for broader, transcultural and transnational approaches. Ditto as concerns

Michael Rothberg's "multidirectional memories," that is to say the study of those memorial constellations that dip into and drawn on disparate cultures, traversing and redirecting memories across different eras and contexts.[9]

These positions have significantly broadened the scope of univocal approaches such as Nora's own, which seem to congeal and monumentalize discrete units of memory in separate, non-dialogical spheres of interest, in mutual isolation and within clearly demarcated national containers. A more flexible approach is called for, to account for the transcultural inflections (or lack thereof) in the construction of the memory process and the flux of memory transfers across space and time. Mnemonic detritus may flow at random, yet its *dérive* is channeled and underpinned by archaeological layering and traceable flows.

In this context, Huyssen's palimpsestual approach seems to me particularly pertinent, in tandem, I would suggest, with the atlases and dynamics of memory mapped within the school of Aby Warburg. Enter Michael Baxandall and his cogent metaphor of the "sand dune." Understood as a selective archive, the memorial process is best understood as a tectonics, a "lamination" underpinned by its malleable, plastic, and morphing architecture. For Baxandall, the memorial process becomes symbolically analogous to the meteorological and geological weathering on a sand dune, a site enduring periodic transformation and slippage under the erosive force of soil and wind, erasing and reconstituting traces time and time again.[10] My suggestion here is that the accent on the ambiguities, metamorphoses, and fragilities, in short on the complexities of the memorial process proposed by Huyssen and Baxandall are particularly pertinent in the light of Trieste's historical and memorial particularity, and especially productive when attempting to unpack the city's memorial landscape, as is evidence in its textual, visual, as well as architectural and monumental, markers.

These theories will assist me here in revisiting memorial sites, both material and immaterial, where Trieste's transcultural memories are embodied and mobilized. These include physical sites scarring the cityscape to this day, such as the Nazi camp Risiera di San Sabba and the geological pits, ditches, and crevasses commonly known as *foibe*. These further consist of literature and film, key memory containers where textual and visual memories are productively intertwined. The latter are no less significant than material sites such as *foibe* and Risiera; indeed these are even more clearly mediated and remediated markers of the city's identity across time, as will be elucidated below. It is useful to mention at this juncture that Trieste's enduring memories, together with the myths and rhetorics progressively acquired in the *longue dureé*, continue to color and inflect political and intellectual debates both locally and more widely to this day. These ossified discourses, veritable semantic palimpsests in themselves, proved to be resilient and enduring, even in the radically mutated and perpetually shifting scenarios of globalization, as I shall observe to in the concluding part of this chapter.

TRANSCULTURAL MEMORIES AND MATERIAL SITES

Trieste's "fractured," disconnected collective memories coagulate in geological and, by now, officially memorialized monumental sites, especially *foibe* and Risiera di San Sabba. These sites have been referred to as symbolic and enigmatic crossroads, faults, Bakhtinian chronotopes.[11] Similarly to infernal black holes, *foibe* and Risiera appear to have swallowed and regurgitated at different times heaps of layered and sectarian memories.[12] These incendiary sites have become ghostly collectors of memories haunting the city to this day, weighing it down in tragic and pernicious memories, miring cultural exchanges and rendering them fragile, brittle, and uncertain.[13] These are liminal, interstitial, or sites of transit: the port, the coastline, the rail station. They are institutional, historical, and industrial buildings, frequently repurposed and converted, for example, initially designed to perform alternative functions and acquiring in time a chaotic multiplicity of contentious signification. *Foibe* and Risiera have, in recent years, gathered together such a cacophony of public and individual memories to merit the appellation of "il più celebre e dibattuto esempio di memoria divisa del Paese."[14]

In these inert and interstitial sites "remediations" and "multidirections" are twisted and confused by sudden ruptures, throw-offs, bifurcations, crystallizing, and displacing memory in erosive, nostalgic, or escapist directions. In border areas, the univocal, opaque, monolithic frameworks of memory constructed around these sites are elusive and unhomogenous rather than dynamic and dialogical. They are "laminated" as Baxandall would have it, and, as such, forever passable of turns, collapses, and tectonic refigurations, plastically reforming time and time again, calling constantly into question their archaeological architecture, as well as pointing to desirable, but invariably displaced and precluded, transcultural exchanges.

In line with their status as reconverted sites—the major *foiba* near the village of Basovizza was originally a coalmine, as John Foot illustrates in chapter 5 of this volume—*foibe*, first and foremost, continue to generate stories, legends, opinions, observations, rhetorics, new facts and figures. *Foibe* are natural ditches and crevasses that punctuate the mountainous and rural Triestine hinterland. While they are part of the geological fabric of the region, their traumatic memorial import increased exponentially after their deployment as sites of torture and disposal of human remains in the context of the violent strife for national prevarication between Italy and Yugoslavia in 1943 and 1945. As such, *foibe* have progressively acquired the status of quintessential "memorial faults" whose symbolic hollowness accommodates a shifting tectonics of irreconcilable and "fractured" memories. *Foibe* stand as perpetual memory machines, churning out a colossal quantity of layered and telluric signification alongside the cubic meters of remains, human, animal, vegetal, and man-made, there uncovered and extracted.

The ancestral terror inspired by these caves, many of which delve deeply into the ground and gather within them intricate and rocky corridors, translated in a copious stream of fiction, both in prose and verse—the novels *Il baratro* (1964) by Enrico Morovich; *La foiba grande* (1992) by Carlo Sgorlon; *Una croce sulla foiba: Il grido delle vittime ritrova la strada della memoria* (1996) by Giuseppe Svalduz; the more recent *Foiba in autunno* (2006) by Ezio Mestrovich; and *Gabbiani sul Carso* (2010) by Giulio Angioni. Short stories and other fiction include Giani Stuparich's "La grotta" (1935), in the collection *Nuovi racconti*, and numerous verse collections by Lina Galli, all of which are a testament to their unabated memorial force.[15]

Foibe's complex historical and ideological configuration, in tandem with their mythic and legendary resonances, has granted them constant attention in the literary culture of the region, and yet this arresting presence is still largely overlooked by critical literature. Theaters of personal and collective tragedies, suicide and political vendettas, *foibe* have gathered together a tangle of anxiety, conflict, and commemoration, evoked in magical realist styles designed to exorcise their malignant and spectral and, to a large extent, enigmatic history.[16]

Stuparich's long story "La grotta" centers on an expedition to the Karst mountains and the tragic downfall of two young men in the abyss. A maternal, uterine symbolism is utilized here to signify redemption for Lucio, the only survivor, in the person of a teacher intervening as helper and protective maternal figure. The symbolic link between *foiba* and maternal uterus is a cliché frequently encountered in this literature. In Sgorlon's *La foiba grande* this becomes combined with an archetypical, legendary aura centered on the aberrations and unspeakable horrors of the *foiba*. An artificial dichotomy between *romanità* and *balcanicità* is emphasized in the switch between an individual and collective first person and an impersonal third person.

At the other end of the ideological spectrum, *Una croce sulla foiba* radicalizes the rift between Catholic fighters and Slav partisans, embracing the cause of the former to the detriment of the latter, easily categorized and dismissed as undesirable.[17] Common to these narratives is the call toward an erosive, laminated and palinsestual memorial framework, pointing to the flaky, slippery, and shifting memorial status of these pits. Transcultural exchanges are stalled here: *foibe* remain monolithic, enigmatic, and thick-skinned memory sites, where the slippage of a laminated memory lead to serial, even chaotic, overlapping, a flotsam and jetsam of signification. Rather like Nora's *lieux*, the *foibe* are not shared transculturally but are, rather, veritable "bastions" propping up the irredeemably split identity of this region.[18]

Borrowing from Jan Assman we can assert that *foibe* and *Risiera* comprise "that body of reusable texts, images, and rituals specific to each society in each epoch, whose 'cultivation' serves to stabilise and convey that society's self-image."[19] In its specificity as national monument and former Nazi extermination and transit camp, Risiera di San Sabba displays a comparable set of memorial ambiguities and entanglements. *Risiera* was set up in 1943 on the model of Treblinka and other successful industries of genocide. Its red brick building was erected in the nineteenth century and served the purpose of a rice-husking factory before it was requisitioned and repurposed by the Nazis who, later, before fleeing the city in the night between April 28 and 29, 1945, burned it down after two years of scrupulous activity, sorting and torturing. The structure and walls survived the blast (the burnt shadow of the crematorium is still visibly imprinting the main wall), however, all contents, furnishings, papers, instruments, uniforms, and, last but not least, the truck that supplied fumes to the underground chamber, went up in smoke.

Ferruccio Folkel's *Olocausto dimenticato* (2000), the first important study of Risiera, blazed a trail and described the site as a Gordian knot of history and memory, crossroads of contradictions and problems where competing ideologies, ethnicities, nationalities and trauma sedimented upon one another without becoming homogenized.[20] A memorial work in progress, whose pivotal location tore up the urban fabric and at the edge of the Balkans, a blood-drenched anti-communist bulwark whose sinister aura was designed to be visible and audible, whose olfactory traces hung on Trieste's sky for days.

In recent years, the site has grown a robust symbolic and literary reputation, driven by literary works emanating from the diverse cultures and languages historically present in the area: Slovenian (e.g., Boris Pahor), Italian (e.g., Ketty Daneo, Mauro Covacich, and Giuseppe O. Longo) and German (e.g., Veit Heineken).[21] More widely, *Risiera*'s symbolic reputation rests on its memorialization as a monumental site in the course of the 1970s. A 1976 trial aiming to bring its perpetrators to justice, later infamously known as a "Nuremberg manqué," constitutes the immediate background of the site's memorialization. The initial indictment of various protagonists of the Triestine Holocaust, including Allers, Hering, Oberhauser, Stangl, and Wirth, gave way to fraught proceedings mired by numerous procedural controversies, not least the arbitrary distinction between "innocent" and "culpable" victims. The trial was brought to a conclusion on April 29, 1976. None other than one life sentence was passed, that to Josef Oberhauser who was not, however, extradited and did not lose his job in a beer Keller of his native Munich.[22] The shedding of blood remained unpunished, the collective memory of those crimes washed down in the non-reparative, non-redemptive null and void of an accidental turn of the judiciary.

The establishment of a Risiera monument seemed to match the traumatic memorial process underpinning the site, its naked structure left behind featureless and "neutered," compounded by the obvious omissions stunting the trial. A "creative restoration" by the architect Romano Boico consisted in the installation of two facing concrete walls to mark the entrance to the site, a visual strategy designed to elicit horror by subtracting rather than adding content, emphasizing the sacral simplicity of the site, inviting respectful silence. It is an abstract, unadorned, brutalist refitting, an attempt to highlight the memorial import of the Risiera through an emphasis on its isolation, vacuity, and decontextualization from its urban surroundings.[23] In this respect, too, Risiera seems to me to exemplify Huyssen's palimpsest and Baxandall's wavering and modular memory, a "delocalized" memory erected not on material supports, which are scarce in any case, but rather underpinned by heterogenous and plastic detritus of signification, appropriated by various interest groups, and heaped up in the course of Trieste's fraught history.[24]

TRANSCULTURAL MEMORIES AND LITERATURE

Does literature allow smooth transcultural memorial vistas denied to the monumental symbols and markers of memory dotting the city and the wider region? Launched by the young scholar Scipio Slataper and his *La Voce*–inspired lyrical novel *Il mio carso* (1912), Triestine literature has undoubtedly acquired unrivaled critical authority in recent decades due to its close connection with the great tradition of modernist writing, from James Joyce to Italo Svevo.

The cosmopolitan flair of its literary production, predicated on commercial affluence and federal Imperial heritage, a Joycean *Nebeneinander* carefully packaged and marketed in the course of the 1980s and 1990s, propelled the reputation of local literati to the pinnacles inhabited by giants of Mitteleuropean literature, from Joseph Roth to Robert Musil.[25] While in his *Giacomo* James Joyce contemplates Trieste through a dusty looking glass, emphasizing the blurred, undetermined contours of this urban culture,[26] much local literature has since embraced the topos (and also, later, the cliché) of an autobiographical "endogamic" (to use Magris's own word) intertextuality anchored to the great tradition of European modernism mentioned above.[27] A handful of writers, with Fulvio Tomizza at their helm, have, on the other hand, stressed the plural identity of Triestine literary culture, its long-standing transcultural exchanges predicated on hybridization and *métissage*, the overlapping of languages, bloods, identities stretching out beyond the Austro-Hungarian area to embrace the Balkans and the European East. Tomizza's Trieste articulates a "neurotic" culture, impermeable, self-determined and self-referential, stalled by ambivalent and conflicting memories of its own making. A culture symbolically assimilated to a vortex, primordial broth, or blood-clotted plasma rather than the layered architecture of a sand dune or a parchment palimpsest.

The history of Triestine literature testifies to these rifts, incommunicability and acts of defiance and resistance to hybridizations, right from the word go. Two impetuous contemporary intellectuals epitomized this trend: the Italian Scipio Slataper (1888–1915) and the Slovenian poet Srečko Kosovel (1904–1926). Slataper and Kosovel grew up in Trieste and the neighbouring Karst village of Sežana respectively, frequenting the same rugged and mountainous landscapes, attending the same theaters, and drawing on the multicultural and multilinguistic heritage of Austria-Hungary. Both were staunchly and ethically pro-European, both died while at the peak of their intellectual activity, standing to this day as heroic and romantic figures wedged at the very core of Triestine and Slovenian literary culture.

Yet, like distant galaxies, Kosovel and Slataper seemed to rotate at cosmic distance from each other, unable (and unwilling to boot) to pursue a transcultural agenda. Kosovel became an expert reader of Italian culture, but only through the mediation of his friend Carlo Curcio, a Neapolitan, the translations of the Slovenian cleric Ivan Trinko and the mediation of his collaborator Fanica Obid. The Irredentist Slataper, who, despite his own maternal Slovenian descent deserted the Austrian Army, volunteered in World War I to "regain" Trieste to the Italian nation, would not have been perceived as a friend, nor a desirable cultural mediator.[28] The lack of convergence the case of Kosovel and Slataper attests to confirms once again the volatile nature of this cultural border, its status as a "crucible manqué" in the words of Apih,[29] a receptacle of divisive cultural and memorial detritus of neighboring cultures dancing alongside one another, experiencing rare encounters, typically leading to tragic and traumatic collision routes.[30]

A partial corrective to the cultural and memorial incommunicability of this region seems to be evidenced in writing by women, both historically and more recently. Triestine women were relatively better educated with comparison to their counterparts in mainland Italy, due to the robust educational legacy of Austria-Hungary,[31] as is reflected in the copious literary production by women, especially in periodical publications throughout the twentieth century. The unrivaled degree of emancipation enjoyed by Triestine women facilitated the blossoming of a tradition of women's writing, typified, in many cases, by awareness of local ethnic, linguistic, and cultural particularities and a more or less latent antagonistic stance with respect to a largely male literary canon.[32] Despite the fascist emphasis on demographic growth and relative social marginalization, women's writing flourished in this period, to include Jewish authors swiftly acquiring national notoriety and reputation, such as Haydée (pseud Ida Finzi; 1867–1946), Pia Rimini (1900–1945), and Willy Dias (pseud Fortuna Morpurgo; 1872–1956).

A further group of women writers were socially and politically engaged, remaining well aware throughout of local specificities. Anita Pittoni (1901–1982), for example, a descendant of the renowned socialist leader Valentino Pittoni, was the most "militant *femme de lettres*" of postwar Trieste in the words of Curci and Ziani,[33] a wide-ranging cultural operator who founded the influential publishing house Lo Zibaldone. Nora Franca Pogliaghi (1900–2001) epitomized a new wave of feminist writing in Trieste. Pogliaghi was well aware of the non-neutral, nor equally distributed, status of collective memories in Trieste, as well as of her own marginal position in the literary field—see especially *Colore di Trieste* (1967).[34] Chronologically closer to us, Marisa Madieri (1938–1996), Susanna Tamaro (b. 1957) and Nelida Milani Kruljac (b. 1939) make up a diverse and nonaligned cluster of writers, whose multilingual, multicultural, and hybridized experience seeped powerfully into their literary works, frequently scrambling and exploding stale and rhetorical *triestinità*. Migrations from the south of the world have even more recently enriched the cultural and linguistic breadth of Triestine literature, as is evidenced in the novels of Lily Amber Laila Wadia (b. 1966) that I shall return to in the concluding pages of this chapter.

TRANSCULTURAL MEMORIES AND FILM

A fragmented layering of memorial signification is forcefully in evidence during the Cold War through the medium of film. Winston Churchill famously invoked Trieste in his "Iron Curtain speech" delivered in Fulton, Missouri on March 5, 1946.[35] Churchill's loaded words were shortly to become prophetic: together with Stettin (now Polish Szczecin), he posited Trieste as the southwestern gatekeeper of the impenetrable Iron Curtain. The city sat then at the uncomfortable interface between the communist east and the western democracies, shortly to become a pawn in a geopolitical game of chess that will keep the entire world waiting with bated breath for a resolution over Trieste's uncertain national and geopolitical status. At this juncture, the city's predicament rose to international attention via the vehicle of film, from sleek Hollywood productions to Slovenian propaganda pieces. A mechanical medium often acting as an echo chamber of literature, predicated on a layering of dissonant memories, cinema seems best placed to capture the contradictory and yet alluring mystique of Trieste at one of the most contested times in modern history.

Typified by the confluence of individual and collective identities along national lines, Slovenian films repeatedly revisited the partisan struggle in memorial function contributing to the founding myth of socialist Yugoslavia, as both Stanković and Pavlaković have shown.[36] Slovenian film tended to view Trieste as a military front, approaching the city almost entirely from a perspective of ethnic and ideological antagonism, forged in the years of active persecution suffered under the Fascist regime.

Trieste does not feature all too frequently in Slovenian film. Nonetheless, the city itself, together with its powerful hold on the Slovenian collective imagination, acts as a memorial device emphasizing the national identity of the protagonist hero propelling and cementing his struggle for a communist Yugoslavia.[37] Together with its alluring mystique, its palimpsestual layering is evidenced, for example, in a compelling shot in France štiglic's *Na svoji zemlji* (On our own land; 1948) featuring the eyes of a young partisan (Little Eagle) lingering longingly, as does the camera, over the gulf of Trieste.[38]

Associated with the crudest Cold War *Realpolitik*, the name itself Trieste acquired suggestive, if ambiguous and fragile, overtones across the western world. This name became virtually ubiquitous and frequently grafted onto the title of films with all but the flimsiest connection with the city at all: for example, the English *Sleeping Car to Trieste*, directed by John Paddy Carstairs, marketed elsewhere under the alternative title *Sleeping Car to Venice*.

A sleek Hollywood production, *Diplomatic Courier* (1951) was directed by Henry Hathaway who translated it into film from a novel by Peter Cheyney titled *Sinister Errand*. The film centers on Mike Kells, a diplomatic agent who becomes embroiled in a covert operation aimed at recovering a top-secret document detailing Stalin's plans to occupy Western Europe. Trieste's perceived exoticism and cosmopolitanism nurture further myths and rhetorics of its multiple, divided, alienating identity. Indeed, Trieste is singled out here as a microcosm of the early Cold War, embodiment of the cast-iron, irreconcilable split between East and West.

Perched at the extremities of the Iron Curtain, this multi-cultural city suffers and contains with difficulty its tectonic shifts, in the manner of a sand dune seeping inexorably toward desertification, the alienation encapsulated in the communist threat.[39] Trieste is not merely the ultimate shore of this divide, but a matrix of the state of the world frozen at this point in time: "The whole world is in one city" stands out as the film's opening statement, referring back to Joyce's *Nebeneinander*, to the "crucible manqué" of Trieste's inhomogeneous, palimpsestual identity.

CONCLUSION

A promise of transcultural redemption seems to emerge within the globalized context we inhabit today. In *Present Pasts* Andreas Huyssen recalls Italo Calvino's invisible cities as a paradigm of the experience of the city as both a real, material, and an imaginary space. The memories discussed here productively demonstrated the extent to which Trieste inhabits this most elusive interstitial space. Unable to shake off once and for all the myths and rhetoric of its skewed, "fractured" history, Trieste and its multilayered, erosive frameworks of memory continue to act as powerful memorial generators. New migrations and novel cultural hybridizations are, however, injecting the city's intransigent, monocultural veins, with the blood of geographically distant cultures, their cosmopolitanism, and memorial set.

Born in Mumbai in 1966 and a resident of Trieste since 1986, Lily-Amber Laila Wadia writes narrative fiction in Italian, her second language. Among other fictional and quasi-fictional works, the exhilarating *Come diventare italiani in 24 ore: Diario di un'aspirante italiana* (How to Become Italian in 24 Hours: Diary of a Would-Be Italian; 2010) is a tongue-in-cheek exposé debunking received local cultural stereotypes. Bypassing are resituating received paradigms, including post-colonial and Mitteleuropean, Wadia's eccentric and successful literary work achieves the goal of exploding the essentialist paradigm of untranslatability of local culture.[40]

Through the medium of irony, Wadia further explodes canonical notions such as center and periphery, national, regional and transnational, monocultural and multicultural, scrambling ossified local binaries, reconfiguring them in mutually intelligible, translatable, and dialogical frameworks. The mnemonic sand dune may finally be spilling over here, allowing for exchanges that, while encompassing local and global, will invite readings in smooth and intelligible transcultural keys.

NOTES

1. A. Huyssen, *Present Pasts. Urban Palimpsests and the Politics of Memory* (Stanford, CA: Stanford University Press, 2003), 101.

2. See especially J. Foot, *Fratture d'Italia* (Milan: Rizzoli, 2009).

3. Elio Apih, *Il ritorno di Giani Stuparich* (Florence: Vallecchi, 1988), 75: "Trieste fu frequentemente crogiolo mancato."

4. See, in particular, the collected essays edited by Pierre Nora, *Les lieux de mémoire* (Paris: Gallimard, 1981–1992).

5. M. Isnenghi, *I luoghi della memoria: Simboli e miti dell'Italia Unita* (Rome-Bari: Laterza, 1998), ix: "regno della storia sociale."

6. J. Winter, *Sites of Memory, Sites of Mourning: The Great War in European Cultural History* (Cambridge: Cambridge University Press, 1998), 10: "[M]y 'sites of memory' are other than Nora's. First, they are international; secondly, they are comparative; thirdly, they are there for their value in answering specific historical questions related to the cultural consequences of the 1914–18 war. That is why my 'sites of memory' are also 'sites of mourning.'"

7. See Alon Confino, "Collective Memory and Cultural History: Problems of Method," *The American Historical Review* 102 (1997): 1386–403.

8. See Cathy Caruth, *Unclaimed Experience: Trauma, Narrative and History* (Baltimore and London: Johns Hopkins University Press, 1996); C. Caruth, *Trauma: Explorations in Memory* (Baltimore: Johns Hopkins University Press, 1995); Dominic LaCapra, *Writing History, Writing Trauma* (Baltimore and London: Johns Hopkins University Press, 2001); Roger Luckhurst, *The Trauma Question* (London: Routledge, 2008); Stef Craps, *Postcolonial Witnessing: Trauma out of Bounds* (New York: Palgrave MacMillan, 2013).

9. See, for example, *Mediation, Remediation and the Dynamics of Cultural Memory,* eds Astrid Erll and Ann Rigney (Berlin and New York: De Gruyter, 2012). Michael Rothberg, *Multidirectional Memory: Remembering the Holocaust in the Age of Decolonization* (Stanford: Stanford University Press, 2009).

10. See the posthumous book Michael Baxandall, *Episodes: A Memory Book* (London: Frances Lincoln, 2010).

11. These are only a handful of the many metaphors utilized by recent and authoritative historiography, part of a truly vast bibliography. The most salient books are John Foot, *Fratture d'Italia* (Milan: Rizzoli, 2009); Pamela Ballinger, *History in Exile: Memory and Identity at the Borders of the Balkans* (Princeton: Princeton University Press, 2003); Raoul Pupo and Roberto Spazzali, *Foibe* (Milan: Bruno Mondadori, 2003); Claudia Cernigoi, *Operazione foibe–Tra storia e mito* (Udine: Kappa Vu, 2005); Katia Pizzi, *Trieste: Italianità, triestinità e male di frontiera* (Bologna: Gedit, 2007); Gianni Oliva, *Foibe: Le stragi negate degli italiani della Venezia Giulia e dell'Istria* (Milan: Mondadori, 2007); Joze Pirjevec, *Foibe: Una storia d'Italia* (Turin: Einaudi, 2009); and so on and so forth.

12. Pizzi, *Trieste,* 166–74. See also K. Pizzi, "Storia e memoria ai confini nordorientali d'Italia," *Italian Studies* 68 (2013): 340–55.

13. See also K. Pizzi, "A Modernist City Resisting Translation? Trieste between Slovenia and Italy," in *Speaking Memory. How Translation Shapes City Life,* ed. Sherry Simon (Montreal and Kingston, London, Chicago: McGill-Queen's University Press, 2016), 45–57.

14. Foot, *Fratture,* 129.

15. Enrico Morovich, *Il baratro* (Padua: Rebellato, 1964); Carlo Sgorlon, *La foiba grande* (Milan: Mondadori, 1992); Giuseppe Svalduz, *Una croce sulla foiba: Il grido delle vittime ritrova la strada della memoria* (Venice: Marsilio, 1996); Ezio Mestrovich, *Foiba in autunno* (Trieste: Il Ramo d'oro, 2006); Giulio Angioni, *Gabbiani sul Carso* (Palermo: Sellerio, 2010); Giani Stuparich, "La grotto," in *Nuovi racconti* (Milan: Treves-Treccani-Tumminelli, 1935); the most recently published collection is Lina Galli, *Nata per il mistero* (Empoli: Ibiskos Editrice Risolo, 2013).

16. Controversies abound over the pits and polemics are particularly fierce as concerns quantitative data (e.g., size, configuration, number of victims)—see the vast bibliography part of which is cited here (footnote n. 11).

17. A detailed examination of these narratives is in Pizzi, *Trieste,* 166–74 and K. Pizzi, *A City in Search of an Author: The Literary Identity of Trieste* (London and New York: Sheffield Academic Press–Continuum, 2001), 91–99.

18. For *lieux de mémoire* as bastions, see Nora, "From between Memory and History: Les Lieux de Memoire," *Representations* 26 (1989): 7–24.

19. Jan Assman, "Collective Memory and Cultural Identity," *New German Critique* 65 (1995): 125–33 (132).

20. Ferruccio Fölkel, *La Risiera di San Sabba: L'Olocausto dimenticato: Trieste e il Litorale Adriatico durante l'occupazione nazista* (Milan: Rizzoli, 2000), esp. 8–9 and *passim*. The book is dedicated to Primo Levi.

21. Boris Pahor and Cristina Batocletti, *Figlio di nessuno: Un'autobiografia senza frontiere* (Milan: Rizzoli, 2012); Mauro Covacich, "La Risiera di San Sabba. Visita a un forno crematorio," in *Trieste sottosopra: Quindici passeggiate nella città del vento* (Rome: GFL Laterza, 2006); Giuseppe O. Longo, "Il reddito della vergogna," in *Il futuro nel sangue: 19 fantapologhi sul potere,* ed. V. Catani ([n.p.]: R & D, 2003); Veit Heineken, *I morti del Carso* (Rome: Edizioni e / o, 2003); Ketty Daneo, *La Risiera di San Sabba* (Trieste: [n.p.], 1970).

22. I draw all information on this trial from the papers published by Adolfo Scalpelli, ed., *San Sabba: Istruttoria e processo per il Lager della Risiera* (Milan: ANED Mondadori, 1988), vol. I and II; see also Folkel.

23. See Massimo Mucci, *La Risiera di San Sabba: Un'architettura per la memoria* (Gorizia: Goriziana, 1999).

24. Francesco Mazzucchelli, "Ricordi innominabili: La ristrutturazione dell'ex campo di concentramento di San Sabba," *Chora* September 16, 2008: 24.

25. Most recently, Kwame Anthony Appiah began and concluded his first BBC4 Reith Lecture 2016 "Mistaken Identities" with reference to Trieste as a case study of the fragmented

status of modern literary culture—see http://www.bbc.co.uk/programmes/b07z43ds (accessed January 27, 2017). The myth of Mitteleuropean Trieste grew largely out of Angelo Ara and Claudio Magris's seminal and pluri-translated volume *Trieste: Un'identità di frontiera* (Turin: Einaudi, 2015), first published in 1982.

26. J. Joyce, *Giacomo Joyce*, ed. Richard Ellmann (Parma: Guanda, 1991).

27. Stelio Mattioni's novel *Il richiamo di Alma* (Milan: Adelphi, 1980) is one of the first examples of this successful strategy, embraced eagerly by local writers subsequently.

28. For an in-depth analysis and further details, see K. Pizzi, "Storia e memoria ai confini nordorientali d'Italia": 340–55 and K. Pizzi, "A Modernist City Resisting Translation? Trieste between Slovenia and Italy," 45–57.

29. See footnote n. 3

30. I am thinking, for example, of the arson attack to the Slovenian Hotel Balkan and Cultural House on July 13, 1920, and the forty days of Yugoslav occupation of Trieste in May-June 1945.

31. The first *Ginnasio Femminile* was established in 1872, followed closely by the first *Liceo Femminile* in 1881.

32. See K. Pizzi, *A City in Search of an Author*, 138–41.

33. Roberto Curci and Gabriella Ziani, *Bianco rosa e verde: Scrittrici a Trieste fra Ottocento e Novecento* (Trieste: Lint, 1993), 375.

34. Nora Franca Pogliaghi, *Colore di Trieste* (Trieste: Società Artistico Letteraria, 1967).

35. Winston Churchill "Sinews of Peace," http://www.youtube.com/watch?v=PJxUAcADV70, accessed February 1, 2017: "From Stettin in the Baltic to Trieste in the Adriatic, an Iron Curtain has descended across the continent. Behind that line, lie all the capitals of the ancient states of central and Eastern Europe. . . . All these famous cities and the populations around them lie in what I must call the Soviet sphere and all are subject in one form or another not only to Soviet influence but to a very high and in some cases increasing measure of control from Moscow." See also K. Pizzi, "Cold War Trieste on Screen: Memory, Identity and Mystique of a City in the Shadow of the Iron Curtain," in *Cold War Cities: History, Culture and Memory*, eds K. Pizzi and M. Hietala (Oxford: Peter Lang, 2016), 75–95.

36. Peter Stanković, "Constructs of Slovenianness in Slovenian Partisan Films," http://hrcak.srce.hr/file/46336, accessed February 1, 2017; orig. Stanković, *Rdeči Trakovi* (Ljubljana: Fakulteta za družbene vede, 2005) and Vjeran Pavlakovič, "Twilight of the Revolutionaries: 'Nasi Spanci' and the End of Yugoslavia," *Europe-Asia Studies* 62 / 7 (2010): 1175–91.

37. Examples include *Na svoji zemlji* (On Our Own Land; 1948) and *Trst* (Trieste; 1951) directed by France štiglic and *Hudodelci* (The Felons; 1987), directed by Franci Slak.

38. See K. Pizzi, "Cold War Trieste on Screen," 84–85.

39. The opening shots feature a dialogue between Mike Kells, traveling by plane to Trieste, and the officer on board. This dialogue prepares the ground for Mike's visit to Trieste, described in terms of Cold War stereotypes.

40. See also K. Pizzi, "A Modernist City Resisting Translation? Trieste between Slovenia and Italy," 45–57.

WORKS CITED

Angioni, Giulio. *Gabbiani sul Carso*. Palermo: Sellerio, 2010.

Apih, Elio. *Il ritorno di Giani Stuparich*. Florence: Vallecchi, 1988.

Appiah, Anthony Kwame. "Mistaken Identities," with reference to Trieste as a case study of the fragmented status of modern literary culture. http://www.bbc.co.uk/programmes/b07z43ds (accessed January 27, 2017).

Ara, Angelo, and Claudio Magris. *Trieste: Un'identità di frontier*. Turin: Einaudi, 2015.

Assman, Jan. "Collective Memory and Cultural Identity." *New German Critique* 65 (1995): 125–33.

Ballinger, Pamela. *History in Exile: Memory and Identity at the Borders of the Balkans*. Princeton: Princeton University Press, 2003.

Baxandall, Michael. *Episodes: A Memory Book*. London: Frances Lincoln, 2010.

Caruth, Cathy. *Trauma: Explorations in Memory.* Baltimore: Johns Hopkins University Press, 1995.

———. *Unclaimed Experience: Trauma, Narrative and History.* Baltimore and London: Johns Hopkins University Press, 1996.

Cernigoi, Claudia. *Operazione foibe–Tra storia e mito.* Udine: Kappa Vu, 2005.

Churchill, Winston. "Sinews of Peace." http://www.youtube.com/watch?v=PJxUAcADV70 (accessed February 1, 2017).

Confino, Alon. "Collective Memory and Cultural History: Problems of Method." *The American Historical Review* 102 (1997): 1386–403.

Covacich, Mauro. "La Risiera di San Sabba: Visita a un forno crematorio." In *Trieste sottosopra: Quindici passeggiate nella città del vento.* Rome: GFL Laterza, 2006.

Craps, Stef. *Postcolonial Witnessing: Trauma out of Bounds.* New York: Palgrave MacMillan, 2013.

Curci, Roberto, and Gabriella Ziani. *Bianco rosa e verde: Scrittrici a Trieste fra Ottocento e Novecento.* Trieste: Lint, 1993.

Daneo, Ketty. *La Risiera di San Sabba.* Trieste: [n.p.], 1970.

Erll, Astrid, and Ann Rigney. *Mediation, Remediation and the Dynamics of Cultural Memory.* Berlin and New York: De Gruyter, 2012.

Fölkel, Ferruccio. *La Risiera di San Sabba: L'Olocausto dimenticato: Trieste e il Litorale Adriatico durante l'occupazione nazista.* Milan: Rizzoli, 2000.

Foot, John. *Fratture d'Italia.* Milan: Rizzoli, 2009.

Galli, Lina. *Nata per il mistero.* Empoli: Ibiskos Editrice Risolo, 2013.

Heineken, Veit. *I morti del Carso.* Rome: Edizioni e / o, 2003.

Huyssen, A. *Present Pasts: Urban Palimpsests and the Politics of Memory.* Stanford, CA: Stanford University Press, 2003.

Isnenghi, M. *I luoghi della memoria: Simboli e miti dell'Italia Unita.* Rome-Bari: Laterza, 1998.

Joyce, James. *Giacomo Joyce*, ed. Richard Ellmann. Parma: Guanda, 1991.

LaCapra, Dominic. *Writing History, Writing Trauma.* Baltimore and London: Johns Hopkins University Press, 2001.

Longo, Giuseppe O. "Il reddito della vergogna." In *Il futuro nel sangue: 19 fantapologhi sul potere*, ed. V. Catani ([n.p.]: R & D, 2003).

Luckhurst, Roger. *The Trauma Question.* London: Routledge, 2008.

Mattioni, Stelio. *Il richiamo di Alma.* Milan: Adelphi, 1980.

Mazzucchelli, Francesco. "Ricordi innominabili: La ristrutturazione dell'ex campo di concentramento di San Sabba." *Choral.* September 16, 2008.

Mestrovich, Ezio. *Foiba in autunno.* Trieste: Il Ramo d'oro, 2006.

Morovich, Enrico. *Il baratro.* Padua: Rebellato, 1964.

Mucci, Massimo. *La Risiera di San Sabba: Un'architettura per la memoria.* Gorizia: Goriziana, 1999.

Nora, Pierre. "From between Memory and History: Les Lieux de Memoire," *Representations* 26 (1989): 7–24.

———. *Les lieux de mémoire.* Paris: Gallimard, 1981–1992.

Oliva, Gianni. *Foibe: Le stragi negate degli italiani della Venezia Giulia e dell'Istria.* Milan: Mondadori, 2007.

Pahor, Boris, and Cristina Batocletti. *Figlio di nessuno: Un'autobiografia senza frontiere.* Milan: Rizzoli, 2012.

Pavlakovič, Vjeran. "Twilight of the Revolutionaries: 'Nasi Spanci' and the End of Yugoslavia." *Europe-Asia Studies* 62 / 7 (2010): 1175–91.

Pirjevec, Joze. *Foibe: Una storia d'Italia.* Turin: Einaudi, 2009.

Pizzi, Katia. *A City in Search of an Author: The Literary Identity of Trieste.* London and New York: Sheffield Academic Press–Continuum, 2001.

———. "Cold War Trieste on Screen: Memory, Identity and Mystique of a City in the Shadow of the Iron Curtain." In *Cold War Cities: History, Culture and Memory*, eds Pizzi and M. Hietala. Oxford: Peter Lang, 2016, 75–95.

————. "A Modernist City Resisting Translation? Trieste between Slovenia and Italy." In *Speaking Memory: How Translation Shapes City Life*, ed. Sherry Simon, 45–57. Montreal: McGill-Queen's University Press, 2016.

————. "Storia e memoria ai confini nordorientali d'Italia." *Italian Studies* 68 (2013): 340–55.

————. *Trieste: Italianità, triestinità e male di frontiera*. Bologna: Gedit, 2007.

Pogliaghi, Nora Franca. *Colore di Trieste*. Trieste: Società Artistico Letteraria, 1967.

Pupo, Raoul, and Roberto Spazzali. *Foibe*. Milan: Bruno Mondadori, 2003.

Rothberg, Michael. *Multidirectional Memory: Remembering the Holocaust in the Age of Decolonization*. Stanford: Stanford University Press, 2009.

Scalpelli, Adolfo, ed. *San Sabba: Istruttoria e processo per il Lager della Risiera*. Milan: ANED Mondadori, 1988, vol. I and II.

Sgorlon, Carlo. *La foiba grande*. Milan: Mondadori, 1992.

Stanković, Peter. "Constructs of Slovenianness in Slovenian Partisan Films," http://hrcak.srce. hr/file/46336(accessed 1 February 2017).

Stuparich, Giani. "La grotto." In *Nuovi racconti*. Milan: Treves-Treccani-Tumminelli, 1935.

Svalduz, Giuseppe. *Una croce sulla foiba: Il grido delle vittime ritrova la strada della memoria*. Venice: Marsilio, 1996.

Todorova, Maria. *Imagining the Balkans*. Oxford: Oxford University Press, 2009.

Winter, J. *Sites of Memory, Sites of Mourning: The Great War in European Cultural History*. Cambridge: Cambridge University Press, 1998.

Chapter Eight

The Trauma of Liberation

Rape, Love, and Violence in Wartime Italy

David W. Ellwood

When the armies of the United Nations landed in Sicily in July 1943, their commanders thought that World War II in Italy would end by the autumn of 1944 at the latest. They were destined to stay in one form or other until the international Peace Treaty of 1946 came into force on January 1, 1947. "By war's end over 1,000,000 troops had served in the peninsula," calculates Isobel Williams.[1] The bulk of the Allied soldiery had gone by the end of 1945, but remnants stayed in the Livorno area—of whom we shall hear more later—and in the city of Trieste. Italy saw the presence of these forces longer than any other west European country. The Italian campaign was a very long-drawn out, bloody, and destructive affair, and an argument sprang up well before the war was over as to whether this was "liberation" or "occupation."[2]

But in Italy's case this distinction between liberation and occupation was radically confused by the lived experience of the war for so many people, the length and breadth of the peninsula. History and common sense confirm that the longer foreign forces stay on invaded territory, the more their presence feels like an occupation, especially if they are not actually in battle. In Italy's case this meant that the south was more or less "occupied" for over two years—the Allies stayed in Naples from October 1, 1943, to January 1, 1946— while the final advance in the spring of 1945 saw the Allies pass through northern Italy's towns and villages in a matter of weeks.

In recent decades the world of official memory in Italy has been re-created in an effort to overcome the painful heritage of war and cold war and give a new, unifying meaning and honor to some of the most bruising episodes in Italian contemporary history.[3] But in all this public effort to reinvent the recent tribulations of the Italian people for the purposes of binding the nation's wounds and giving its traumas moral meaning, no one has ever proposed erecting a monument to the Allies. The reasons why not will become clear in the pages to come, but one conspicuous result of this neglect has been to leave the spontaneous, unofficial world of memory entirely free to elaborate its own versions of the liberation/occupation experience. Over the years an impressive array of novelists and filmmakers have taken advantage of this space to propose a variety of reconstructions. A few have achieved canonical status in Italian film, theatrical, and literary history.

Before proceeding, an observation on one memory "reality" that strikes anyone who takes the long view of all that has been written, filmed, or spoken about the Allies in the decades since they left. *The only ones who count are the Americans*. The others—and they were many—are barely to be seen.[4] In the two most recent films, which deal with the landings in Sicily— *Un amore in guerra* (Emanuele Diliberto, 2016) and Giuseppe Tornatore's *Baarìa* of 2009—the Allied soldiery is exclusively American, even though of the seven divisions which arrived in July 1943, only three were from the United States. In fact the armies of sixteen nations took part in this military campaign. The 5th American Army included Phillipinos, Brazilians, Hawaiians, and others. The British 8th Army included a wide selection of units from the Dominions and the Empire: Australians, New Zealanders, and Canadians, but also Indians, Gurkhas, and men from Mauritius.

Other forces were supplied by the Free French; they included a battalion of Moroccans who would acquire permanent notoriety because their wild rampages of pillaging in general and rape in particular, to which we shall return. The free Poles acquired battle honors in Italy, but their contribution has been almost entirely forgotten outside the cities where their cemeteries are to be found. Popular history and memory, fictional or otherwise, has also chosen to overlook the fact that it was mostly British generals and political figures who ran the Italian campaign. In contrast, it was the Americans who over the years supplied the most telling fictional accounts, in written and cinematic form. Here though, our concern is with the legacy of Italian narratives, not those of the Anglo-Americans and their fellow "liberators."

This Italian heritage has been transformed over recent years. New generations of young men and women have arisen intent on displaying their own, original varieties of social and historical protagonism, and often profoundly skeptical of the dogmas and conventional wisdom about liberation and occupation they inherited from their forebears. This has radically changed the terrain where memory and history meet. Nothing has contributed more to the evolution of historical studies in this area—as in so many others—than the rise of memory research and women's studies. It hardly seems an exaggeration to say that the *only* significant and substantial new contribution in recent decades to historical understanding of what happened in Italy during the World War II experience has come from women's studies.[5]

This is not just a product of intellectual fashion. As many women historians have noted, the kinds of violence to which women were exposed during the war invariably involved their sexuality and left indelible senses of violation and shame, memories which the passage of time has confirmed as authentic traumas. To bear witness or discuss in public such experiences was prevented by taboos of all sorts, and a natural, generalized reticence sustained unquestioningly by formal and informal custom.[6] The sexual violence of war can only begin to be discussed today, more than seventy years later, when most grief has perhaps been absorbed, and when general standards of *pudore* (decency and chasteness, dignity and modesty) have evolved radically in comparison to those still prevailing in the war years. Even so, says Chiara Fantozzi in a pioneering study of an area in Tuscany that became infamous for the mass prostitution it witnessed, there are still disproportions: far more studies of soldier rape in Italy and Europe have been produced so far, she says, than those dedicated to sex as a stake in a deeply unequal power relationship between foreign soldiers and local women.[7]

THE FIFTIETH ANNIVERSARY

Up and down Italy every tenth anniversary of the Liberation produces its national and local outpouring of speeches and editorials, marches, celebrations, and TV debates. But the fiftieth occasion in 1995 was particularly significant from the point of view of any attempt to study collective memory. In Bologna the inheritors of the Communist tradition, which had crowned that city and its region as their showpiece administration, published a supplement to their party newspaper, still called—as in the days of the old party— *Unità*. The supplement dwelt on "the symbolic renewal of life" the Americans had brought, with music and dancing, baseball and Camel cigarettes, the color-filled images of a renewed way of life and an undreamt of prosperity. Staying in Bologna only six weeks, the Allies included Poles and Brits, but it was the Americans who had left the memories, as one may read in the testimony—reproduced in the *Unità* supplement—from a young woman who had witnessed the city's liberation:

> "[C]orremmo anche noi verso la piazza a vedere gli americani. Ce n'erano di tutte le razze, bianchi, neri, indiani. Erano la nostra salvezza. Erano simpatici, come nei loro film. Non si atteggiavano da liberatori. . . . Erano uomini liberi, venivano da un paese dove la vita non era mai stata interrotta e si vedeva. Erano pieni di energia, di allegria. Come noi, ma la nostra era un'allegria che esplodeva dopo vent'anni di terrore. Mamma si mise a cantare a squarciagola Bandiera rossa. Come quando, da piccola, imparava le note dell'Internazionale dal cugino prete.[8]

(We all ran out to see the Americans arrive. There were all sorts of colors,
whites, blacks, Indians. They were our salvation. They were nice and friendly,
just like in their films. They didn't act like liberators. They were free men, they
came from a country where life had never been interrupted [by war] and you
could tell. They were full of energy and cheer. Like us, but ours was a cheer-
fulness which exploded after twenty years of terror. Mamma suddenly started
singing *Red Flag* at the top of her voice. Just like when we were kids, when we
learned to sing the *International* from a priest who was our cousin.)

In those joyous days you could be Communist, Catholic, and pro-American,
at least in Bologna.

How very different was the account supplied in the same months of 1995
by a quite different Communist source, the journalist and writer Ermanno
Rea, a long-time observer of the Neapolitan scene and member of the party in
that city for decades. Rea's semi-fictional "diary" is titled *Mistero napoletano: Vita e passione di un comunista negli anni della guerra fredda* (Neapolitan Mystery: The Life and Passion of a Communist in the Years of the Cold
War). At first sight the Allies of the war years appear to offer only a back-
drop to Rea's emotional search for the reasons a much-loved colleague and
fellow comrade, Francesca, had committed suicide in 1961. The context is all
political: for Rea, the war had turned out to be just the first in an ineluctable
chain of events that propelled the American military to supreme power in the
city. The local ruling boss, a shipping tycoon who had survived Fascism
intact, had sold out Naples to NATO, according to Rea, and the military had
quickly turned the place into their Mediterranean command base, the focal
point of the Cold War in southern Europe. And in so doing, insisted this
witness, they had suffocated its potential for development, if not modernity.
The powerful local Communist Party, to which Francesca was passionately
devoted, stood little chance of making an impact.[9]

But the excerpts from Francesca's wartime diary offered by Rea concentrate on her experience of the shock of Fascism's collapse, the arrival of two
fighting armies where she is living, and her solitary efforts to protect her sons
(their father had gone off to join Mussolini in the north). At the start of her
account, states Rea, the noblest sentiments are expressed, then material reality takes over and her words express all the anguish of her situation. The day
the Allies land in Sicily, July 7, 1943, she writes,

Ecco, invadono la Sicilia. Ma dio mio, Dunque ci siamo! Pare incredibile. E
quanta legerezza, quanto poco senso di Patria nella massa. "Patria"—che vuole
dire? Io non lo so, ma si può superare il senso di Patria solo col senso *vero*
[sic] di carità umana—col senso di Cristo. Se non si è a quel punto, patria è
ancora la carità più vasta che possiamo sentire. E io ora che farò? I bambini,
non posso tenerli qui. Dove li porterò? E la roba? Queste notti –brevi notti
estive, ma lunghe per l'apprensione snervante. Allarmi, esercitazioni, non è
possibile dormire.[10]

(So, Sicily is invaded. My God, this is where we've got to. Seems incredible. And what superficiality, what scarce sense of patriotism you see in the masses. "Patria"—what does it mean? I don't know, but you can only put patriotism behind you with the *true* [*sic*] sense of human charity—the Christian sense. If we haven't got there yet, "patria" is the widest form of charity which we can still feel. . . . And now what am I going to do? I can't keep the kids here. Where will I take them? And my stuff? These nights—these short summer nights, so long in nervous tension. Air-raid alarms, troop movements, sleep is impossible.)

By the time Italy officially surrenders on September 8, Francesca has taken her children to Latina, a small town north of Naples. She characterizes the armistice as "honourable,"[11] but then describes the vicious reaction of the Nazi armies, who have immediately taken over the local area. She recalls the contempt she has always felt for them when Italy was allied with Nazi Germany. Now she feels just powerless, and her scorn is directed at the politicians and military men in Rome, who have handed everything over to the Germans without firing a shot: "[P]osso solo piangere, piangere di aver trasmesso ai miei figli questa Italia"[12] (I can only weep, weep at handing over to my children this Italy). Overcome by "guerra, distruzione, rovina, terrore, crudeltà, sfacelo, disonore, vergogna"[13] (war, destruction, ruins, terror, cruelty, chaos, shame), the diary comes to a halt when the bombing and fighting reach Latina. When it starts again in May 1945 she has become a devoted Communist, and there is no space for reflection on the meaning of the war, the liberation and all Naples has passed through.[14] Rea fills the gap with his own, highly politicized, 1995 interpretation of it all.

NAPLES

Liberated Naples presented the Allies and the city's inhabitants with a challenge of coexistence that they had never imagined and would never encounter again, in all its destruction from war, its scabrous misery and derelict vitality. The sheer scale of the Allied presence was overwhelming. The British army alone numbered over 199,000 men.[15] The records of that experience from all sides—official material, memoirs, diaries, films, plays, novels—portray something like a clash of civilizations erupting along with Vesuvius in the old Bourbon city. For the American soldiery, the bombed out, starving metropolis allegedly represented everything they hated about the Old World. "In August, 1944, the port of Naples was a flytrap of bustle and efficiency and robbery in the midst of ruin and panic," wrote the American novelist John Horne Burns in his postwar masterpiece *The Gallery*, set in the city. Looking at the rubbish floating in the sea water, one of his soldier characters remarks simply, "Europe drains into the Bay of Naples."[16] The soldiers "figured it this way," wrote Burns,

> These Ginsoes have made war on us; so it doesn't matter what we do to them, boost their prices, shatter their economy, and shack up with their women. [17]

In their desperate struggle for survival, many Neapolitans seemed to take pride in flaunting their anti-modernism. The British diarist Lewis claimed, with ample evidence, that the war had pushed them "back into the Middle Ages."[18] Yet the playwright Eduardo De Filippo took a different view. His celebrated play *Napoli milionaria*, written and set during the liberation/occupation experience, became a triumphant symbol of the Neapolitan spirit in adversity, and made him a national hero. Later he recalled,

> The new century, this twentieth century did not reach Naples until the arrival of the Allies; here in Naples, it seems to me, the Second World War made a hundred years pass overnight. [19]

One of the greatest Italian novels of the war, Curzio Malaparte's *La Pelle*, of 1948, also set largely in Naples, emphasized instead national abjection. In Malaparte's deeply pessimistic world view, self-abasement turns into a form of exhibitionism. As such it denotes a generalized defiance of the Anglo-Americans' logic of liberation, especially their bizarre blend of moralism and materialism. Malaparte rejected the conventional definitions of victory and defeat, liberation and occupation. Once an unorthodox Fascist, now a liaison officer between the Allies and the remains of the Italian armies, the writer declared that the Neapolitans, with all their centuries of foreign invasions, were never likely to feel *defeated* just because a new invader had arrived. As for these Allied armies, it was useless for them to claim to liberate people and at the same time want to make them feel defeated. Either they were free or they were defeated. In truth, claimed Malaparte, the Neapolitans felt neither.[20]

As in all the liberated territories of Europe, it was women who bore the brunt of the paradoxes and contradictions the Allies brought with them. At the beginning, every kind of collaboration was on display between the newly arrived soldiery and local women, as the Neapolitan historian Maria Porzio observes: "[D]a quelle positive—frequentazioni, fidanzamenti, matrimoni— a quelle illecite, come il diffusissimo commercio clandestino di merci alleate" [21] (From the positive sort—dates, engagements, marriages—to the illegal kind, centered on the ever-swelling market in Allied goods). The Americans' opulence and generosity conquered many a heart, and made up in some way for the recent bombardments and the plague of requisitioning: local men thought "their" women had been requisitioned. But within months it was these same Americans who had set in motion and come to dominate vast markets in sex, war materials, and crime. The armies sent by the United States were supposed to be agents of the American versions of modernity, but the profoundly ambiguous destiny of this message in wartime Naples comes out unmistakably in Porzio's pages. On the one hand was its total irrelevance and uselessness in the chaos and misery left by the Nazis and by Allied bombardments; on the other was the desire it provoked of flight *to* America. The misery and degradation of all concerned in the carnival of sex is confirmed yet again.

Yet the illusion persisted of a standard of living in the Promised Land far superior to anything Italy could ever provide, a vision to be grasped through marriage with the very men bringing all the chaos, men who, in spite of everything, were *different*. The experience of a range of Neapolitan women caught up in this contradiction is documented very strikingly in Porzio's book, with reference to specific cases. One said,

> La guerra è stato un disastro, ma anche dopo, anche quando se ne andarono i tedeschi Napoli era rovinata, non si poteva vivere, c'era la fame ... (. . .). Però se ci penso ... è strano, non lo so spiegare, ma se qualcuno mi domanda: 'vuoi cancellare la guerra?' io non direi sì. A me la guerra ha portato anche il bene, se non scoppiava la guerra on sarebbero venuti gli americani e non avrei conosciuto John.[22]

> (The war was a disaster, but even afterward, when the Germans had gone, Naples was ruined, life was impossible, there was starvation. . . . And yet, if I think about it . . . it's strange, but if someone asked me, 'Want to cancel the war?, I wouldn't say yes. The war brought good things too; if the war hadn't broken out, the Americans would never have come and I'd never have known John.)

Echoes of all these experiences could be heard and seen throughout the postwar years. When it came to depicting the war, nothing like wartime Naples captured the imagination of the Italian film industry. Roberto Rossellini's second neo-realist classic, *Paisà*, of 1946, portrays the liberation/occupation story in a series of six episodes, offering a fictional narrative—linked by newsreel sequences and a voice-over—stretching from Sicily to the Po delta in winter 1944. But it's the Neapolitan sequence that offers the most complex depiction of local responses to the Allied presence. The protagonists are the street kids, a swarming mass of urchins whose newly adapted arts of survival capture a drunken Afro-American soldier and exploit him for all the trappings he brings, from his harmonica to his boots. A deeply unhappy soul, he crashes a (highly allegorical) puppet show, and ends up on a pile of rubble singing the blues to the kid who's dragged him through the streets. The next day though his dignity is restored with a proper uniform and the jeep of a military policeman. He sees the same street urchin again and forces him to go to the child's home in the hope of recovering his stolen property. When the soldier discovers this is a warren of caves inhabited by a crowd of dispossessed and afflicted people, a sense of stupor silently overtakes him: there are human beings in the world much worse off than him.

Paisà remains the most striking cinematic tribute to the extraordinary ambivalence of the Allied impact. It shows Italians who sacrifice themselves for the Allies—a girl in Sicily who, at the cost of her life, warns an American patrol of approaching Germans—and Anglo-American individuals who risk their lives for the Italians: including a British nurse taking care of wounded partisans in Florence, and an OSS officer who stays with his partisan group until they are rounded up by the enemy (though apparently only the partisans are executed).

In the central episode, set in Rome, six months of liberation transform the heroes from the tanks into a drunken mob, and a shy middle-class young lady into a street prostitute, whose last illusion is shattered. The roughness and squalor of war, the destruction of every basic standard and asset of life, the upheaval of values, are transmitted through grainy, black-and-white imagery that seems intended to supply a permanent repertoire of memories from a situation all involved knew to be ephemeral, fleeting. [23]

By 1985 color and a certain *allegria* had returned to Naples, and one of the best-known of the postwar film directors, Ettore Scola, produced *Maccheroni*, a light-hearted play on those stereotypes of the wartime Italian-American encounter that had survived the passage of time. The production brought two leading men from Cinecittà and Hollywood together: Marcello Mastroanni and Jack Lemmon. The former plays a humble bank functionary, the latter Mr. Travers, the chief executive of a grand U.S. aerospace company. During the war, when a simple soldier, Travers had captured the heart of a young woman of Naples. Afterward her brother Antonio (Mastroianni), in order to console her, had dedicated himself to years of writing fake letters from her American idol, portraying him as a hero of modern adventures all over the world but forever devoted to his Maria. When Mr. Travers does eventually return to Naples, he is indeed a great personage but with no memory at all of his wartime affair. How then to reconcile myth and reality?

The film offers an easy way out: the winning stereotypes are those that confront the ancient (Antonio is a scribe in the historical archive of his Neapolitan bank) and the modern (Mr. Travers, captain of a high-tech industry, with all his American neuroses, haste, indifference to the past, and conviction that everything can be bought with credit cards). But such is the force of local superstition and folklore, as deployed by Antonio that in the end Mr. Travers becomes *de-Americanized*, and can finally start to enjoy life. (Maria, meanwhile, a silent, imposing matriarch, has been left behind by both men.)

ELSEWHERE IN THE SOUTH

Decades later certain authoritative reflections claimed that the arrival of the Allies in the south of Italy set in motion aspirations for movement and change that would find their full expression in the mass migrations from the southern countryside to the northern industrial cities characteristic of the 1950s.[24] Curzio Malaparte's short story "Il compagno di viaggio" ("Travelling Companion"), written just before his death in 1957, argued that the Fascism's collapse in 1943 had set in motion an exodus from Sicily, led by women, who saw in it a chance to escape from misery in search of a land that would give them prosperity, justice, law and order, and dignity. Malaparte, however, did not attribute this phenomenon to the arrival of the Allies, but to an ancient, deep-rooted impulse that saw every destruction of the existing system as an "opportunity for liberty" for the poorest people.[25]

Using a wide variety of local and Anglo-American documentation, Isobel Williams has presented in detail the forms of disorder the Allied soldiery brought with them after pushing out the enemy, behind the fighting lines. "The trouble often occurred," she writes, because the soldiers were, as one report put it, "in cerca di vino e signorine," ("in search of wine and women"), and "having found and drunk the wine were not particularly sensitive about how they found the young ladies. In addition, the soldiers were armed, which added another element to incidents, as the means were available for them to cause much greater physical harm than otherwise."[26] Looting, street theft, traffic accidents, fights and brawls between Allied soldiers, and between them and local men were very often uncontrolled by Allied police, and could not be stopped by Italian police forces, at least in the early stages, since they had no authority over Allied servicemen. All this meant, as Williams puts it, that "there was a certain element of fear in the relationship between soldier and civilian."[27]

Against such a background the question of sexual violence takes on a particularly dramatic profile. Williams's account places the southern Italian experience in its European context and comments, "It seems that soldier rape was common, widespread and not taken particularly seriously by the high military command," although a few Allied soldiers in southern Italy were in fact executed for particularly brutal assaults. Her "guess-timate" is that probably about 660 soldier rapes took place in the south in the 1943–1945 period.[28]

An even more abhorrent picture is presented by the behavior of the Moroccan "Goumiers," irregular mountain troops of the French Expeditionary Forces. Their record of pillage and rape puts them in a category that left their victims certain that they had been much better treated by the Germans than by their French "liberators." Williams calculates that the 15,000 Goums—out of a total of more than 1 million Allied soldiers—were responsible for 90 percent of the over one thousand rapes officially reported by the Italian authorities.[29]

Ever-increasing reports of terror and atrocities from "liberated" towns and villages south of Rome in the Spring of 1944 produced a flood of denunciations from local Italian authorities at every level to the Allied command.[30] But, as Williams makes clear, the British and Americans knew that the French military had nothing but contempt for the Italians, and until very late in the war had no problem in turning a blind eye to this form of vengeance for Fascism's "stab in the back"—the invasion of France in 1940.[31] A 2003 interview with the former Algerian president Ben Bella by an Italian historian confirms that colonial troops were promised "carte blanche" on arrival in Italy by their French commanders.[32]

As many Italian observers have noted, this story was for a long time confined to the shadows, displaced by other contingencies, not least the forms of "political correctness" associated with the dogma of Liberation, which discouraged all forms of criticism of the Allies and dwelt exclusively on what happened in the north.[33] Only gradually was the radical sense of outrage and shame felt by the victims reconstructed by historians, together with the feelings of bewilderment that arose as one force of male terrorists in uniform gave way immediately, in some places, to another. These were "liberators" that no authority local or Allied seemed able or willing to control or even restrain.[34]

Beyond all this, says Michela Ponzani, the surviving accounts always emphasize the extra-dimension of terror that accompanied the presence, whether violent or not, of "coloured" troops, with the result that all—whether Indian, Asian, or African—become subsumed under the collective title of "Moroccans." Worse would come later, says Ponzani, when in many cases the victims found themselves repudiated not just by their own menfolk, but even by their local communities, under the sway of "credenze popolari e canoni legati alla religione e alla superstizione " (popular beliefs and standards distilled from religion and superstition), of the kind that attributed diabolical origins to the appearance and behavior of the "Moroccans," and stigmatized anyone who had come into contact with them, no matter what the circumstances.[35]

MOVING NORTH

Among the many recollections of the moment when the liberators arrived in a town or village, this one, deposited in the *Archivio diaristico nazionale di Pieve di Santo Stefano* (National Diary Archive), sums up well its delights but also something of its ambiguities:

Cantando, gridando, smanacciando, ridendo, i soldati gettavano alla folla ai lati della strada, cioccolate, scatolette, pacchetti di cigarette e tutti ad azzuffarsi per raccoglierle. Sarei sprofondata dalla vergogna. Neppure se si fosse trattato di pane e avessi avuto una fame da morire mi sarei degnata di raccoglierlo così indecorosamente tirato, peggio che ai cani. Per cose superflue, poi, non trovavo nessuna giustificazione. Addio dignità di un popolo! Facevamo la figura degli accattoni al passaggio di gran signori. [36]

(Singing, shouting, waving, laughing, the soldiers threw chocolates, tins of food, cigarette packets to the crowds lining the streets, and people fell over themselves to pick them up. I felt covered in shame. Not even if they'd been throwing bread and I was dying of hunger would I have deigned to take stuff thrown at us like that, as if we were dogs. But for all that rubbish . . . no excuse. So much for the dignity of a people! We looked like beggars when some grand lord passed by.)

Not everyone was so troubled:

E giunse il 23 Aprile 1945 quando arrivarono finalmente, gli americani nella Valle del Lucido. Fu per tutti una gioia indicibile. Molti erano soldati di colore e ci portavano cioccolate, biscotti, gomme da masticare, ma soprattutto ci portavano la pace. Si poteva tornare a casa. Nella propria casa. [37]

(Then the 23rd April 1945 came, when at long last the Americans arrived in the Valle del Lucido. Limitless joy for everyone. There was a lot of colored soldiers and they brought chocolate, biscuits, chewing gum, but above all they brought peace. We could go home. To our own houses.)

Many women remember the dancing that always broke out wherever the Americans went, and how the local men looked on with suspicion and jealousy as their wives, girlfriends, and sisters instantly responded to the call of "these big blonde boys with their bags full of chocolate, chewing-gum and cigarettes, terrific boogie-woogie dancers." A dance scene is the central happening in Luigi Zampa's *Un americano in vacanza*, of 1946, made "with the collaboration of the Allied authorities," as announced in the opening frames. In this Cinderella-style fable, a pretty young school-teacher, working with her little pupils in the ruins of her village, is taken up by two GIs on leave. She captures the heart of one of them, who takes her to a ball in Rome "in honour of the Allies," where she is dressed in the finest style by one of the matrons present. All the while she reminds her admirer that while he is on holiday, she has to worry about how to find the means to start rebuilding at home. The film makes very clear, with nice, honest soldiers, references to U.S. aid, and tributes to the flag, that it is to America that Italy would be looking for the way to recovery and reconstruction. The implication is that memories of the war must be left behind and politics set aside.

Whatever the legacy of images, emotions, and agitated hearts in many places, it was the quite colossal amount of war materials the U.S. armies abandoned after the end of hostilities that struck some communities most forcefully, not just Naples. This immense store of discarded industrial production lies at the heart of Giorgio Ferroni's *Tombolo, paradiso nero*, of 1947, a lesser sub-product of neo-realism whose historical significance lies in the reflection it offers on a true story.

Behind the beaches stretching from Livorno to Pisa and beyond lay a wooded territory where for over two years a sub-world of deserters, racketeers, bandits, prostitutes, and hangers-on survived, living on the profits from the illegal and dangerous sale of stuff from the huge dumps of war surplus. The GIs were from the "Buffalo" infantry division, the only unit in Italy composed entirely of Afro-Americans, and in the film it is one of them who acts as the linchpin between local petty criminals and the outlaw world of the woods, a place where drinking, dancing, and womanizing are depicted as free and easy.

As Chiara Fantozzi has shown, the Livorno experience adds another dimension of evidence to the liberation/occupation story, but also to local and national responses to the scene. In *Tombolo, paradiso nero* the local men come over, once more, at best feckless, at worst scavengers: only the male protagonist, a middle-aged ex-policeman lives and dies the death of the one individual able to maintain his integrity amid the physical and moral ruins. The women are almost all engaged in prostitution, either from necessity or attracted by the atmosphere of fun and the easy money. But Fantozzi proposes, not surprisingly, a more complex analysis.

Because of the scale of the illegal phenomena associated with it, the area attracted a widespread notoriety that lasted well after the end of the war. Moralists of every stripe dedicated films and novels to it, down to 1965.[38] Local and national honor was said to be affronted by the persistence of the outlawed territory, with the women involved posing threats to public health—through the spread of sexually transmitted diseases—and law and order. A heritage of rules, legislation, and moral codes surrounding prostitution was felt to be under threat.[39] The response was every kind of repression, detention, and hospitalization of the women of the sex market, a number thought to total about eight thousand between 1944 and 1947, when the last American soldiers left.

Livorno/Tombolo provoked a sense of moral offense across every ideological and ethical boundary: on those women, says Fantozzi, was projected "una colpa insanabile, che sublimava in sé i mali dell'occupazione straniera, primo tra tutti l'offesa all'onore della comunità"[40] (a form of guilt which could not be canceled, a sublimation of the evils of occupation, above all the violation of the sense of honor of the [national] community). A left-wing sociologist, Franco Ferrarotti, who would later achieve national distinction, after visiting Tombolo and its female inhabitants, spoke of "a morale fatigue, a longing for a more prosperous life":

> Queste ragazze, proseguiva, «sono l'espressione d'una stanchezza morale, di un desiderio di vita più ricca» e della «tragedia di noi italiani,» «che per liberarci dai fascisti e dai tedeschi, abbiamo avuto bisogno di lui, di Johnny. E lui regalerà alle donne che lo aspettano lungo la strada un piccino color caffe-latte.» [41]

> (These girls, he would carry on, "are symbols of a morale fatigue, a longing for a more prosperous life" and of "our Italian tragedy," which has meant that in order to get rid of the Fascists and the Germans, we have had to rely on him, Johnny. And as a gift to those who wait for him in the streets, he will present a little coffee-coloured infant.")

A fictionalized version of the story of one innocent girl who falls victim to the Tombolo scenario, written by a local Communist working man, Urano Sarti, in his *Livorno città . . . aperta: Romanzo in vernacolo livornese, Società editrice italiana* discussed by Fantozzi, blames the war and the Americans for her downfall. Up to this point a familiar refrain from that ideological point of view; but in emphasizing at the end that the girl's sacrifice and death are the only roads to *redemption*, the full repertoire of patriotic and Catholic values come into play, and the story takes its place in a long-established tradition of bourgeois moralizing, with the role of the foreigner as the only novelty. Fantozzi comments, "E proprio la forza e l'uniformità del discorso favoriscono la sua lunga persistenza, che si protrae ben oltre la scomparsa delle «donne degli americani» dagli scenari del dopoguerra" (it is the force and uniformity of the discourse which explains its persistence in time, long after the "women of the Americans" disappear from the postwar scene). [42] Stereotypes had taken root, and mechanisms of consolation, which would accompany Italy's postwar reconstruction for decades.

CONCLUSION: REMEMBERING AND FORGETTING

The liberation/occupation experience was bearable because of three factors that have now lost all their potency in official as well as popular memory. First there was the enormous wave of relief and joy the end of fighting brought, the prospect of no more terror, starvation, ruins, rags; the hope of life restored and renewed. Secondly was the certainty that the war would end before long, (even though "long" turned out be much longer than anyone imagined, a torment mentioned by many witnesses, fictional and otherwise). When the Allies had arrived in July 1943, the turning point of the war was well behind them and the collapse of Fascism only confirmed it for the mass of Italians. As the leading British figure among the Allied authorities remarked later, the Italians listened to them and appeared grateful, "but [they] were waiting for us to leave."[43]

Finally there was what a Rome intellectual Enzo Forcella later called the "American Dream": the conviction, partly encouraged by propaganda but also by the "soft power" of all those goods, all that optimism, that the violent destruction of half of Italy would be compensated by a new kind of salvation, made-in-the-USA.[44] Practical experience of "the Dream" was deeply equivocal, as we have seen, and yet it persisted, reinforced by the return of Hollywood and "the revolution of rising expectations" that America's participation in the war, on its terms, had legitimized around the globe. Given Hollywood's historic attention to its female audience, and all the more superficial attributes of the GIs, it was no surprise that young women in Italy were far more sensitive to "the Dream's" allure than local men, who felt often deeply alienated, humiliated even, by this spectacle.[45]

These pages have drawn attention to some of the historical research that in recent years has made possible a gendered history of the Allied soldiery's impact and reception in Italy, in the time of liberation/occupation. Equally striking, and not unrelated, has been the research carried out by Gabriella Gribaudi and others dedicated to the effects of Anglo-American aerial bombing campaigns on civilians up and down the peninsula. A vast array of new facts has emerged: it has not been difficult to show that in a variety of places as many human beings were killed or injured by Allied bombs as by Nazi atrocities of one sort or another. But many other considerations come into play. Gribaudi says,

> Sono soprattutto le donne a mettere l'accento.. sulla sospensione dei valori morali in guerra, sull'impossibilità di trovare delle ragioni alla violenza, sia alleata, quando il bombardamento coglie un piccolo paese inoffensivo o dei contadini che stanno lavorando la terra, o quando le truppe marocchine vengono lasciate libere di stuprare, uccidere, saccheggiare in massa, sia tedesca, quando colpisce alla cieca donne, bambini, famiglie intere.[46]

> (It was women above all who drew attention to the [moral nihilism] of war, to the suspension of all moral values, to the totally incomprehensible origins of all the violence, whether Allied—when a bombardment wipes out a harmless village or some peasants working their land—or when Moroccan troops *en masse* are left free to rape, kill, pillage, or when the Germans lash out blindly at women, children, entire families.)

It was not by chance that postwar Italian cinema was not made for fun, or escapism. Instead it played a fundamental role in what the sociologist Ann Kaplan calls "the ethical imperative of creating witness," a "cultural working through of past catastrophes."[47] If there is an underlying impulse in so many of the films and novels, it is to show the persistence of strains of individual humanity that survived all the torments: an urge to avoid sentimentalism but express instead compassion toward all the victims of the war, even *pietà*. This Italian legacy demonstrates no interest whatsoever in the Allied military as such, either collectively or individually, the exact opposite of how Hollywood and the British film industry treated the war.[48] Roberto Rossellini expressed a powerful strain of postwar feeling and memory when, in a 1960 radio interview on his *Paisà*, he stated,

> [A]lla fine non c'erano più né vincitori né vinti; restava solo l'eroismo quotidiano dell'uomo che si aggrappa alla vita. E che vive, pro e contro tutto, che faccia parte dei vincitori o dei vinti.[49]

> (In the end there were no victors and no defeated; all that remained was the daily heroism of people clinging on to life. And who survived, in spite of everything, whether on the winning side or that of the losers.)

Today, in Italy as elsewhere, it is historians, institutions, and media who do the remembering, while everyone else does the forgetting, as long as they are left free to do so. And the energies of the former, no matter how sincere and well-intentioned, are as nothing compared to the massive effort of displacement and removal that a people must undertake to recover from a national catastrophe such as Italy's experience of World War II on its own territory. While official institutions and the media selectively produce morals and myths for their respective publics, historians try to remind people of things that should not thoughtlessly be pushed over the border from memory to history. This is just one achievement of the work of women's history in recent decades, looking unambiguously at Italy's deeply ambiguous experience of World War II.

NOTES

1. Isobel Williams, *Allies and Italians under Occupation: Sicily and Southern Italy 1943–45* (London: Palgrave Macmillan, 2013), 31.

2. It is worth rereading accounts of the military struggle in order to be reminded of just how hard fought and destructive the Italian war was; for example, see James Holland, *Italy's Sorrow: A Year of War 1944–45* (London: Harper Press, 2008).

3. Giovanni, De Luna, "La repubblica del dolore," *Passato e Presente* 82 (2011): 5–6.

4. This impression is confirmed by Maria Porzio: Maria Porzio, *Arrivano gli Alleati! Amori e violenze nell'Italia liberata* (Bari: Laterza, 2011), 66.

5. The origins of this shift are traced in Maria Grazia Camilletti, "'Esistere da donne in tempo di guerra': Come interpretare i mutamenti: un problema aperto." In *Guerra, Resistenza, Politica: Storie di donne*, edited by Dianella Gagliani (Reggio Emilia: Alberti editore, 2006), 141–43; see also "Donne, guerra, Resistenza: Silenzi e presenze nella storiografia italiana," in the same volume.

6. Patrizia, Gabrielli, *Scenari di guerra, parole di donne: Diari e memorie nell'Italia della seconda guerra mondiale* (Bologna: il Mulino, 2007), 128–29; Cinzia Venturoli, "Abusi e

molestie sessuali lungo la Linea Gotica," in *Guerra, Resistenza, Politica. Storie di donne*, edited by Dianella Gagliani, 79–83 (Reggio Emilia: Alberti editore, 2006).

7. Michela Ponzani, *Guerra alle donne: Partigiani, vittime di stupro, "amanti del nemico" 1940–45* (Turin: Einaudi, 2012), 227; Chiara Fantozzi, "L'onore violato: Stupri, prostituzione e occupazione alleata (Livorno 1944–47)," *Passato e Presente* 99 (2016): 88.

8. *L'Unità*, April 21, 1995, 10. The "symbolic renewal of life" is celebrated in many ways in all accounts of the immediate arrival of Allied forces (e.g., Ponzani 2012, 223–26).

9. Emanuele Rea, *Mistero napoletano: Vita e passione di un comunista negli anni della guerra fredda* (Turin: Einaudi, 1995), 61, 66–67. Rea suggests Naples could never have embraced modernity as commonly understood.

10. Rea 1995, 140.

11. Ibid., 141, ("un gesto necessario che serba l'onore.").

12. Ibid., 143.

13. Ibidem.

14. Ibid., 148.

15. Williams 2013, 181.

16. John Horne Burns, *The Gallery* (New York: Bantam Books, 1947), 223.

17. Ibidem.

18. Norman Lewis, *Naples '44* (London: Collins, 1978), 108, 132, 145, 151.

19. Cited in *Italy and America 1943–44*, 442 (quoted in English here); on the play, see Gribaudi, in ibid., 303–5; the piece was written from direct experience and first staged in May 1945.

20. Curzio Malaparte, *La pelle* (Milan: Adelphi, 2015), 4; full discussion of Malaparte, Burns, Lewis, and others in John Gatt-Rutter, "Naples 1944: Liberation and Literature," in *Italy and America 1943–44: Italian, American and Italian American Experiences of the Liberation of the Mezzogiorno*, edited by John A. Davis, 55–97 (Naples: La città del sole, 1997).

21. Porzio 2011, 66; similar recollections cited in Ponzani 2012, 226.

22. Porzio 2011, 142–43. Porzio calculates that in spite of the many official obstacles placed in their way, over two thousand Neapolitan women married Allied soldiers of all levels in the years 1944–1947, of which 1,446 involved U.S. servicemen.

23. The film, its evolution, laborious production, and ambiguous critical reception—at the time—are amply discussed in Adriano Arpà, *Il dopoguerra di Rossellini* (Rome: Cinettà International), 1995; and Stefania Parigi, *'Paisà': Analisi del film* (Padua: Marsilio, 2005).

24. Eugenio Scalfari, *L'autunno delle Repubblica* (Milan: Etas Kompass, 1969), 95–96.

25. Curzio Malaparte, *Il compagno di viaggio* (Milan: Excelsior 1881, 2007), 74–75.

26. Williams 2013, 33.

27. Ibid., 35.

28. Ibid., 40–41.

29. Different figures are reported by Ponzani 2012, 235–36; both authors insist that the real numbers must have been much higher than those officially recorded, for obvious reasons.

30. For similar reports from the Isle of Elba, also "liberated" by French colonial troops, Chiara Fantozzi, "L'onore violato: Stupri, prostituzione e occupazione alleata (Livorno 1944–47)," *Passato e Presente* 99 (2016): 87–1193.

31. Ibid., 52–53. "Stab in the back" was the phrase used by President Roosevelt to describe Italian Fascism's unprovoked attack and invasion of southern France in June 1940.

32. Frezza in Gagliani 2006, 76. The author notes that before participating in the liberation of the south of France, the commander of the *goumiers* was obliged to swear to de Gaulle that nothing could happen to French women of the sort seen in Italy; ibidem, 77. She also states that an important gesture of apology was offered by the president of the National Association of Moroccan Veterans at an academic conference in Italy in 2004; ibidem, 78, n.7.

33. Ponzani 2012, 234, 247, 248–49.

34. On the "displacement" of the story, Guido Crainz, *L'Ombra della Guerra: Il 1945, l'Italia* (Rome: Donzelli editore, 2007), 19; on the indifference of Allied commands, and the interchangeability of violence against women, see Ponzani 2012, 228, 234.

35. Ponzani 2012, chapter 8, quote at p. 241; cf. Gabrielli 2007, 136.

36. Quoted in Gabrielli 2007, 148.

37. Ibid.

38. List in Chiara Fantozzi, "L'onore violato: Stupri, prostituzione e occupazione alleata (Livorno 1944–47)," *Passato e Presente* 99 (2016): 95.

39. Ibid., 95–96.

40. Ibid., 101.

41. Franco Ferrarotti, quoted in Fantozzi,102. The use of stereotyped racial language was considered totally normal at this time, as Silvana Patriarca has documented (Patriarca 2015). The article describes the widespread "anxieties of racial contamination" that the phenomenon of mixed-race babies produced up and down society, and how the various authorities, particularly the Catholic Church, set out to reconcile this unwanted legacy of liberation/occupation with the prejudices of the day.

42. Fantozzi 2016, 103–6.

43. Harold Macmillan, president of the Allied Control Commission, in a newspaper article of 1948; quoted in Ellwood 1985, 137.

44. Forcella quoted in Crainz 2007, 8–9.

45. I have analyzed the weight of myths and promises the Americans brought with them in Ellwood 2012, chapter 7. This discussion includes comparisons of the responses of women in Britain, Italy, France, Austria, and Germany.

46. Cit. in Gabrielli 2007, 56–57. On the bombardments, see Gribaudi 2005.

47. Ann E. Kaplan, "Trauma Studies Moving Forward: Interdisciplinary Perspectives," *Journal of Dramatic Theory and Criticism* 27/2 (2013): 55.

48. Cf. Ellwood, 2014.

49. Cited in Arpà 1995, 104; on the sense of natural catastrophe, see Ponzani 2012, 232; the damage done to masculine,—and hence national—pride by the failure of men to protect female and racial "honour" in the rape and pillage phases, see Gabrielli 2007, 136.

WORKS CITED

Arpà, Adriano. *Il dopoguerra di Rossellini*. Rome: Cinettà International, 1995.

Burns, John Horne. *The Gallery*. New York: Bantam Books, 1947.

Camilletti, Maria Grazia. "'Esistere da donne in tempo di guerra'. Come interpretare i mutamenti: Un problema aperto." In *Guerra, Resistenza, Politica: Storie di donne* edited by Dianella Gagliani, 141–50. Reggio Emilia: Alberti editore, 2006.

Crainz, Guido. *L'Ombra della Guerra: Il 1945, l'Italia*. Rome: Donzelli editore, 2007.

De Luna, Giovanni. "La repubblica del dolore." *Passato e Presente* 82 (2011): 5–19.

Ellwood, David W. *Italy 1943–1945. The Politics of Liberation*. Leicester: Leicester University Press, 1985.

———. "Per capire l'impatto degli americani in Italia nella Seconda guerra mondiale non c'è niente di meglio del cinema." *Da Venezia al mondo intero. Scritti per Gian Piero Brunetta*, edited by his pupils, 55–68. Venice: Marsilio, 2014.

———. *The Shock of America. Europe and the Challenge of the Century*. Oxford: Oxford University Press, 2012.

Fantozzi, Chiara. "L'onore violato: Stupri, prostituzione e occupazione alleata (Livorno 1944–47)," in *Passato e Presente* 99 (2016): 87–111.

Frezza, Daria. "La popolazione civile del Basso Lazio e le truppe coloniali francesi nella campagna d'Italia (1943–44)." In *Guerra, Resistenza, Politica: Storie di donne*, edited by Dianella Gagliani, 72–79. Reggio Emilia: Aliberti editore, 2006.

Gabrielli, Patrizia. *Scenari di guerra, parole di donne: Diari e memorie nell'Italia della seconda guerra mondiale*. Bologna: il Mulino, 2007.

Gatt-Rutter, John. "Naples 1944: Liberation and Literature." In *Italy and America 1943–44: Italian, American and Italian American Experiences of the Liberation of the Mezzogiorno*, edited by John A. Davis, 55–97. Naples: La città del sole, 1997.

Gribaudi, Gabriella. "Napoli 1943–45: La costruzione di un'epopea." In *Italy and America 1943-44: Italian, American and Italian American Experiences of the Liberation of the Mezzogiorno*, edited by John A. Davis, 303–35. Naples: La città del sole, 1997.

Gribaudi, Gabriella. *Guerra totale: Tra bombardamenti alleati e violenze naziste: Napoli e il fronte meridionale 1940–44*. Turin: Bollati Boringhieri, 2005.

Holland, James. *Italy's Sorrow: A Year of War 1944–45*. London: Harper Press, 2008.

Kaplan, E. Ann. "Trauma Studies Moving Forward: Interdisciplinary Perspectives." In *Journal of Dramatic Theory and Criticism* 27/2 (2013): 53–63.

Lewis, Norman. *Naples '44*. London: Collins, 1978.

Malaparte, Curzio. *Il compagno di viaggio*. Milan: Excelsior 1881, 2007.

Malaparte, Curzio. *La pelle*. Milan: Adelphi, 2015 (first edition: Milan 1949).

Parigi, Stefania. *'Paisà': Analisi del film*. Padua: Marsilia, 2005.

Patriarca, Silvana. "Fear of Small Numbers: 'Brown Babies' in Postwar Italy." In *Contemporanea* 18 (2015): 537–67.

Ponzani, Michela. *Guerra alle donne: Partigiani, vittime di stupro, "amanti del nemico" 1940–45*. Turin: Einaudi. 2012.

Porzio, Maria. *Arrivano gli Alleati! Amori e violenze nell'Italia liberata*. Bari: Laterza, 2011.

Rea, Emanuele. *Mistero napoletano: Vita e passione di un comunista negli anni della guerra fredda*. Turin: Einaudi, 1995.

Scalfari, Eugenio. *L'autunno delle Repubblica*. Milan: Etas Kompass, 1969.

Venturoli, Cinzia. "Abusi e molestie sessuali lungo la Linea Gotica." In *Guerra, Resistenza, Politica: Storie di donne*, edited by Dianella Gagliani. Reggio Emilia: Alberti editore, 2006.

Williams, Isobel. *Allies and Italians under Occupation. Sicily and Southern Italy 1943–45*. London: Palgrave Macmillan, 2013.

Chapter Nine

Between Past and Present, Self and Other

Liminality and the Transmission of Traumatic Memory in Elena Ferrante's La figlia oscura

Torunn Haaland

In a recent study into post-traumatic subjectivity and cultural narratives, Robert Luckhurst observes how trauma opens "passageways between systems that were once discrete, making unforeseen connections that distress or confound. Trauma," he continues, "also appears to be worryingly transmissible: it leaks between . . . victims and their listeners or viewers."[1] This conceptualization of cognitive and emotional distress captures the way physical and psychological violations will recur as nightmares, flashbacks, and repeated actions if they were too shattering to be elaborated or acknowledged at the time. Genocide, slavery, and war would typically create such experiences, but singular or repeated exposure to abuse, assault, and abandonment may also leave an open "wound," as the Greek term trauma implies, on the victim's mind.[2] Although the original event is unlikely to be forgotten or disassociated from consciousness, the memories generated are alterable[3] and may be so intrusive as to alter or altogether undermine current experiences.[4] Luckhurst's description of an uncontainable transmissibility evokes both the violent recurrence of such memories and the exigency they create to be articulated.[5] Crucially, as Cathy Caruth has illustrated, for the sufferer to take possession of haunting memories, she must relive and transform it into narrative memory: the therapeutic imperative promotes therefore the one of recording collective and individual trauma.[6] Considering, however, that recovery can only take place retrospectively, when fragmentary recollections are holistically examined, the victim's narrative will unfold, anachronistically, along lines of temporal disruptions and transgressed borders that severely challenge "the capacities of narrative knowledge."[7]

What narrative dimensions post-traumatic stress disorder present has been amply demonstrated since the diagnosis was recognized and scientifically elaborated in the 1980s and 1990s.[8] The clinical and theoretical examinations conducted at the time resonated in creative and critical responses to the "post-traumatic culture" of the late twentieth century: on the one hand, a wave of memoir writing[9] as well as fiction that in particular uncovered the dilemma of articulating unspeakable experiences,[10] on the other, a series of studies that fused psychoanalytical and literary perspectives.[11] An emblematic example of this interdisciplinary form of critical reception was Dori Laube and Daniel Podell's prescriptive assessment of the "art of trauma."[12] Testimonial narratives are not merely marked by the lack of adequate words or forms available and the "absence" that may obfuscate the original violations, but also by the particular viewpoint from which the sufferer addresses herself and her interlocutor. To communicate these aspects, narrative and figurative representations of trauma must be indirect, aestheticized, and dialogic.[13] Considering the non-mimetic strategies required to represent extreme realities, Michael Rothberg speaks of "traumatic realism" as strategies adopted to make the event epistemologically accessible and to confront readers with their relation to post-traumatic culture.[14] Several recent readings of trauma narratives have elaborated this view,[15] identifying the function modernist and postmodernist characteristics such as intertextuality, repetitions, fragmentation, and broken chronologies have in encouraging a critical engagement. Rather than identifying with the sufferer, the reader is compelled to develop the type of "empathetic unsettlement" that, according to Dominick LaCapra, allows for "an affective relation, rapport, or bond with the other recognized and respected as other."[16]

The understanding of a dialogic art apt to stir emphatic reactions beg several ethical considerations that Susana Onega and Jean-Michel Ganteau have usefully related to Emmanuel Lévinas' "ethics of alterity." Drawing on Lévinas' concept of *excendance*—or the self's need to evade Being by reaching out toward an internal and/or an external Other—they see trauma narratives as unleashing a "discursive ethics" or a "liminal ethics" in which the sufferer's testimony not only *reacts* to but also *performs* "an openness to the wound [and] to the Other's wound."[17] Anchored, as it is, to a dialogic and intermittent mode that implicates the interlocutor in an exchange of empathy and alienation rather than identification, the elaboration of trauma does not merely unite "the principle and the concern of the ethics of form and the ethics of affects," but it crucially also challenges "the teleological discourse of history" by bringing the story toward the limits both of the Self and of narrative art.[18] The relational foundations and implications involved in the essentially liminal nature of trauma narratives may usefully be illustrated with reference to Elena Ferrante's *La figlia oscura* (2006). Constructed as a journey of revisitation, the novel follows Leda's temporary return from her life as an academic in central Italy to ambiances associated with her Neapolitan background. Readers of Ferrante's first works *Amore molesto* (1992) and *I giorni dell'abbandono* (2002), as well as of her widely celebrated tetralogy *L'amica geniale* (2011–2014), will recognize the thematics, but whereas the former follow solipsist and claustrophobic paths and the latter outlines centrifugal lines of individual and collective history, *La figlia oscura* accentuates the relational process of confronting and transmitting traumas and inner contradictions. An ethical reading of Leda's narrative will account for the role natural and social circumstances play in triggering traumas endured as daughter and mother, and in intensifying the sense she still has of standing between two female universes—one associated with her Neapolitan mother, the other with her cosmopolitan daughters. As intrusive recurrences blur borders between past and present and between mental and physical realities, Leda enters a critical liminal state that, as we shall see, makes her reach for the Other as a witness to the most vulnerable parts of herself.

That Leda's story is retrospective and marked by breaks of nonlinearity is anticipated by a prologue in which she outlines two thematically interconnected and partly merged narrative paths: one reconstructs recently occurred events, the other re-evokes more or less removed incidents and circumstances. The prologue itself relates the chronologically last of the events to be told: a car accident Leda brought herself into but cannot remember. Instead, what she recalls is the sudden faintness and disorientation that made her forget being on the road and imagine herself at the seaside: the beach was deserted and the water was calm, but as the red flag was raised, nonetheless, she resisted the temptation to take a bath. The undue apprehensiveness demonstrates the lasting effect, Leda explains, of her mother's repeated warnings, and the childhood memory is emphasized by the sense she had, during this moment of mental dislocation, of hearing her mother scream from behind the sandbanks: "Leda, che fai, l'hai vista la bandiera rossa?" (Leda, what are you doing, did you see the red flag?).[19] Although this fantasy has canceled the accident from Leda's mind, she clearly remembers its underlying causes. Contrary to what she has told her daughters and ex-husband, in fact, what made her drive off the road was not sleepiness but, she confesses,

> un mio gesto privo di senso e proprio perché era insensato decisi subito di non parlarne con nessuno. Le cose più difficili da raccontare sono quelle che noi stessi non riusciamo a capire.[20]

> (a gesture of mine deprived of sense, and precisely because it was senseless I immediately decided not to talk about it with anyone. The hardest things to narrate are the ones we ourselves fail to understand.)

To understand not merely this but also other aspects of herself would be the primarily reason why Leda determines to confront what escapes logical explanations, but as she acknowledges the difficulties involved in such a narrative and anticipates the scarcely formative objective of deciphering a senseless act, she seems to aim for something more extensive and inclusive than a therapeutic exposure of herself.

As we shall see, the prologue prepares the listener for an episode in which she loses stability and leaves her normal pattern of behavior. In Ferrante's world, this sense of abandonment is known as "frantumaglia," but we may also consider it a form of evasion or excess. In fact, the exigency Leda has to confront her essentially gendered sense of difference makes her acknowledge the Other in herself and, by extension, reach for the Other both within the world revisited and among her hypothetical interlocutors. Considering the vulnerability to which Leda admits and the implicit appeal she makes to the reader for empathy and acceptance of her limits and imperfections, the attempt at taking narrative possession of unresolved tensions and conflicts appear as an invitation to a dialogue whereby personal memory may be transmitted and transformed into collective history.

Having premised the motivation for her narrative, Leda describes her current situation as a divorced, middle-aged, university professor in Florence. As her adult daughters have recently moved to their father in Toronto, she finds herself relieved from maternal concerns and obligations and seizes the moment of rejuvenation and autonomy to spend some solitary weeks on the Ionic coast. Halfway to destination, however, Leda regrets having left her quiet and air-conditioned home: the thought of going to the seaside makes her anxious, and the place she has booked will likely be nasty, hot, and exposed to nocturnal noise.

Once she arrives, these presentiments are confirmed with grotesque variations: what welcomes her at the apartment is a tray of perished fruit and a cicada on her pillow disturbs her first night's sleep. Surely, her vacation takes a disquieting start, but the impression we get is that the underlying and partly subconscious objective of this journey is neither to recharge energies, nor, indeed, to celebrate her resituated independence. Rather, the natural and human realities she seeks seem to be selected for their power to bring forth conflicting sentiments and moments of pain.

The next morning, Leda walks through a pine forest whose distinct scent evokes childhood summers spent along beaches before, she reflects, the Camorra buried them in concrete. Loaded with sensual signals and personal significance, the pine forest may offer a transitory retrieval of a childhood idyll and even allow a nostalgic look back at natural treasures not-yet-subjected to ferocious exploitations. Certain particulars in the arid terrain provoke, however, far less harmonious circumstances: in the crunching sounds of pinecones and in the color of pine nuts, Leda has stored unmistakable images of her mother's mouth smiling while unshelling the small golden kernels:

> Li dà da mangiare alle mie sorelle che li pretendono chiassosamente, a me che taccio in attesa, o li mangia lei stessa . . . dicendo, per insegnarmi a essere meno timida: va', a te niente, sei peggio di una pigna verde. [21]

> (She gives them to eat to my sisters who demand them noisily, to me who wait quietly, or she eats them herself . . . saying, to teach me to be less shy: there, none for you, you are worse than a green pine.)

The experiences evoked as an effect of revisiting a familiar landscape encapsulate the tendency of traumatic memories to be state dependent and activated by environmental stimuli. Crucially, the understanding of trauma as an incontrollable force implies that the original violation is brought forth in response to external factors and with such abruptness that they merge with or eclipse entirely the present. [22]

What unchain the intrusive return of the past are the unique proprieties of the pine forest; a trigger of associations so strong and complex that it leads from a déjà vu of aromatic delight to a moment of maternal critique and humiliation. The continuity Leda establishes between these conflicting sensations suggests that the experience of disparagement reflects a general and repeated scenario and that her childhood may have been marked by a fear of shortcoming and of being a disappointment to her scarcely sensitive mother. Reassuming tensions and a sense of anguish Leda introduced in the prologue, this re-encounter with a motherland abandoned decades earlier unfolds as a retrieval of occurrences that can only be relived within the ambiance in which they originally occurred.

Seen in light of the experimental nature of trauma fiction, the immersion into the Mediterranean landscape presents first and foremost a break in narrative chronology. We recognize the temporal incongruence from the seaside fantasy, but the effect this time is even more disruptive, since part of the episode presents a return of the past within a present moment that restores the circumstances of the original experience. Interrupting the retrospective narration to assume the dual perspective of a dismissed little girl and of the adult who relives this trauma, Leda constructs a double present that gives insight into her mental life without, however, encouraging an uncritical identification either with the neglected child or the troubled middle-aged woman. Rather, by dramatizing the nature of intrusive recollections as brought forth by contextual associations, the fragmentation distances the reader from the character's suffering and draws attention, instead, to the interaction that unfolds between physical conditions and mental realities.

The defamiliarizing qualities intrinsic to the time space of trauma are reinforced by the indirect and liminal way in which Leda relates her past.

While the context of her current life is outlined, few and only elusive antecedents are given for the events recalled and the tensions and confrontations she relives in suspense and reassumed in successive moments. Instinctively conducted for the sake of self-clarity but also to engage the listener, the account demands that the temporal order and chain of cause and effects be reconstructed and partly inferred. What shapes Leda's dialogic mode is, exactly, a reliance on the reader's engagement and capacity to piece together the fragments she presents while she, for her sake, reaches the holistic view of memories she does not yet fully possess.

To what extent the process of reliving a haunting past is contextual and largely dependent on a confrontation with the external world appears more clearly from several key scenes set to the seaside. The observations and interactions in which Leda engages at the beach unfold, significantly, as a re-encounter, in so far as the area she chooses for sunbathing is dominated by an extended family whose obnoxious presence denounces unmistakable Neapolitan origins: the jokes, the sentimentalisms, and the anger—it is all part of Leda's childhood. If it was the diffusion of distinct odors, in particular, that uncovered memories embedded in the pine forest, in front of this human landscape it is largely auditory impressions that reactualize realities she thought she had left behind.

The pervasive tones of laughter, cries, exclamations, and arguments recall not merely Leda's own childhood vacations, but an entire sociocultural world in whose vernacular expressivity she discerns miserable lives, crude behaviors and inconsiderate, presumptuous attitudes. Indicative is, in this sense, the jovial assertiveness with which the Neapolitans convince other beachgoers to relocate so as to accommodate new arrivals of friends and relatives. It is mainly to showcase her competency, that Leda accepts to translate their request to some Dutch visitors, but she soon regrets having acted as a mediator for such villainy and refuses categorically to renounce her spot in the sand.

The stubborn opposition to whims she knows all too well presents a more overarching stance of resistance that partly illuminates Leda's previous observation regarding the camorra's gradual destruction of the coastline. The group composed of kinship and friendship is indicatively referred to as a "clan," and in emphasizing their claim to an assumed natural dominance over other visitors, Leda seems to imply an affinity with this criminal underworld. What more profoundly incites her aversion and, at the same time, her attentive observation of the group is, however, the awareness of having grown up in an all too similar ambiance: "i miei zii, i miei cugini, mio padre erano così," (my uncles, my cousins, my father, were like this), she recalls, "di prepotente cordialità" (overbearingly cordial).[23] Although the attitudes and behaviors she so much detests are perceived as quintessentially male, the memories they evoke involve her mother and her failed attempts, more specifically, to distinguish herself from Leda's plebeian father. Despite the efforts to dress well and show noble sentiments, at the first rise of conflict, her mother would submerge to the destructive ways of her surroundings:

> La osservavo meravigliata e delusa, e progettavo di non assomigliarle, di diventare io diversa davvero. . . . Come soffrivo per lei e per me, come mi vergognavo di essere uscita dalla sua pancia di persona scontenta. Quel pensiero, lì nel disordine della spiaggia, mi innervosì ulteriormente e crebbe il dispetto per i modi di quella gente, insieme a un filo di angoscia.[24]

> (I observed here astonished and disappointed, and planned not to resemble her, to become different for real. . . . How I suffered for her and for myself, how ashamed I was over having come out of her discontent person's belly. That thought, there in the mess of the beach, made me even more nervous, and my irritation over the ways of those people increased along with a hint of anguish.)

Inherent in this image of a child so painfully disappointed that her mother can offer nothing but a negative example, we seem to identify a larger context for the tensions, anxieties, and resentments evoked previously. The confrontations that so far have been presented as interpersonal and rooted in her mother's nature appear partly to be a matter of ambiance and social conditions. Furthermore, when Leda observes that her present nervousness and disdain are reinforced by the thought of the shame her mother caused, she indirectly confesses how alive some of her traumas still are. In fact, the vein of anguish she feels rise in front of the Neapolitans' tones and modes uncovers not merely a revival of past suffering but, crucially also, a doubt as to whether she has actually succeeded in becoming different.

Just as the testimony Leda composes is dialogically engaging the reader's empathy and capacity to interconnect her recollections and infer omitted particulars, so does the gradual confrontation of her own ambivalent identity unfold along senses of alterity that provoke and are in turn accentuated by intrusive recollections from the past. Contradictory sensations of identification and superiority, of nostalgia and anguish, appear in relation to the Neapolitan women. In the unashamed and obese Rosaria who carries her pregnancy with boasting pride, Leda recognizes the very incarnation of collective ills and vices, whereas Rosaria's refined and beautiful sister-in-law, Nina, forms an anomaly in the group.

Detached from and apparently unaffected by the others, she spends entire days at the waterfront with her little daughter, Elena. From behind her books, Leda observes the young mother's grace, her apparent calm as she plays with the girl and her doll, and her intonation. So different from the rest of the family, whose dialectal expressivity compliments their brusque and vulgar ways, Nina speaks with a tender Neapolitan cadence Leda associates with a world of play and sweetness. Just like the pine forest, her speech is so distinct and enchanting as to re-evoke the very myth of childhood.

Linguistic and dialectal usages is a recurrent concern in Ferrante's works, which all testify to an educated Neapolitan woman's experience of having acquired not merely a sophisticated Italian but also the knowledge of classical as well as modern languages. According to Laura Benedetti, this linguistic discourse tends to complicate conventional views of the dialect as a vehicle of affection and authenticity. For Ferrante's troubled and educated characters, Neapolitan is something one endures; it transmits "quella 'verità sfacciata' contro cui il soggetto si trova senza difese" (that insolent truth against which the subject finds herself defenseless), whereas the acquisition of the national language constitutes a passageway to emancipation.[25] Leda will soon discover that Nina is neither as calm as she appears nor immune from violent and vulgar forms of expression, but in these moments of unworried play, she is able to reclaim the dialect as the very language of maternal tenderness.

The dichotomic conception of linguistic suppression and emancipation usefully illuminates the "catena di donne mute o stizzose" (chain of muted or peevish women) from which Leda determined to free herself in order, eventually, to build an academic career.[26] Her mother, on the other hand, would have been irremediably caught among the second category of supressed women and the sweetness in her speech was, consequently, always at risk of declining into its violent antithesis:

> [R]icordo il dialetto nella bocca di mia madre quando smarriva la cadenza dolce e ci strillava, intossicata dallo scontento, non ce la faccio più con voi, non ce la faccio più. [27]

> (I remember the dialect in the mouth of my mother when she lost her sweet cadence and she yelled at us, intoxicated by discontent, I can't stand you anymore, I can't stand it.)

Brought forth by contrast to Nina's interaction with her daughter, the memory of her mother burdened by a discontent so deep and perennial that it could only be channeled into verbal abuse and empty threats seems to form the very origin of Leda's traumas. As is the case with the previous circumstances evoked—the apprehensiveness in front of the sea, the lack of recognition, and the shame and disappointment over her mother's weak character—the intimidation to leave reoccurred over time, and although her mother was always there, the repeated threats created a fear of abandonment that intruded into and prevailed over the nostalgic experience of rehearing and reliving the gentle tones of childhood play and intimacy. The testimony Leda composes would primarily serve to control these intrusive memories, but no less imperative is it to confront the implications of having left Napoli "come un'ustionata" (as a woman injured by fire) who in tearing her skin off thinks she can remove the burn itself.[28] The existential dilemma she faces consists not only and perhaps not even principally in the pain of intrusive memories, but in having to acknowledge that the conflicts and the conditions she escaped at the age of eighteen are still part of her.

Alongside the exigency to confront an ambivalent sense of self as well as painfully lingering memories, the solitary return to spaces of the past also reactivates more recent conflicts endured as an emancipated woman and mother. The ambivalences developed in front of the Neapolitans women are crucially mirrored in her attitudes toward friends and colleagues and, more importantly, toward her daughters. Modern and sophisticated, Marta and Bianca make fun of her English and her Neapolitan intonation and are perfectly at ease in the cosmopolitan circles encountered in Canada.

Despite Leda's devotion and constant concern for her daughters, she finds them ungrateful, selfish, and superficial, and resents their tendency to blame her for their trivial misfortunes while refusing to discuss the one responsibility she does have: that of having left them with their father when they were small, without warning or threats. At the time, to seek freedom was the only way she could avoid abandoning herself and letting excessive maternal love bring her back into the chain of repressed women. However, when Leda returned after three years, divorcing her almost-perfect husband and caring for Marta and Bianca as if they were hers alone, her attempts at reestablishing relations were hampered not merely by the abandonment committed, but also by her tendency to project her own sensitivities—in particular the aversion and resolute fear of degradation that had driven her away from her mother's world—onto their lives. Leda recalls, for instance, that when the girls fell behind in school as a result of disorientation, she sought to motivate their studies but ended up tormenting them about the direction in which they seemingly were headed:

> [V]olete tornare indietro, degradarvi, abolire tutti gli sforzi che abbiamo fatto vostro padre e io, tornare a com'è vostra nonna, che ha solo la licenza elementare."[29]

> (Do you want to turn back, degrade yourself, abolish all the efforts your father and I have done, turn to what your grandmother is like, who has only an elementary school diploma.)

This recollection is emblematic of the confessional mode Leda adopts and the indirect association it establishes between violations she herself has undergone and those she would have inflicted on others. By composing a comparative and holistic account of the traumas she relives, an empathetic listener will, in this case, discern a conflict spanning three generations that may usefully be illuminated by more general aspects of mother-daughter relations. According to Sara Ruddick, in societies in which maternal work is defined in terms of consuming sacrifices, "the ideology of mother*hood*" will be experienced as oppressive to women and create ambivalences that may or may not be neutralized by the power and pleasures of maternal love and competence.[30]

The exigency to conform to this repressive and degrading identity—an imperative significantly perpetuated among and between women—will be particularly strong in societies where, as Adrienne Rich writes, "it is the mother through whom patriarchy early teaches the small female her proper expectations." Mother-daughter relations in patriarchal societies will, consequently, often be shaped by the daughter's resentment toward her mother for having passively accepted her own humiliation and victimization.[31] It is, as we have seen, out of rage toward her mother's weakness and against the degrading social laws she could never resist that Leda has rebelled, firstly by seeking emancipating forms of life and, secondly, by refusing the role of the self-denying mother. Unable, however, to step definitively out of one world and one form of motherhood to assume, unreservedly, the laws and ways of another, Leda has lived, and finds herself still, in an in-between position that sees her mediate anxieties and ambivalences, reproaches and resentments, and in her efforts to free the girls from her line of female descent, she may, in effect, have removed them from herself.

Considering the interrelated violations Leda lives and relives—the anxiety and shame in front of her mother's neglect and lack of discipline, the fear of abandonment and awareness of having abandoned, the vain search for filial approval and misconceived parental guidance—we can perceive of the enragement that builds up in her and the point of gravitations it finds in Nina and Elena. It may be an effect of poor sleep or negative thoughts, Leda confesses, but all of a sudden their mother-daughter unity starts to annoy her. The playfulness she initially admired appears so artificially staged that she would tell them to stop and she also finds the little girl repulses whereas Nina appears less beautiful than she initially thought. These negative sentiments would reflect an increasing nervousness over being at a crowded beach on the weekend when the extended family gets even larger, but the aggravation over Nina and Elena seems, more specifically, to betray a resentment over the harmony she never had either as daughter or as mother, and a suspicion that something more troublesome lingers beneath this dyad's undisturbed intimacy.

When, at a certain point, Leda sees the girl's doll abandoned in the sand and notices that Nina is walking exasperatedly around herself, these ambivalent attitudes reach a juncture. Elena has disappeared, and as the Neapolitans spread and create a turmoil of terrified looks and futile calls, three relatable moments intrude into Leda's present: her constant fear that her mother would leave; her own tendency—forgotten but testified to her by her mother—to disappear as a child; and, lastly, a moment when Bianca disappeared on the beach. In that moment, Leda searched equally frantically for her daughter, and like Nina, she dared not even look toward the water. Now, when Leda starts to look for Elena, these separate incidents merge to form one experience of frightening disorientation:

> Mi sembrava di essere Elena, o Bianca quando si era persa, ma forse ero solo io stessa da piccola che stavo risalendo dall'oblio. La bambina che si perde tra la folla sulla spiaggia vede ogni cosa immutata e tuttavia non riconosce più niente. . . . Bianca piangeva . . . quando me la riportarono. Piangevo anche io, per la felicità, per il sollievo, ma intanto gridavo di rabbia—come mia madre.[32]

> (It seemed to me that I was Elena, or Bianca when she was lost, but perhaps was it just myself as a child who was reascending from oblivion. The girl who gets lost among the crowd on the beach sees everything unchanged and yet she does not recognize anything anymore. . . . Bianca cried . . . when they brought her back to me. I cried to, out of happiness, of relief, but meanwhile I yelled in anger—like my mother.)

An emblematic example of the tendency Leda's liminal and indirect narrative has to superimpose temporal perspectives and combine levels of memories, the episode conveys the cumulative effect of recalling separate incidents of fright and reliving the terror of a lost child, while also realizing that she has replicated her mother's errors in front of her daughter. The essentially subjective mode prepares the listener for an act Leda cannot even identify with herself, but around which she seeks to establish an emphatic dialogue. Perfectly capable of imagining Elena's state of mind, Leda locates her at the waterfront where she is crying, desperately, as she can no longer find her doll. When the Neapolitans celebrate the girl's safe return, Leda leaves the beach, the doll furtively hidden in her bag. Inexplicably, it is as if it happened to her, and yet this senseless act synthesizes the effect the return South has had of making her revision her rational, measured, and reserved self.

Leda subsequently recalls having acted as a doll for her daughters' amusement—a pleasure her mother never conceded her—and having had a doll as a child that she later handed over to Bianca in an attempt to bring the girl closer to her. Far from creating the desired gratitude, however, the gift had only provoked disdain and a manifest inconsideration to which Leda, for her sake, had reacted with equal destructiveness. Two decades later, the painful disappointment she felt at the time fades behind her failure to handle the insensitivity of a three-year-old girl.[33]

The disconcerting memory illuminates but does not logically explain either the theft and failure to immediately return the doll, despite the suffering and tensions this incident creates for Elena and her mother, nor indeed

Leda's impulse to purchase cloths and dress the doll. Rather, the senseless act may be seen as symptomatic of a state of being that Leda's narrative identifies by two distinct modes of expression. The first—"the chill of the crooked wing"[34] —is a literary citation she and her daughter would evoke as a way to insinuate unease, displeasure, or moodiness. Now, standing underneath a cold shower that cannot wash away the theft she has just committed, Leda is reminded of this code phrase and it occurs to her how she has imposed her cultured sensitivities on her daughters—even on their "lessico familiare" (family lexicon).[35]

As it appears, the verse is a citation from the English poet W. H. Auden's poem "They," a composition originally titled "The Crisis" and that, written in 1939, refers unequivocally to the imminent war and the German occupation of Great Britain. The underlying theme is, however, a spiritual crisis Auden perceives as divisions between heart and reason, individual and collective, liberal and brutal.[36] As the poem makes clear, the crisis asks to recognize the enemy in oneself, and it is likely this aspect that resonates with Leda who is brought to acknowledge how much of her past she still carries with her and how much of herself is anchored to behaviors she has strived to leave behind as well as to acts and sentiments that do not belong to her.

This literary key to Leda's crisis has an oral counterpart that is expressed in one of her conversations with Nina. Exasperated and exhausted from innumerable attempts to remediate for the lost doll, Nina discloses the frustration and uncertainties she faces both as a mother and as a wife controlled by her husband's family. At a certain point, she asks whether "lo scombussolamento" (the upheaval) will ever end, and Leda translates the expression into what her mother used to call "frantumaglia." It was, precisely, this transient and entirely incontrollable a form of existential suffering Ferrante had in mind when, solicited by her editors, she gathered the extensive commentaries she had composed in response to questions from readers and critics and titled the collection *Frantumaglia*. As is the case with Leda, the term belongs to the "lessico familiare" (family lexicon) Ferrante inherited from her mother[37] and indexes a feeling of losing ground and sense of self so overwhelming and deep-going that it overturns the subject's sense of time:

L'insorgere della sofferrenza annulla il tempo lineare, lo spezza. . . . La notte dei tempi si raccoglie ai bordi dell'aurora d'oggi e di domani. . . . I sentimenti forti sono così, fanno saltare la cronologia. [38]

(The outbreak of suffering cancels linear time, it breaks it up. . . . The beginning of time curls up on the edges of today's and tomorrow's dawn. . . . Strong sentiments are like that, they set off chronology.)

As moments of a remote past intrude into and collide with recent and present experiences, time builds up in layers of recollections and creates an entirely subjective dimension void of order and limits. Bringing the subject ambiguously and painfully from before to after and from here to there, the *frantumaglia* unfolds as a traumatic in-between state that in many ways captures this journey of revisitation and the effect it has of accentuating Leda's conflicting sentiments. The feeling of instability and turbulence may, in particular, explain the ambiguity of Leda's gendered identity and her changing attitudes not merely toward Nina and Elena but also to Rosaria.

In Nina's sister-in-law, Leda identifies at first only a vulgar and unattractive appearance, but later, she looks at her with empathy and starts to scrutinize her own sense of superiority. While blaming herself for having favored Nina just because she is physically more akin to herself, Leda opens her eyes to Rosaria and acknowledges that, far from repulsive, the pompously expecting woman manifests her own beauty and form of determination. As we have seen, similar ambivalences are associated with Bianca and Marta. In front of her daughters, Leda feels culturally inferior, even though she was the one who pestered them about their schoolwork and gave them opportunities of education and refinement.

Now, considering her position in relation to the respective women who all embody an essential part of herself, Leda must acknowledge that to fall back, in time as well as in manners and visions, and reenter into Rosaria's world would come far easier to her than to venture into her daughter's exclusive realm. The complete disassociation she aimed toward but never quite achieved, Bianca and Marta have, in fact, completed, and the effect is, Leda reflects, that they belong within a future to which she has no access.

This part of Leda's testimony demonstrates how vulnerable she may make herself once she starts to relive and examine failures and disappointments undergone both as a mother and as a woman of very specific sociocultural aspirations. As she exposes her darkest sides, it becomes clear that her difference resides neither in the insuperable distance to her daughters nor in her undesirable affinity with her mother, but in a general sense of alienation or non-belonging that leaves her caught between these two worlds.

The tendency of her social self to linger on and around limits resonates in the way she transgresses borders of time and physical realities, as well as in the narrative reconstruction of these experiences, and both compel a study of liminality. Etymologically rooted in "limen," the Latin and Greek term for threshold and harbor respectively, the anthropological concept of the "liminal phase" originated in Arnold van Gennep's pioneering comparative studies of rites of passage in stateless societies.[39] His understanding that the change in status or in time represents a potentially risky transition between two secure states of being, was significantly elaborated by Victor Turner's thesis that although the suspension of norms and structures will ultimately reconfirm the very status quo that the ritual is set in to challenge, the "*communitas*" built among the ritual subjects is a dialectical force invested not merely by temporary "interrelatedness" but also by a "potentiality" for creativity and social change.[40]

That certain liminal situations may assume more fixed forms, transpired from Turner's later studies of the pilgrimage in Christian culture, and it is this particular insight that, as Bjørn Thomassen observes, resonates in more recent theories of liminality and the modern condition.[41] When physical and mental limits collide and the very structures of social life disintegrate, transitions may, according to Arpad Szakolczai, become infinite and cause "an anguishing state of permanent liminality" from which there is no logical return.[42] Whether the experience is that of a "'time stood still'" or a "void," or of inhabiting the very "realm of the absurd," it is not to reason that we shall look for a point of stability, Szakolczai underlines, but to our heart, and hence, to feelings and actions apt to interrupt the slumber of modern life.[43]

Seen in light of the unresolved ambivalences and the intrusive memories that leave Leda on the threshold between two female universes and between then and now, here and there, the chances that reason may interfere to resolve her social and mental liminal phase are rather scarce. Both the timelessness of her revisitation, the senselessness shaping certain aspects of her behavior, and the void in which she dwells as a woman suggest, rather, that hers is a case of the permanent liminality Szakolczai sees as the essence of modern life. After a tense confrontation with Nina in which Leda restitutes the much sought-after doll, causing a surprising reaction of violence in the young mother's speech and acts, Leda anticipates her return to Florence and articulates a sense of relief. The accident she subsequently undergoes as an effect, precisely, of losing anchorage and being brought away by a form of mental dislocation do, however, not mark the end to a crisis but rather the circular mechanics of an eternal return.

Symptomatically, Leda has previously explained to Nina that although the *frantumaglia* will never end, you can live well with it, and her trauma appears, in similar ways, to be an unresolvable but ultimately manageable component of a permanent existential condition. In this sense, the decision to revisit and articulate the past in a testimony has seemingly not led to a possession either of unsettled tensions or her uncontrollable memories. Rather, the act of revisitation have positioned her in ways that evoke the collective nature of the liminal phase, insofar as the in-betweenness Leda confronts at several levels of experience unfolds along a dimension of alterity. If her story manifests a strong sense of evasion—an experience she expresses in terms of being "senza contorni" (without contours) and that leads to the critical point of *frantumaglia*—it is, in particular, for the effect moments of abandonments and disorientation have in opening her eyes to the Other's face.[44]

Levinas speaks, crucially, about an "l'epiphanie du visage" (epiphany of the face) that resides in a look "qui supplie et exige"(that begs and demands), and Leda's response to the Other's begging demand for recognition unfolds as a total reconsideration that uncovers her contradictions and challenges her self-assurance.[45] The function of this epiphany is, Levinas explains, to question "le monde possedé par moi" (the world possessed by me), and as the confrontation with the Other opens up to an entire new perspective, "un point du vue indépendant de la position égoïste" (a point of view independent from an egoistic position); it becomes the very basis for all social relations.[46]

Forced as she is to acknowledge her own difference and permanent non-belonging, Leda also recognizes the Other within and outside of herself, and between the traumas relived and the senseless act committed, the destructive forces she carries in her have become the basis for an a transformational exchange. Significantly, in sharing the repositioning she undergoes from aversion, and alienation, to a reconsideration of two opposed female universes, Leda confirms not merely that the relation between teller and listener is gendered, but also that the transmission of trauma and its transformation into cultural memory is a process of interdependence wherein which the Other encountered and the Other addressed operate as witnesses and agents.[47] It is in this way that trauma, both as an inner process of revisioning and as a narrative of essentially empathetic presuppositions, becomes a relational process that may not reach individual recovery but that in the perspective of alterity has contributed to larger objective of solidarity and understanding across apparently insuperable borders and divisions.

NOTES

1. Roger Luckhurst, *The Trauma Question* (London: Rutledge, 2008), 3.

2. Catherine Caruth, *Unclaimed Experience: Trauma, Narrative, and History* (Baltimore: Johns Hopkins, 1996), 3, 7.

3. Richard J. McNally, "Debunking Myths about Trauma and Memory," *The Canadian Journal of Psychiatry* 50 (2005): 821.

4. Bessel A. Van der Kolk and Otto Van der Hart, "The Intrusive Past: The Flexibility of Memory and the Engraving of Trauma," in *Trauma: Explorations in Memory*, ed. Cathy Caruth (Baltimore: Johns Hopkins, 1995), 174–75.

5. Luckhurst, *The Trauma Question*, 3.

6. Cathy Caruth, "Introduction: Part II: Recapturing the Past," in *Trauma: Explorations in Memory*, ed. Cathy Caruth (Baltimore: Johns Hopkins, 1995), 153.

7. Luckhurst, *The Trauma Question*, 79.

8. Chris Brewin and Emily Holmes, "Psychological Theories of Posttraumatic Stress Disorder," *Clinical Psychology Review* 23 (2003): 339–40.

9. Leigh Gilmore, *The Limits of Autobiography: Trauma and Testimony* (Ithaca: Cornell University Press, 2001), 3.

10. Luckhurst, *The Trauma Question*, 118.

11. Emblematic examples of this critical approach are Shoshona Felman and Dori Laube, *Testimony: Crisis of Witnessing in Literature, Psychoanalysis and History* (New York: Routledge, 1992); Dominick LaCapra, *Writing History, Writing Trauma* (Baltimore: Johns Hopkins, 2001); and Cathy Caruth, ed, *Trauma: Explorations in Memory* (Baltimore: Johns Hopkins, 1995a); and Cathy Caruth, *Unclaimed Experience*.

12. Dori Laub and Daniell Podell, "Art and Trauma," *International Journal of Psychoanalysis* 76 (1995): 992.

13. Ibid., 994–96.

14. Michael Rothberg, *Traumatic Realism: The Demands of Holocaust Representation*, (Minneapolis: University of Minnesota Press, 2000), 109.

15. See, in particular, Luckhurst, *The Trauma Question*; Anne Whitehead, *Trauma Fiction* (Edinburgh: Edinburgh University Press, 2004); Laurie Vickroy, *Reading Trauma Narratives: The Contemporary Novel and the Psychology of Oppression* (Charlottesville: University of Virginia Press, 2015); and Laurie Vickroy, *Trauma and Survival in Contemporary Fiction* (Charlottesville: University of Virginia Press, 2001).

16. Dominick LaCapra, *Writing History, Writing Trauma*, xxxi, 21.

17. Susana Onega and Jean-Michel Ganteau, "Introduction: Performing the Void: Liminality and the Ethics of Form in Contemporary Trauma Narratives," in *Contemporary Trauma Narratives: Liminality and the Ethics of Form*, ed. Susana Onega and Jean-Michel Ganteau (London: Routledge, 2014), 5, 8, 10.

18. Ibid., 11, 7.

19. Elena Ferrante, "La figlia oscura," in *Cronache del mal d'amore*, Elena Ferrante (Roma: e/o, 2011), 379. All translation are mine unless otherwise stated.

20. Ibid., 379.

21. Ibid.

22. Bessel A. Van der Kolk and Otto Van der Hart, "The Intrusive Past," 173–75.

23. Ferrante, "La figlia oscura," 395.

24. Ibid.

25. Laura Benedetti, "Il linguaggio dell'amicizia e della città: *L'amica geniale* di Elena Ferrante tra continuità e cambiamento," *Quaderni d'italianistica* 33 (2012): 179–80.

26. Ferrante, "La figlia oscura," 440.

27. Ibid. 390.

28. Ibid., 456.

29. Ibid., 458.

30. Sara Ruddick, *Maternal Thinking: Toward a Politics of Peace* (Boston: Beacon, 1995), 29.

31. Adrienne Rich, *Of Woman Born: Motherhood as Experience and Institution* (New York: Norton, 1986), 243.

32. Ferrante, "La figlia oscura," 411.

33. A topus of dramatic and metaphorical value in Ferrante's works, the figure of the doll figures prominently in her children's book *La spiaggia di notte* (Roma: e/o, 2007), and the first volume of her tetralogy *L'amica geniale* (Roma: o/e, 2011).

34. Ferrante, "La figlia oscura," 468. In Auden's original poem "They," the line quoted reads as "the chill of their crooked wing." W. H. Auden, *Collected Poems*, ed. Edward Mendelson (New York: Vintage, 1991), 253–54.

35. Ferrante, "La figlia oscura," 470.

36. James Fenton, "Auden at Home."

37. Elena Ferrante, *La frantumaglia* (Roma: e/o, 2007), 97.

38. Ibid., 102.

39. Alan Roughley, "Liminal Paperspaces: Writing between Derrida and Joyce and Being and Writing," in *Mapping Liminalities: Thresholds in Cultural and Literary Texts*, ed Lucy Kay et al., (Bern: Peter Lang, 2007), 209.

40. Victor Turner, *The Ritual Process: Structure and Anti-Structure* (Ithaca: Cornell, 1969), 107–9.

41. Bjørn Thomassen, *Liminality and the Modern: Living through the In-Between* (London: Routledge, 2014), 82–83.

42. Arpad Szakolczai, "Living Permanent Liminality: The Recent Transition Experience in Ireland," *Irish Journal of Sociology* 22 (2014): 46

43. Ibid., 34, 46–47.

44. Ibid., 384.

45. Emmanuel Lévinas, *Totalité et infini: Essai sur l'exteriorite* (Paris: Le livre de poche, 1991), 73.
46. Ibid., 234.
47. Marianne Hirsch and Valerie Smith, "Feminism and Cultural Memory: An Introduction," *Signs* 28 (2002): 7–8.

WORKS CITED

Auden, W. H. *Collected Poems*, edited by Edward Mendelson. New York: Vintage, 1991.
Benedetti, Laura. "Il linguaggio dell'amicizia e della città: *L'amica geniale* di Elena Ferrante tra continuità e cambiamento," *Quaderni d'italianistica* 33 (2012): 171–87.
Brewin, Chris, and Emily Holmes. "Psychological Theories of Posttraumatic Stress Disorder." *Clinical Psychology Review* 23 (2003): 339–76.
Caruth, Cathy. "Introduction. Part II: Recapturing the Past." *Trauma: Explorations in Memory,* edited by Cathy Caruth, 151–57. Baltimore: Johns Hopkins, 1995.
———, ed. *Trauma: Explorations in Memory.* Baltimore: Johns Hopkins, 1995.
———. *Unclaimed Experience. Trauma, Narrative, and History.* Baltimore: Johns Hopkins, 1996.
Felman, Shoshona, and Dori Laube. *Testimony: Crisis of Witnessing in Literature, Psychoanalysis and History.* New York: Routledge, 1992.
Fenton, James. "Auden at Home," *The New York Review of Books* 47 (2000). Accessed January 3, 2017. http://www.nybooks.com/articles/2000/04/27/auden-at-home/?printpage=true.
Ferrante, Elena. *L'amica geniale.* Volume primo. Roma: e/o, 2011.
———. "La figlia oscura." *Cronache del mal d'amore.* Roma: e/o, 2011.
———. *La frantumaglia.* Roma: e/o, 2007.
———. *La spiaggia di notte.* Roma: e/o, 2007.
Gilmore, Leigh. *The Limits of Autobiography: Trauma and Testimony.* Ithaca: Cornell University Press, 2001.
Hirsch, Marianne, and Valerie Smith. "Feminism and Cultural Memory: An Introduction." *Signs* 28 (2002): 1–19.
LaCapra, Dominick. *Representing the Holocaust. History, Theory, Trauma.* Ithaca: Cornell University Press, 1994.
———. *Writing History, Writing Trauma.* Baltimore: Johns Hopkins, 2001.
Lévinas, Emmanuel. *Totalité et infini: Essai sur l'exteriorite.* Paris: Le livre de poche, 1991.
Laub, Dori, and Daniell Podell. "Art and Trauma." *International Journal of Psychoanalysis* 76 (1995): 991–1005.
Luckhurst, Roger. *The Trauma Question.* London, Rutledge, 2008.
McNally, Richard J. "Debunking Myths about Trauma and Memory." *The Canadian Journal of Psychiatry* 50 (2005): 817–22.
Onega, Susana, and Jean-Michel Ganteau. "Introduction: Performing the Void: Liminality and the Ethics of Form in Contemporary Trauma Narratives." In *Contemporary Trauma Narratives: Liminality and the Ethics of Form*, edited by Susana Onega and Jean-Michel Ganteau, 1–18. London: Routledge, 2014.
Rich, Adrienne. *Of Woman Born: Motherhood as Experience and Institution.* New York: Norton, 1986.
Rothberg, Michael. *Traumatic Realism: The Demands of Holocaust Representation.* Minneapolis: University of Minnesota Press, 2000.
Roughley, Alan. "Liminal Paperspaces: Writing between Derrida and Joyce and Being and Writing." In *Mapping Liminalities: Thresholds in Cultural and Literary Texts*, edited by Lucy Kay et al., 209–26. Bern: Peter Lang, 2007.
Ruddick, Sara. *Maternal Thinking: Toward a Politics of Peace.* Boston: Beacon, 1995.
Szakolczai, Arpad. "Living Permanent Liminality: The Recent Transition Experience in Ireland." *Irish Journal of Sociology* 22 (2014): 28–50.
Tal, Kali. *Worlds of Hurt: Reading the Literatures of Trauma.* Cambridge: Cambridge University Press, 1996.

Thomassen, Bjørn. *Liminality and the Modern: Living through the In-Between*. London: Routledge, 2014.

Turner, Victor. *The Ritual Process: Structure and Anti-Structure*. Ithaca: Cornell, 1969.

Van der Kolk, Bessel A., and Otto Van der Hart. "The Intrusive Past: The Flexibility of Memory and the Engraving of Trauma." In *Trauma: Explorations in Memory*, edited by Cathy Caruth, 158–83. Baltimore: Johns Hopkins, 1995.

Vickroy, Laurie. *Reading Trauma Narratives. The Contemporary Novel and the Psychology of Oppression*. Charlottesville: University of Virginia Press, 2015.

———. *Trauma and Survival in Contemporary Fiction*. Charlottesville: University of Virginia Press, 2001.

Whitehead, Anne. *Trauma Fiction*. Edinburgh: Edinburgh University Press, 2004.

Section III

Memory as Nostalgia

Chapter Ten

Mother-Daughter Nostalgia in the Abruzzi of Donatella Di Pietrantonio

Patrizia Sambuco

From a marginal beginning, as an outsider to the Italian literary panorama, Donatella Di Pietrantonio is showing herself to be one of the most interesting voices of contemporary Italian fiction. A children's dentist with a passion for writing, Di Pietrantonio approached the publication of her debut novel *Mia madre è un fiume* (2011) with humility and even incredulity, judging from the words she uses in her acknowledgments at the end of the novel. She admits to not having believed in her own writing and defines herself as "un'esordiente nascosta nella provincia italiana"[1] (a beginner hiding in provincial Italy). Luckily for us, rather than being an isolated achievement of an inexperienced author, her first novel has marked the beginning of a career successful with both public and critics. This led to her second book, *Bella mia* (2014), being nominated for the Premio Strega—the most prestigious Italian literary prize. Her third novel, *L'Arminuta* (2017), was published with Michela Murgia's endorsement on the dust cover; it reads, "Donatella Di Pietrantonio è una delle più importanti scrittrici italiane" (Donatella Di Pietrantonio is one of the most important Italian writers). The book won the Premio Campiello (2017), the Segafredo Zanetti, Un libro per il cinema prize, and the Premio Alassio.

In this chapter I analyze the themes of memory emerging from the plot in Di Pietrantonio's first novel, and in particular her use of a distinctive shade of nostalgia as an emotion that renegotiates present and past rather than a backward-looking perception of the past. In reality, all her three novels are imbued, in one way or another, with themes of memory: the reconstruction of a bygone agricultural Abruzzi in *Mia madre è un fiume*, the elaboration of the trauma of the 2009 earthquake in L'Aquila in her second novel *Bella mia*, and the ambivalence of the sense of origin and her past on the part of the teenage protagonist of *L'Arminuta*.

Another characteristic of Di Pietrantonio's narrative (so far) is its setting in the region of Abruzzi. Probably there had not been such a sustained emphasis on a remote Abruzzi since Ignazio Silone's trilogy. The setting of Di Pietrantonio's novels is fundamental for the understanding of the psychological development of the characters. Affection, the lack of it, and family relationships are very much determined by the cultural and historical settings. Therefore Di Pietrantonio's novels, in their working on memory, become both a testimony to personal memory (the reconstruction of past events affecting the characters) and to public memory (the reconstruction of aspects of the history of the Abruzzi). This is explicit in the case of the first novel, where the story of the narrator's mother recreates the life of a small village in the North sub-Appennine area of the Abruzzi, in the province of Teramo, from World War II to the present day.

Mia madre è un fiume (2011) has sailed through regional and national literary prizes,[2] good reviews, and translations into English and German despite the sensitive topic—the loss of memory, through Alzheimer's disease, by the mother of the daughter-narrator—and the setting in a remote agricultural Abruzzi. All the reviews agree on the poetic qualities of Di Pietrantonio's writing, and on the delicate treatment of complex themes, undoubted strengths of the book. Beyond the fine rendition of a troubled daughter-mother relationship, of the psychological and emotional devastation of Alzheimer's, and of forgotten ways of living and traditions, the book employs a system of techniques to discuss personal and public memory.

In this chapter I argue that a particular use of nostalgia, understood as an emotion that helps the revisitation of past and present—rather than a sense of yearning for the past perceived from an impoverished present—is at the core of the renegotiation of the daughter-mother relationship. The agricultural setting and the reconstruction of the way of living of the little village on the mountains around Teramo are part of the textual devices employed to give voice to a mother-daughter bond until then unexpressed. Far from being the appreciation of a lost naturalistic pure past and of mother as Nature, the archaic setting emerges in its bitter reality of poverty and violence, of strenuous everyday struggles, as key to the understanding and negotiation of a relationship with the mother that is also bitter and difficult.

A corpus of fiction by women writers in Italy, and in other literatures, has dealt with conflicting mother-daughter relationships, for which the daughter-narrator seeks a resolution in the reconstruction of her mother's past and of her own bond with her.[3] If this has been a trend or direction of women writers' fiction in the second part of the twentieth century, it has proved to remain a recurrent theme among women writers of the twenty-first century.[4]

Mia madre è un fiume therefore connects to and enters into conversation with a substantial tradition of women's literature.

The topic of the mother-daughter relationship often opens reflections and comparisons on the sociohistorical context of past generations, or of particular complex knots of history. Abyssal was the generational distance between mothers and daughters of post–World War II Italian culture, between women who had experienced lack of freedom, poverty, and war, and daughters who were able to enjoy civil rights, sexual freedom, and wealthier conditions. Complex and contrasted mother and daughter relationships, like the one between Esperina and her daughter, find a congenial setting in that context. The rural location, the daily struggle of the early years of the mother's life, and its distance from the more progressive way of living of the daughter contain echoes of other successful novels such as Michela Murgia's *Accabadora*, Elena Ferrante's *L'amore molesto*, and Francesca Sanvitale's *Madre e figlia*, yet the peculiarity of *Mia madre è un fiume* lies in the particular treatment of the distance between past and present.

Although in novels like *L'amore molesto* and *Madre e figlia* the distance between past and present at times collapses, bringing epiphanies for the daughter's understanding of her relationship with her mother,[5] fundamentally the daughter's point of view stands in a more educated, more modern society where the mother's knowledge is seen as more limited. In Di Pietrantonio's book, although the mother belongs to a more archaic world—a time when people were employed in rural occupations that today have disappeared, and where collective activities marked the annual cycle, she is part of social evolution and progress as much as the daughter. It is the manipulation of memory and of nostalgia that allows Di Pietrantonio to make the past relevant to the present and to untie the knots of the troubled mother-daughter relationship.

The novel presents itself as the daughter Tina's narration of the mother Esperina's life at the time when the onset of Alzheimer's disease becomes visible but has not reached a drastic stage. The story is constructed by two separate sets of narrations: the first addresses the mother in the second person "tu" form and is therefore the narration that the daughter is offering to the mother to help her remember her life at the time when memory has started abandoning her. This is both an exercise in personal and in collective memory, as it is the life of the small sub-mountainous village of the Abruzzi Apennines that emerges distinctively in the narration. In this sense Alzheimer's appears as a metaphor for the loss of memory of collective local identities that have remained marginal in historiography. In addition to this account, there is also the narration that the daughter conducts about the mother, where it is the daughter's experience that prevails and where the mother is referred to in the third person. It is in this line of narration that the daughter's troubled relationship with her mother is expressed. Two episodes recounted by the daughter both to the mother and to herself clearly show the discrepancies between the two parallel narrations and help understand the knots around the daughter's perspective, the first step before analyzing the deployment of nostalgia as a technique to renegotiate the daughter's relation with the mother and the rural village.

In the first part of the novel, when the daughter's narration to Esperina is still focusing on her mother's adolescence and young adulthood, a section on the daughter's pregnancy and her giving birth to her first and only child reveals her anger toward her insensitive, unemotional mother who manages to spoil that special day, and even falls asleep forgetting to care for her daughter:

> Tremavo, di rabbia e del freddo che mi veniva da quel sonno senza riguardi, dalla consumata esperienza di essere insieme invadente e lontana. Mi sono indignata per come aveva profanato il momento facendomi notare ancora sulla porta la camicia e il lenzuolo macchiati di sangue, che andavano cambiati. Non glielo racconterò mai, mai così.[6]

> (I shivered, with the rage and cold I felt at that inconsiderate sleep, the consummate skill in being both intrusive and distant. I was indignant at the way she'd spoiled the moment by making me notice, when she was barely through the door, that my nightdress and sheet were stained with blood and needed changing. I'll never tell her, not like that.[7])

And in fact, toward the end of the novel, the narration of the same night that the daughter offers to her mother depicts mother and daughter in mutual understanding and support. Care, affection, and empathy are, this time, the ingredients of the night of the daughter's giving birth:

> Avevo la camicia macchiata di sangue, hai detto non fa niente, non cambiarla, perché tremavo, di freddo e di gioia.[8]

> (My nightshirt was stained with blood, never mind you said, no need to change it, because I was trembling, with cold and with joy.[9])

It is a romanticized reimagining and retelling of the event. A similar treatment is given to a dream where the daughter's revisitation transforms the image of the mother. This time the daughter's two narrations, the one to herself and the one to the mother, are juxtaposed to one another: the dream of the mother vanishing into the grass, symbolizing her death, is turned into the image of the mother appearing from the hill like a sun rising (65–66).

These revised versions of events are generated not only by the desire to give back an affectionate story to the weakening mother but to alleviate the daughter's sense of guilt. The anger she has experienced, and still feels toward her mother now crashes in front of the image of the frail, disoriented human being that she has become. Emotional deprivation is at the basis of the daughter's progressive detachment from her mother; the daughter's resentment for her uncaring and hardworking mother, is now turned, in the face of the effects of Alzheimer's disease, into a sense of guilt ("Le visite di controllo servono a me. Mi rassicurano, non l'ho ammalata io"[10] (The check-ups are for my benefit. They reassure me; it wasn't I who made her sick[11]).

As the opening sentences make clear, Alzheimer's disease is perceived first of all as an illness affecting the mother's emotional responses, and this already suggests that emotions are central in the narration ("Certi giorni la malattia si mangia anche i sentimenti. . . . [Il corpo] Ha perso la capacità di provare"[12] (Some days the illness eats away at her emotions too. . . . It [the body] loses the ability to feel[13]).

It is the double function of the narrator as both affectionate and uncaring daughter that encourages speculation on nostalgia. I argue that it is a particular shade of nostalgia that contributes to mending the daughter-mother relationship. The relationship is not brought to a resolution through the daughter's revisitation of her life with the mother, as in *L'amore molesto*, nor does the daughter's narration lead to an imagined resolution as in *Madre e figlia*.[14] It is the structure of the text, in fact the two lines of narration and the particular use of rural metaphors in the description of the mother that create a resolution through the evocation of a nostalgic emotion. The rural setting plays a role in the resolution.

To clarify the dynamics of nostalgia within the mother-daughter relationship depicted in *Mia madre è un fiume*, it is pertinent to discuss what is actually meant by nostalgia, and how nostalgia is seen in current theorization. I am keen to define it now because the fact that Di Pietrantonio's novel deals with a remote rural village—and there are many references to lost traditions—may lead to a perception of nostalgia as the loss of an antiquated but happier time, compared to modernity, which is certainly not the case.

The word nostalgia dates back to the seventeenth century when it was coined to signify the suffering experienced by the person away from their homeland, as the etymology of the word indicates ("nostos" as return to the homeland and "algos" as pain).[15] As Jean Starobinski reports, the word was coined in 1688 by Johannes Hofer in his medical doctoral dissertation on the suffering experienced by Swiss mercenaries away from home.[16] Nostalgia continues to be treated as a medical disease in the eighteenth and nineteenth centuries, when it was studied as an illness affecting soldiers away from home.[17] For an interpretation of nostalgia outside the medical framework and, as an emotion that deals with the relationship between past and present, not only at the individual level but as a collective response, we have to wait for the work of the American sociologist Fred Davis, who in 1979 published *Yearning for Yesterday*.

As Patrick Hutton explains, the fundamental innovation of Davis's groundbreaking work was to identify that in the course of the nineteenth century, nostalgia began to be seen not only as a medical condition but as an emotion affecting the daily lives of ordinary people.[18] In modern times, the technological changes in communication and mass media made images of the past available to everyone, and in so doing determined that the individual nostalgic response widened into a collective response.[19]

Moving from a medical to a sociophilosophical interpretation of nostalgia has a relevance on how the emotion of yearning for the past is valued and judged. Undoubtedly nostalgia is commonly connected to reactionary ideas and politics, originating from dissatisfaction with the present, from the perception of the poverty of the present. As Stuart Tannock summarizes, typical elements of the nostalgic rhetoric are "a Golden Age and the subsequent Fall, the story of the Homecoming, and the pastoral."[20]

Politically, nostalgia is often seen as a reactionary movement that obstructs social progress. Within feminist critique, nostalgia has been analyzed by Janice Doane and Devon Hodges (1987) as a move toward the desire to go back to traditional roles for women, as they highlight in their analysis of American novels.[21] Linda Hutcheon mentions not only several instances of feminist critique of nostalgia that see feminism as a progressive force with no possibility for nostalgic interpretation, but also feminist criticism of utopian perspectives that bring back nostalgic flavors.[22]

Stuart Tannock opens his article criticizing Gayle Greene's assumption that feminist fiction always aims at changes and is not reconcilable with nostalgia and with the search for stable meanings. Greene, argues Tannock, is showing herself to be nostalgic for feminist fiction.[23] The point that Tannock makes is that there can, in fact, be different types of nostalgia and that it is possible to feel nostalgic for progress or for stability.[24] More importantly, Tannock argues that in nostalgic representations the sense of retreat and retrieval cannot be really separated, as a nostalgic text can open up new readings and access to ignored forms of resistance. In his words,

> nostalgia should unquestionably be challenged and critiqued for the distortions, misunderstandings, and limitations it may place on effective historical interpretation and action; but, in the modern West at least, nostalgia should equally be recognized as a valid way of constructing and approaching the past—recognized, that is, as a general structure of feeling, present in, and important to individuals and communities of all social groups.[25]

The definition of nostalgia as an emotion at the junction between past and present is echoed by many other contemporary analyses. With his reading of Proustian nostalgia, Scott Alexander Howard highlights that the relation between past and present in the inception of nostalgia must also be redefined: as the involuntary Proustian recollection shows, nostalgia does not necessarily derive from the poverty of the present. Considering nostalgia as an affective experience rather than a fascination with the past, as Howard does, leads him to conclude that nostalgia may be triggered by an unrecoverable past perceived, in that specific moment, as deserving desire, "for its bittersweet affective character [rather] than for the sort of past it is directed toward or the relationship that obtains between that time and now."[26]

David Gerber's recent article on nineteenth-century British immigrant personal correspondence follows this same line of thought. In his case study of letters written to family in Britain by three immigrants from different social milieux, he argues that the nostalgic attachment expressed in various degrees in these letters can be interpreted as a process, through which the immigrant subjects elaborate their relationship to their past in their home country and their new present life in America. Nostalgia is therefore an emotion psychologically significant to the migrant subject at the moment of adjusting her- or himself to new identities.[27]

Similar interpretation of nostalgia, no longer as fascination or obsession with the past but as an emotion that has a bearing on the interpretation of the present, is shared by the articles collected in the Fall 2004 issue of the *Iowa Journal of Cultural Studies*. Sean Scanlan summarizes in his introduction to the journal issue that "nostalgia may be a style or design or narrative that serves to comment on how memory works. Rather than an end reaction to yearning, it is understood as a technique for provoking a secondary reaction."[28]

The influential interpretation by Svetlana Boym in the *Future of Nostalgia* (2001) also draws on an idea of nostalgia as fruitful for the future, rather than as a dead-end illusory fascination. Her theorization of restorative and reflective nostalgia clearly highlights the relevance that the emotion can have for the subject's development, where reflective nostalgia weaves together even discarded elements of the past to create an idea of the past useful for the future.

In the analysis of *Mia madre è un fiume*, I am helped by some of the aspects emerging from the theories highlighted. Particularly illuminating is the idea that nostalgia is an affective process focused on the moment when it takes place rather than on the past itself, as the Proustian analysis of Scott Alexander Howard and David Gerber's reading of immigrant letters show. A second important element for my reading is Sean Scanlan's view of nostalgia, again as a process, and one that generates secondary reactions rather than a desire fixed to a circumscribed past.

In *Mia madre è un fiume*, narrating is far from being perceived by the daughter as an action of love. It is a technique of detached care where the daughter is offering her mother a recollection, but not love; it is rather a purely medical and antiseptic approach, a simple addition to the medical treatment (68). Yet the narration of the story of the rural village intertwined with that of Esperina's life ends up generating other reactions in the daughter's psychology, as we will see.

After the first admission of the daughter's sense of guilt, the narration moves to the story of Esperina's life in the remote village near the mountains; in fact the first three short chapters focus, almost entirely, on the story of the remote Abruzzi village, on the mountains around Teramo, in the 1940s and 1950s, through the life of Fioravante, Esperina's father, and her sisters. The novel unwinds as a narration of a preindustrial rural society, where the Viola family lived in a dignified poverty but was able to produce by themselves all the food they needed and was also able to offer support to evacuees of the area. It is an enclosed community, where the possibility of experiencing the world outside came to Fioravante only during the war, through his time in Yugoslavia as a soldier. World War II, Fioravante's difficult character, and his leave periods at home, each of which produced a daughter, are narrated in the first chapters.[29]

The simplicity of the Viola family and their environment does not resemble the simplicity of the peasants of Silone's Abruzzi. The story of the village is inserted into a line of progress, so that it reads as a story of social development, where the mass media, the radio first and the television later, are introduced in fact by Fioravante "troppo curioso del Progresso"[30] (also earnest about Progress[31]). Likewise Esperina, rather than being represented as a woman of a past generation with ideals and beliefs detached from the present—as she could have been, given the disparity between the social and civil achievements of her generation and those of her daughter's—is perfectly in tune with a historical vision of social development. As a child, she embraces the changes represented by school and the radio, first opportunities to confront realities outside her isolated and limited experience. Electricity and a new road connect the village with the rest of the world and give the opportunity to Esperina, by now married with a daughter, of radical changes. Finally they move away from the mountains to live in easier conditions on the hills near the sea. It is possible to see the unfolding of the story within an idea of history as a progressive phenomenon, where historiography is seen as the dominant framework; in fact the narration moves from the war to the economic improvements of the 1950s and 1960s to emigration and new agricultural legislation in the 1980s. Despite this clear emphasis on progress, nostalgia—not as a return to a lost Golden Age, but as an emotion that helps negotiate the past and the present—becomes interwoven with the daughter-narrator present.

In relation to the childhood home, the adult daughter tells of a recent occasion when, together with her son, she goes back to the childhood home in the woods. Having walked through the paths and fields of her childhood and seen the derelict houses where nature has repossessed what had been modeled by man, the narrator remembers the harsh winters, when her father would walk first in the snowy path to the school so that the little girl would not fall deep in the snow. A sudden pang of nostalgia strikes the daughter at this point:

> Non so come mai ci penso ora e mi escono le lacrime, sarà la nostalgia. Di papà che rompeva la neve per me. Non gli ho mai detto grazie. Non era necessario.[32]

> (I don't know why I think of that now, and tears come, it must be nostalgia. Dad treading down the snow for me. I never said thank you. There was no need.[33])

Nostalgia is not felt for the place or the rural setting, but for emotions that at that time in the past were not even appreciated or understood. The daughter's nostalgic revisitation establishes an emphasis on the present desire to experience an emotion yearned for its bittersweet flavor or for making sense of the present, as in the discussion by Howard and Gerber. The scene tells us something about the present and the emotions, that is about the need of an affective relationship with the past that the daughter's detachment from her mother has caused.

The mother's relationship with her daughter, as well as the daughter's relation with her own sense of the past are tinged with this particular shade of nostalgia. The emotional attachment between mother and daughter is a desire for a tender relationship they have never had. Nostalgia is understood in the narration as an emotion that, while moving away from reality, comments on unexpressed desires, it is a process of revisitation of the past rather than an attachment to the past as it has been lived. Two revealing moments of this shade of meaning of nostalgia are attributed both to the mother and to the daughter. Despite having been an absent and uncaring mother, there are moments when Esperina indulges in a closeness unknown to the daughter:

> Mia madre mi tocca la gamba all'improvviso e parla di questa mia gonna così morbida. È nuova? Apprezza la stoffa con le dita deformi e intanto ho la mano addosso. Quello, cerca. Vuole me. Spesso lo fa con le maglie. . . . Si attarda sulla lana, si stacca con un movimento lungo dalla spalla verso il polso, come una carezza, una nostalgia.[34]

> (My mother suddenly touches my leg and asks about my skirt, so soft. Is it new? Her misshapen fingers appraise the fabric, all the time with her hand on me. That's what she wants. She wants me. She does that often with my tops. . . . She lingers on the wool, moves away, sliding her hand slowly from shoulder to wrist, like a caress, a wistfulness.[35])

When the fear of contracting the same illness as her mother strikes her unexpectedly, the narrator imagines herself at the age of her mother: "Ho nostalgia di quello che dimenticherò. Ho nostalgia di chi sarò stata"[36] (I am already wistful for what I will have forgotten. I long for the person I will have been[37]). Nostalgia is therefore an undefined feeling, an emotion that characterizes a sense of attachment for something that cannot even be defined or remembered. In this sense nostalgia counteracts the effect of Alzheimer's defined at the onset of the novel, as a disease of the emotions. It functions therefore, as Tannock has put it, "as a general structure of feeling" relevant to the subject and to social groups.

What does this shade of nostalgia add to the daughter's relationship with her mother and to the perception of the history of the rural community? The shorter sections appearing as narrator's comments in the last part of the novel clarify the development of the daughter's relationship to the mother. These scattered pages intersect with the two main lines of narration and cannot be inscribed into that subdivision. It is in these sections that it is possible to detect a re-elaboration of rural images. This time, though, these short pieces have nothing to do with the mother's life story nor with the daughter's anger and resentment. They are rather an appropriation of rural images in sections of writing that express the attachment of the daughter to the mother as well as to those traditions and environments.

Significantly, it is after the much shorter section on the new life away from the mountains that the first of these very brief comments by the narrator on her mother appears. Only at the time in the narration when the distance from the rural past is acknowledged does the narrator's desire to reconnect to that reality manifest itself as if determined by the acquired distance, and therefore by a loss of that experience in the present. These isolated half pages synthesize in a sometimes more lyrical way, the daughter's love for her mother, her contrasting feelings, her present disorientation for the deterioration of her mother's condition.

More than the double narration that the daughter has conducted so far, these short pieces are meaningful because they encapsulate the emotion of attachment and conflict regarding the mother through a series of metaphors that echo the natural world of the remote Apennine village. The first section is the one that gives the novel its title, where Esperina's whole life is synthesized in less than a page by comparing the different stages of her life to a river. Esperina is a river because her long, black hair appeared as a phenomenon of stunning beauty to the little girl, when, in the evenings, Esperina would let it hang loose and comb it. The river, "fluttuante nel vento"[38] (fluttering in the wind[39]), soon becomes a stream, reminder of the one not far from their home in the mountains. The metaphor of the river extends to represent Esperina's deteriorating memory: "è un fiume di vecchi ricordi salvati"[40] (she is a river of salvaged old memories[41]), and again un "fiume di parole" (a river of words), because indeed she was a clever storyteller, but now only the holder of a limited number of stereotyped phrases. The page concludes stretching the metaphor to indicate the progressive deterioration and the imminent death:

> È un fiume in secca, la neve dei pioppi lo sorvola. L'ombra dei sassi cade sul letto bianco, crepato. Qua e là una pozza d'acqua ancora, ferma e densa, lambita dagli insetti.
> Fa odore di morte.[42]

> (She is a dried-up river, a blizzard of poplar flakes blowing over [it]. The rocks cast their shadow on the bleached, broken bed. Here and there a few puddles still, the water stagnant, murky, insects skimming the surface.
> It smells of death.[43])

The whole description draws images from a rural landscape, harsh and unattractive, where a drought has marked the riverbed, and where dead water attracts insects. Yet making a direct connection between the mother and the rural Abruzzi village would lead to a perception of the mother as a place in the past, that is, as a custodian of an immobile time. And Di Pietrantonio, as we have seen, hardly wants to emphasize the image of the mother as a metaphor for an idea of stability against progress, or as a haven of peace and tranquillity in an idyllic setting.

In *Mia madre è un fiume*, the relationship with the mother and the rural past appears as a language that allows the recuperation of elements of the past in the present. The loss of emotions and the guilt with which the novel begins find the attempt at a resolution in the lyrical commentary sections that enrich the last part of the book. The mother is a river and soon after is seen as a tree, covered with purple flowers, "viola" like her surname, and finally her surname is a musical instrument. She is given eternal life through the comparison with natural elements, and in turn nature becomes the matter of emotions.

It must not be forgotten that Di Pietrantonio makes clear gruesome aspects of Esperina's life. These are the harassments suffered by Esperina from her own father, Fioravante. A brief mention in the daughter's narration reflects the synthetic and matter of fact confession of the mother to the daughter, some years back. Using an echo of Ferrante's narrative, Di Pietrantonio defines the harassment suffered by Esperina as "amore molesto"[44] (troubling love), but it remains a feeble and uncertain explanation of Esperina's lack of maternal care.

Yet the rural past is fundamental not only to a portrayal of the love for the mother but for its value that the daughter appropriates for herself. The short lyrical pages just seen are an example of the value the rural setting has acquired for the daughter narrator, as a language able to re-elaborate emotions. The rural setting demonstrates an attachment to emotions of the past that become significant in the present.

Another example of attachment to the past re-elaborated for the present is given by a chapter on the ritual of the killing of a pig for the preparation of winter provisions that suddenly breaks the narration of the first forty pages on the village life of six decades before. A tradition of rural communities, the section is not related to Esperina's past but is rather an account of this activity as it is done today. The section is all in the present tense. As a consequence, the reader is brought from the narration of the village life in the past to the one of present rural activities through a zooming effect. Contrary to ideas of domesticity that such traditional and rural activities may evoke, the narrator emphasizes how those provisions become advantageous when, in present daily life, for example, one does not feel like cooking. Continuity between the rural past and the present is established, one that underlines the positive elements of the remaining traditions of that lost society. It is an attachment to an idea of the past, which as Sean Scanlan summarizes in his already quoted introduction, tells us more about the process of memory, about the desire and its secondary reactions. If the yearning for a loving mother-daughter relationship that never existed is an indication of the emotional need felt in the present, the nostalgic manipulation of images of the rural landscape and of the mother, as well as the representation of traditional rural activities as useful for the present, are evidence of the process that aims at generating the resolution of contradictory feelings.

The knots that did exist in the daughter's private life (her resentment over her mother's lack of care, the horrid and violent aspects suffered by the child Esperina) are not resolved or untied, but the relevance of a social rural community that has also generated those aberrations is taken to the present. As a result, local and forgotten social entities are given a value within the linear progress that could have easily hidden them from history. In this sense, if Alzheimer's can be seen as a metaphor for the loss of memory of collective local identities marginal to historiography, then the nostalgic manipulation of rural images has the power to counteract that amnesia.

In the relationship with the old rural village as well as in her relationship with her mother, the narrator does not express a desire for an idyllic past or for an idealized relationship seen as locus of stability. Yet nostalgia is present in the novel both for the old village and for the complex relationship with a much loved and hated mother. In both cases it is experienced as an emotion that helps the renegotiation and the dialogue between present and past and is part of the narrator's active attempt to create a more empowering future.

NOTES

1. Donatella Di Pietrantonio, *Mia madre è un fiume* (Roma: Elliot Edizioni, 2011), 179.
2. The novel was awarded the Premio di Letteratura Naturalistica Majella 2011; Premio Letterario Nazionale Tropea 2011; Premio Lamerica 2011; Verga d'Argento 2011; Premio

John Fante Opera prima 2012. It was also runner-up for the Premio Rapallo Carige 2011 and received special mention at Premio Alziator 2011.

3. See Brenda Daly and Maureen T. Reddy, *Narrating Mothers*; Cathy Davidson and Esther M. Broner, *The Lost Tradition*; Mickey Pearlman, *Mother Puzzles*; Adalgisa Giorgio, *Writing Mothers and Daughters*; Patrizia Sambuco, *Corporeal Bonds: The Daughter-Mother Bond in 20th-Century Italian Women's Writing*.

4. Among twenty-first-century Italian fiction on the topic of the mother-daughter relationship, see Francesca Melandri, *Eva dorme* (2011); Elisabetta Rasy, *L'estranea* (2007): Daria Bignardi, *Non vi lascer ò orfani* (2009); and Igiaba Scego, *Oltre Babilonia* (2008).

5. In *L'amore molesto* this happens when, by putting on her mother's dress, the daughter perceives the truth about her mother's past through the materiality of her clothes; in *Madre e figlia* the daughter's dreams are often a way to make sense of troubled situations and, hence, to have a present understanding of the past.

6. Donatella Di Pietrantonio, *Mia madre è un fiume* (Roma: Elliot Edizioni, 2011), 41–42.

7. Donatella Di Pietrantonio, *My Mother Is a River*, trans. Franca Scurti Simpson (Folkeston: Calisi Press, 2015), 41–42.

8. *Mia madre è un fiume*, 143.

9. *My Mother*, 135.

10. *Mia madre è un fiume*, 9.

11. *My Mother Is a River*, 13.

12. *Mia madre è un fiume*, 9.

13. *My Mother Is a River*, 13.

14. For a thorough discussion of the daughter's re-elaboration of her relationship with her mother in *Madre e figlia* and *L'amore molesto*, see chapters 3 and 5 of my *Corporeal Bonds: The Daughter-Mother Relationship in Twentieth-Century Italian Women's Writing* (Toronto: University of Toronto Press, 2012).

15. Damien Reid, "Nostalgia," *British Medical Journal* 323 (2001): 496.

16. Jean Starobinski, "On Nostalgia," in *The Emotional Power of Music: Interdisciplinary Perspectives on Musical Arousal, Expression and Social Control*, ed. Tom Cochrane, Bernardino Fantini, and Klaus R. Scherer (Oxford: Oxford University Press, 2013), 329–40, 329. Antonio Prete had included an extract of Hofer's dissertation in his 1992 volume *Nostalgia* (Milan: Raffaello Cortina Editore, 1992).

17. Ibidem 336–38.

18. Patrick Hutton, "Preface: Reconsideration of the Idea of Nostalgia in Contemporary Historical Writing," *Historical Reflections* 39 (2013): 1–9, 2.

19. Ibidem.

20. Stuart Tannock, "Nostalgia Critique," *Cultural Studies* 9 (1995): 453–64, 454.

21. Janice Doane and Devon Hodges, *Nostalgia and Sexual Difference* (New York: Methuen, 1987).

22. This is the case of the works by Michael Fisher (1994) and by Kathe Devis Finney (1983), as reported in Linda Hutcheon's "Irony, Nostalgia and the Postmodern" in *Methods for the Study of Literature as Cultural Memory*, ed. Raymond Vervliet and Annemarie Estor (Amsterdam: Rodopi, 2000), 200. For a discussion of feminist nostalgia and nostalgia for feminism within the Italian context, see Andrea Hajek's chapter in this volume.

23. Tannock, 453.

24. Tannock, 455.

25. Tannock, 461.

26. Scott Alexander Howard, "Nostalgia," *Analysis* 72 (2012): 641–50, 647.

27. David A. Gerber, "Moving Backward and Moving On: Nostalgia, Significant Others, and Social Reintegration in Nineteenth-Century British Immigrant Personal Correspondence," *The History of the Family* 21 (2016): 291–314, 310.

28. Sean Scalan, "Introduction," *Iowa Journal of Cultural Studies* 5 (2004): 3–9, 4.

29. From the political point of view though, Di Pietrantonio portrays a naïf environment. John Foot's chapter in this volume explains the complexity of World War II in the Eastern borders; having that knowledge it becomes perplexing to read the evolution of political belief in the character of Fioravanti. He leaves his village as a soldier of the Fascist government, escapes

execution, and finally returns home as a convinced Communist and an admirer of Tito. An unusual outcome from the historical point of view, that testifies the complexity of cultural memory, but is useful for the characterization of an impulsive and boisterous protagonist.

30. *Mia madre*, 13.
31. *My Mother*, 17.
32. *Mia madre*, 110.
33. *My Mother*, 103.
34. *Mia madre*, 117–18.
35. *My Mother*, 111–12.
36. *Mia madre*, 118.
37. *My Mother*, 112.
38. *Mia madre*, 133.
39. *My Mother*, 127.
40. *Mia madre*, 133.
41. *My Mother*, 127.
42. *Mia madre*, 133.
43. *My Mother*, 127.
44. *Mia madre*, 37. It must also be noted that in Ferrante's novel the sexual harassment of the child daughter is key in the development of the story.

WORKS CITED

Daly, Brenda, and Maureen T. Reddy, *Narrating Mothers: Theorising Maternal Subjectivity*. Knoxville: University of Tennessee Press, 1991.
Davidson, Cathy, and E. N. Broner. *The Lost Tradition: Mother and Daughters in Literature*. New York: Frederick Ungar Publishing, 1980.
Di Pietrantonio, Donatella. *L'Arminuta*. Turin: Einaudi, 2017.
———. *Bella mia*. Rome: Elliot Edizioni, 2014.
———. *Mia madre è un fiume*. Rome: Elliot Edizioni, 2011.
———. *My Mother Is a River*. Translated by Franca Scurti Simpson. Folkestone: Calisi Press, 2015.
Doane, Janice, and Devon Hodges. *Nostalgia and Sexual Difference*. New York: Methuen, 1987.
Gerber, David A. "Moving Backward and Moving On: Nostalgia, Significant Others, and Social Reintegration in Nineteenth-Century British Immigrant Personal Correspondence." *The History of the Family* 21 (2016): 291–314.
Giorgio, Adalgisa. *Writing Mothers and Daughters*. Oxford: Berghahn Books, 2002.
Howard, Scott Alexander. "Nostalgia." *Analysis* 72 (2012): 641–50.
Hutcheon, Linda. "Irony, Nostalgia and the Postmodern." In *Methods for the Study of Literature as Cultural Memory*, edited by Raymond Vervliet and Annemarie Estor, Amsterdam: Rodopi, 2000.
Hutton, Patrick. "Preface: Reconsideration of the Idea of Nostalgia in Contemporary Historical Writing." *Historical Reflections* 39 (2013): 1–9.
Pearlman, Mickey. *Mother Puzzles*. New York: Greenwood Press, 1989.
Prete, Antonio. *Nostalgia*. Milan: Raffaello Cortina Editore, 1992.
Redstone, Susan. *The Sexual Politics of Time: Confession, Nostalgia, Memory*. London: Routledge, 2008.
Reid, Damien. "Nostalgia." *British Medical Journal* 323 (2001): 496.
Sambuco, Patrizia. *Corporeal Bonds: The Daughter-Mother Bond in 20th-Century Italian Women's Writing*. Toronto: University of Toronto Press, 2012.
Scalan, Sean. "Introduction." *Iowa Journal of Cultural Studies* 5 (2004), 3–9.
Starobinski, Jean, "On Nostalgia." In *The Emotional Power of Music: Interdisciplinary Perspectives on Musical Arousal, Expression and Social Control*, edited by Tom Cochrane, Bernardino Fantini, and Klaus R. Scherer, 329–40. Oxford: Oxford University Press, 2013.
Tannock, Stuart. "Nostalgia Critique." *Cultural Studies* 9 (1995): 453–64.

Chapter Eleven

A Future without Nostalgia

Remembering Second-Wave Feminism in Mia madre femminista *and* Fra me e te

Andrea Hajek

EXPIRED FEMINISM

Avevo vent'anni.
Volevamo solo cambiare il mondo.
"70," gli anni in cui il futuro incominciò.

These are the titles of three publications that call back more or less nostalgic and celebrative memories of the 1970s, much in contrast with the predominantly negative public image of the so-called *anni di piombo* (years of lead).[1] One is an autobiographical collection of testimonies by the former members of a student collective in 1977, when Italy witnessed a revival of the student protests that had arisen a decade before;[2] the second text is a photographic chronology or *romanzo fotografico* of the 1970s;[3] the third is a supplement in twelve issues that was published together with the daily *Liberazione*, which—again using personal testimonies and photography—aimed to tell a history of the 1970s from a different perspective, "un ripensamento di quella stagione che smonti il cliché conformista degli anni di piombo" [4] (a reassessment of that season which may dismantle the conformist cliché of the years of lead).

Nostalgia for these years of protest and social uprising, especially among younger generations of activists, is common.[5] This cannot be said for the memory of the women's movement, which manifested itself alongside other social movements in the 1970s, and which has suffered a strong backlash in the 1990s and beyond. Nostalgia for feminism is almost a taboo in the present, and this contribution, then, offers an exploration of the role of nostalgia—its limitations and potentials—in reflections about feminist legacies in contemporary Italy, and by these feminist legacies I refer to the feminist generation of the late 1960s and 1970s, that is, second-wave feminists. By making a distinction between nostalgia *for* feminism, a backward-looking, melancholic approach that draws on a linear and progressive idea of time, and *feminist* nostalgia, which is instead prospective and implies a nonlinear progression, I demonstrate how the former is not so much a longing for the loss of the 1970s women's movement (among second-wave feminists), but is translated into a desire to preserve, revitalize, and give *continuity* to this feminist past by passing it on to future generations.

This approach, however, fails to acknowledge the existence of new feminist subjectivities and to engage with issues that fall outside of the temporal scope of second-wave feminism, and risks turning this nostalgia for feminism into a dead end. I will illustrate my findings by comparing two apparently similar, yet very different texts that engage in generational discourses: *Fra me e te: Madre e figlia si scrivono: Pensieri, passioni, femminismi* (Between you and me: Mother and daughter write to each other: Thoughts, passions, feminisms) by Mariella Gramaglia and Maddalena Vianello; and Marina Santini and Luciana Tavernini's *Mia madre femminista: Voci di una rivoluzione che continua* (My feminist mother: Voices of a revolution that continues).

NOSTALGIA FOR FEMINISM, FEMINIST NOSTALGIA

In her essay on "post-ness" and nostalgia in contemporary feminist thought, Kate Eichhorn observed how nostalgia is often a taboo subject amongst feminists.[6] Indeed, her analysis of three recent studies of feminist and queer histories reveal that it is best to avoid or distance oneself from nostalgia.[7] This is largely because nostalgia, which derives from the Greek *nostos*, to return home, is normally seen in a negative way, that is, as a sentimental, melancholic longing for a past that is no more and which takes on a "backwards-looking stance" and "a defeatist attitude to present and future."[8] From this follows that nostalgia is a construction in the present, and as such reflective more of the present than of the past. In fact, nostalgia always occurs in view of present fears, discontents, anxieties, and uncertainties that pose a threat of discontinuity to our present identity.[9]

Pickering and Keightley argue, however, that there is a second, "utopian" side to nostalgia, where the latter reflects a desire not to return to an earlier state or idealized past but "to recognize aspects of the past as the basis of renewal and satisfaction in the future."[10] It is a "prospective" nostalgia, one "that enables the future."[11] Feminist nostalgia is therefore nostalgia not for a failed project in the past, but rather nostalgia "as the grounds for a feminist project not yet realised" in the present:

> [T]he preoccupation with the past in contemporary feminist thought and cultural production, with its post-ness, may point to a type of nostalgia that does not necessarily exhibit nostalgia's typical markers. Feminist nostalgia is not about longing for some thing, time or place but rather about longing for the very possibility of living in a landscape where the past held little promise, little revolutionary potential, and the future was the only place where possibility dwelled. What makes feminist nostalgia unique, then, is that it is not nostalgia for something tangible but rather for the conditions under which there was nothing for a feminist to be nostalgic about. [12]

This conception of nostalgia not as a backward-looking, melancholic longing for something that is no more but as a prospective and positive move toward a better future, resounds in Victoria Browne's invitation to rethink the history of feminism not as "an endless spiralling between the forward movement of linear progress and the backsliding movement of repetition forced by backlash politics," but as an "untimely" and *nonlinear* progression, where "the idea that feminist histories are 'untimely' may help to bring energy and hope to the process of repeating: 'recollecting forwards' and reactivating the radicality of challenges that have long been forgotten, misunderstood, taken for granted, or simply not seen or heard." [13]

Browne—as many other contemporary (feminist) scholars [14] —rejects the linear perspective on feminist history that has long been applied even by feminist historians themselves; instead, she argues for an alternative, nonlinear approach to historical time that is multilinear and multidirectional, and most importantly, which should be understood as a form of lived time and as polytemporal. [15] By this she means that the way we live time does not conform to a teleological, past-present-future chronology but is constructed from memories and expectations, retention and anticipation. In other words, there is a dynamic interplay at hand where past, present, and future contribute to create a "composite" time, "generated through the interweaving of different temporal layers and strands." [16]

As such Browne dismisses the idea of time as a progressive series of successive waves in feminist history writing, which suggest a graduated progression of feminist thought and present "an integrated account of 'feminist history' *as a whole*." [17] This results in a hegemonic model that "severely curtails the ways in which diverse feminist histories can be mapped and understood, as it functions by blocking out or distorting trajectories which do not fit into the dominant frame." [18]

This interpretation of history not only entails the presence of a hegemonic model and successive waves, which moreover privileges Western European and North American feminism, but also builds on narratives of progress, loss, and return.[19] Loss narratives in particular are driven by feelings of nostalgia, even if this is never explicitly acknowledged. Claire Hemmings, in her analysis of what she calls the political grammar of feminist theory,[20] observes that narratives of progress—with regard to feminism in the 1970s—are positive, forward-looking stories of success, a "hopeful orientation to future,"[21] whereas loss narratives—regarding the development of feminism in the 1990s and beyond (the 1980s are usually described as a period of transition)—represent a loss of the potential of previous women's movements, and subsequently the death of feminism, thus calling for a return to feminist politics as practiced previously.

Thus we could say that in contemporary histories of Western second-wave feminism, progress narratives reflect the rupture (with the past) and gains (in the present and for the future) of the women's movement in the 1970s, whereas loss narratives relate to later periods in which, according to the texts studied by Hemmings, there is an alleged move away from practice toward theory, from activist to professional concerns.[22] They reflect an apolitical present which is dominated by an institutionalized and academic type of feminism, where younger cohorts of feminists are brought to feminism through the text rather than through political practice.[23] Here feminism is presented as dead or expired, and a desire is expressed to "retain a static and familiar object to be lamented," hence nostalgia. This is to ensure that one does not encounter that object in the present, "in order to imagine a future in which that familiar feminism can be recovered by the same subjects as those who keen for its current internment."[24] Eventually, these loss narratives call, in fact, for a return to feminism as experience and practice, rather than as text.[25]

Progress, loss, and return narratives are made possible through the application of linear time, which allows for the existence of a hegemonic model in the present through which the past is totalized—this is the static and familiar object to be lamented, described above. Accordingly, this implies a graduated progression of feminist thought, where a series of successive determinations negates and overtakes the former.[26] In these loss narratives we are therefore not dealing with feminist nostalgia but with nostalgia *for* feminism, which risks becoming an end in itself; thus it is limited to only certain parts of society, excluding for example migrant women, and does not take into consideration different needs, which evolve over time and therefore need continuous reactivation.[27] This type of nostalgia makes feminism dead.

Alessandra Gribaldo and Giovanna Zapperi call instead for an appropriation, in the present, of the conflictuality expressed in other historical periods, by way of a "processo di attualizzazione che è anche trasformazione" (process of actualization which is also transformation).[28] As Browne puts it, feminism is "untimely" and requires that we reactivate the radicality of past moments of feminist struggle.

WE WERE BORN AFTER, BUT WE DON'T FEEL POST

The rejection of linear time and graduated progression is illustrated by the following extract, taken from the *manifesto* of a contemporary Italian feminist collective, the Femministe Nove:

> Siamo nate dopo. Dopo la nominazione di sé come soggetti, dopo la decostruzione dell'universale donna. Dopo l'emancipazione, l'autocoscienza, la liberazione, la differenza. Siamo già state donne e lesbiche, nelle frontiere e ai margini, cyborg e queer, irrappresentabili e rappresentate. Ma non ci sentiamo affatto post. Sentiamo il femminismo come una metamorfosi che ci attraversa, un cambiamento che pensiamo e agiamo attraverso il corpo. Non siamo staffette, siamo partigiane. [29]

> (We were born after. After the self-appointment as subjects, after the deconstruction of the universal woman. After emancipation, *autocoscienza*, liberation, difference. We have already been women and lesbians, at the borders and margins, cyborg and queer, unrepresentable and represented. But we don't feel "post." We feel feminism as a metamorphosis that runs through us, a change that we feel and act through the body. We are not couriers, we are partisans).

In this polemical rejection of the idea of progressive time and successive waves—elegantly illustrated here in the reference to the female heroes of the Italian Resistance against Fascism, whose fighting spirit and leading role are contrasted with the more traditional role of couriers[30] —is implicit also a rejection of nostalgia for those previous manifestations of feminists that present themselves as dominant in the public narrative, which is made clear in the following paragraph:

> Riconosciamo il valore fondativo delle nostre genealogie nel pensiero e nelle pratiche femministe. E non vogliamo vivere il confronto fra generazioni femministe né nell'asimmetria di potere e di autorità né nell'invidia dell'epica di una stagione aurorale.

> (We acknowledge the fundamental value of our genealogies in feminist thought and practice. And we wish to live the confrontation between feminist generations neither in the asymmetry of power and authority nor with envy of the epic dawning of a new decade .)

Yet, by acknowledging the importance of feminist genealogies (which is implied again in the historical reference to and identification with the "partigiane"), the Femministe Nove don't do away with the concepts of linear time, generation, and hegemonic feminism altogether. Moreover, they are clearly indebted to the feminist culture of the past, given the importance placed on the role of the body, for example. However, this is not nostalgia;

perhaps it is simply the due respect for an important legacy that cannot be discarded. In fact, I would argue that contemporary feminists are "conditioned" by the continued presence and activism of second-wave feminists in contemporary society, better known in Italy with the totalizing expression "historical" feminists. Thus any previous "waves" of feminism are canceled out as the 1970s generation is presented as *the* feminist movement of the past. In other words, the historical" feminists lay claim to the title of a hegemonic feminist model, which inevitably calls for respect.

This relationship of authority and recognition is reflected, to some extent, in the theories of disparity and *affidamento* ("trust") that have been carried forward mostly by the women's bookshop in Milan, the Libreria delle donne di Milano, in part as a reaction to the politics of gender equality that developed in the 1980s, which only served to make women equal to men and as such canceled out female subjectivities. *Affidamento* implies the creation of a relationship between two women who are different, in the sense of a kind of mother-daughter relationship where an older woman brings in a knowledge that the younger woman lacks:

> La pratica dell' "affidamento" tra donne viene proposta come una relazione politica privilegiata tra due donne che non si definiscono uguali in termini di sorrellanza ma somiglianti, diverse e dispari e dove il "di più" della disparità funge da mediazione che veicola significati nuovi nel rapporto tra donne, estranei sia all'identificazione che alla rivalità. [31]

> (The practice of "trust" between women is presented as a privileged political relation between two women who do not consider each other as equals in terms of sisterhood, but as alike, diverse and unequal where the "moreness" of the disparity functions as mediation, which transmits new meanings in the relationship between women, unrelated to both identification and rivalry.)

Although the theories of *affidamento* and disparity among women have been accused of creating hierarchies and power imbalances, they have left a strong mark on Italian feminist theory, while the idea of passing knowledge on to younger generations has become something of an obsession for Italian second-wave feminists. Thus as the women's movement started to decline, many women's archives, documentary centers and cultural associations arose, expressing a general anxiety to safeguard the feminist legacy and pass it on to future generations. This is illustrated by the opening sentences of a 1980s retrospective issue on the 1970s in the feminist journal *Memoria*, the aim of which was to

> travalicare la trasmissione orale, pure preziosa, tra donne che comunicano le une alle altre fatti da loro conosciuti o vissuti fornendo con un materiale scritto una prima ricostruzione di pezzi sul movimento femminista, rendendolo così più accessibile alle nuove generazioni. [32]

(overstep oral transmission, as precious as it is, among women who communicate to one another facts known or lived by them, by virtue of written material which may offer an initial reconstruction of parts of the feminist movement, thus making it more accessible to new generations.)

An anxiety which has continued up to the present, as "historical" feminist Emma Baeri demonstrates when she explains why she engaged with two younger feminists in her recent book about feminism: "Ossessionata dal timore di disperdere le fonti di una storia che considero 'bene comune,' e curiosa di una loro attuale interpretazione, ho voluto girare la questione a due giovani femministe" [33] (Obsessed by the fear to disperse the sources of a history that I consider "common good," and curious to see their current interpretation, I decided to confront two young feminists with the issue).

This anxiety is undoubtedly a reaction to the institutionalization of and backlash against feminism in the 1980s and 1990s, and a natural response to the overall process of forgetting or marginalization of women's history over the past four decades, as feminist scholars have often lamented.[34] We could call this a subaltern memory, which is defined as the "informal, communal projects of remembrance, particularly among subordinate or marginal groups and in cases where that group memory has not readily been legitimated by more rigid kinds of historiographic understanding."[35] Three questions arise at this point: *how* does nostalgia for Italian feminism manifest itself in the construction of this subaltern memory; *what* is the object of this nostalgia; and finally, *who* is the nostalgic subject?

REINTERROGATING THE PAST

As we have seen at the beginning, nostalgia occurs in view of present fears, discontents, anxieties, and uncertainties that pose a threat of discontinuity to our present identity, and the contemporary situation in Italy then offers a perfect basis for nostalgia.[36] However, this nostalgia is not to be sought among younger generations of feminists, as the *manifesto* of the Femministe Nove has clearly demonstrated. Rather, nostalgia allows older generations to claim authority on the basis of an experience and knowledge that younger generations lack, and is therefore more common among the older cohorts.

Thus in her autobiographical account of the women's movement in 1970s' Turin, Maria Schiavo laments the contemporary situation and expresses the need for the women's movement to make its voice heard again: "[I]l movimento delle donne, disorientato dai profondi cambiamenti intervenuti, e indebolito dal prevalere dei rapporti di forza sul piano politico e culturale, non è ancora riuscito a trovare una parola significativa, a far sentire in modo autorevole ed efficace la sua voce" [37] (The women's movement, disoriented by profound changes that have occurred, and weakened by the prevalence of power relations at political and cultural level, has not yet succeeded in finding a significant word, in making its voice heard in an influential and forceful manner). Hence, it is only through an intense "intreccio di voci singole e di coralità" (weaving of single and choral voices) that the past can relive and "re-interrogate" the present.[38] Here we clearly have before us a loss narrative, where second-wave feminism is presented as the dominant model of feminism, and its protagonists called to reinvigorate its causes, now that it is more necessary than ever. Hence, nostalgia is definitely present and further still, a powerful tool in the claiming of authority and through this, the transmission of experiences to new generations.

Nostalgia as a tool for transmission manifests itself most evidently through the media that are used for this transmission, mostly autobiographies, memoirs, and oral testimonies.[39] Documentaries about feminism are much rarer and a relatively recent phenomenon, as are photographic publications.[40] There have been some photographic exhibitions but mostly held in concomitance with the fortieth anniversary of 1968. Indeed, public remembrance activities have been far more prolific for other social movements of the 1970s, such as the memorable 1968 protests or indeed the 1977 student movement with which I opened this chapter.[41]

What interests us most here is what the object of nostalgia is. For Eichhorn feminist nostalgia is "the grounds for a feminist project not yet realised," a longing "for the very possibility of living in a landscape where the past held little promise, little revolutionary potential, and the future was the only place where possibility dwelled."[42] It is the realistic possibility and the prospective of radical change and progress that is evoked; it is therefore a narrative of progress as opposed to loss, which is characteristic instead of nostalgia *for* feminism.

The latter is motivated by present discontents and anxieties yet remains firmly connected to the past, as it laments a contemporary age where yes, some progress has been made, but many of the gains of second-wave feminism are incomplete or continuously put at risk. Hence nostalgia *for* feminism is nostalgia not simply for something that is no more, but for something that once was and then was undone or forgotten, and as such marks a failed revolution that is particularly hard to accept for the protagonists of this revolution: "un 'lutto' che ancora ostacola il lavoro di conoscenza"[43] (a "grief" which continues to hinder the work of knowledge).

In other words, the feminist revolution was interrupted or remained incomplete, transformed into equality politics at best, vilified by the sexual politics of the neoliberal era at worst, all the while the women's liberation process was substituted with emancipation rhetoric. In the eyes of the older generation, then, it is only by transmitting (personal and collective) experiences of this past to younger generations that the legacy of the women's movement of the 1970s—damaged by the institutionalization of feminism, in the 1980s, and the backlash of the 1990s and 2000s—can be retrieved, restored, and handed down to the feminists of the day, and the revolution can be continued.

This however requires that we see history in terms of linear time and graduated progress, with successive waves of feminism acting simply as successors to a legacy, who continue a battle that was temporarily suspended, and do so by absorbing the lessons of the previous generation.[44] Younger feminists, in reality, tend to resist the generational logic present in this relationship between generations of feminists, and are more focused instead on creating changes in the present, as we have seen in the *manifesto* written by the Femministe Nove: "Vogliamo partire dalle nostre vite, dal presente che ci accomuna, per costruire pratiche di potenziamento reciproco nel desiderio condiviso di cambiamento, di liberazione dall'oppressione materiale e simbolica" (We want to start with our own lives, with the present that unites us, in order to construct practices of reciprocal strengthening in a shared desire for change and liberation from material and symbolical oppression). There is not much space for nostalgia here, in the sense at least of a backward-looking, melancholic desire for the lost gains of the 1970s generation.

Hemmings summarizes the situation as follows: "Feminism is thus locked into a psychoanalytic dynamic of vigorous supersession (by the younger) and melancholic nostalgia (of the older),"[45] which takes the shape of a "family drama," as mothers and daughters are bound in an antagonistic relation or, at the very best, a relation of "mothering" where the mother figure mentors the daughter, while the latter expresses recognition and respect. In both cases, the generational logic cannot escape a sense of progression in time, and more importantly, a subject passing on the history to a successor who recognizes that history. As such it imposes a singular, dominant story that is fixed in (past) time as shared, rather than a common attachment or interest *across* time. The fact that the Femministe Nove reject any nostalgic "invidia dell'epica di una stagione aurorale" (envy of the epic dawning of a new decade) , and therefore also the hostile confrontation with the protagonists of this near mythical past, is perhaps best illustrated in the claim that they, too, are "historical" feminists: "Siamo femministe storiche: il tempo presente ci fa orrore" (We are historical feminists: present times horrify us).

"POVERA, POVERA MAMMA"

In this final section we will consider two recent publications that both attempt to develop a generational dialogue among women using a seemingly similar technique though with quite different outcomes. Marina Santini and Luciana Tavernini's *Mia madre femminista: Voci di una rivoluzione che continua* (My feminist mother: Voices of a revolution that continues) is presented as a dialogue between a feminist mother and her daughter. Published by Il Poligrafo in 2015 in the series "Soggetti rivelati: Ritratti, storie, scritture di donne" (Revealed subjects: Portraits, stories, women's writing), it writes itself into the idea of linear time and progression described above, as we can deduct from the description of the series: "La storia delle donne è anche la storia di una progressiva, inarrestabile *rivelazione*" (The history of women is also the history of a progressive, unstoppable *revelation*).

The book's subtitle reflects this idea even better, with its reference to the continuity of the feminist revolution brought forward by the generation of the 1970s, which is made explicit through the black and white photograph on the front cover; a mother shows her toddler child (it is not clear whether it is a boy or a girl) how to put his or her hands together in order to form the iconic feminist gesture of the vagina. She is literally showing, and therefore, teaching the child the feminist gesture and thus symbolically passing on her feminism to the next generation, which is in fact the theme of the book. Although it is the daughter's perspective that is written into the title, "my feminist mother," the main theme of the book is the mother and the transmission of her feminist experience to a daughter who initially is critical to feminism; "Ma doveva proprio capitarmi una madre femminista?" (Did a feminist mother really have to happen to me?) is the provocative rebuke that the daughter figure launches at her mother, at the beginning of the book.

The importance of creating a dialogue between women is motivated by the claim that feminism cannot be taught or studied: "Ma il femminismo non si può insegnare. Non è un oggetto di studio. Trasforma se ci si lascia toccare. Dopo, il mondo non è più lo stesso" [46] (But you cannot teach feminism to others. It is not an object of study. It changes you if you let it touch you. After that the world is not the same anymore). In other words, such a radical transformation cannot be taught by academics or learned by reading books; it can only be narrated by those who have *lived* this change. Thus the book "originates within feminism and there is nothing there that hasn't been lived."

Once again second-wave feminism is presented as the dominant model of feminist thought and political practice, firmly located in a past and therefore unattainable for successive generations to whom this past can be transmitted only through the narration of lived experience. The editors acknowledge that in doing so they aren't presenting any complete and exhaustive history of feminism, but this carries the risk of turning it into something static or dead: "Il femminismo è vivo ed è pericoloso farne un monumento" [47] (Feminism is alive and it is dangerous to turn it into a monument).

Nevertheless, if Santini and Tavernini reject the idea of teaching feminism and writing its history, the book makes, first of all, a very clear claim to completeness as it is set to transmit a collective story that covers important themes of feminism,[48] and draws on a wide range of data provided by other women who took part in the women's movement. In fact, in addition to the generational dialogue that makes up the main text, the book contains brief testimonies by other feminist women mostly of the 1970s generation, who offer supplementary information on issues that are raised in the main text. These are the actual "voices" mentioned in the book's subtitle. The testimonies, which are scattered throughout the book and accompanied by photographs, interrupt the main text in a random way, so that the narration is not limited to the experience of one person but builds on the assembly of lived experiences, thus developing an "organic narrative."[49]

Secondly and most importantly, although *Mia madre femminista* is presented as a letter exchange between a mother and daughter, in reality it is a monologue where the feminist mother figure *is* teaching something to her (initially) uninterested daughter. Thus we are offered a chronological panorama of second-wave feminism and its key events, groups, practices, publications, and laws, complete with key words typed in capital letters, while the brief testimonies with supplementary information that frequently interrupt the flow of the text recall the learning boxes that are used in some school textbooks.

The daughter's voice is heard only indirectly throughout the book, in the mother's letters where she reports the daughter's reactions to previous letters. It isn't until the fourth and last section, on the theme of work, that we finally read a letter written directly by the daughter, who seems to have been converted by her mother's teachings, as she closes her letter with a rhetorical question: "Sono forse diventata femminista?" [50] (Have I perhaps become a feminist?). This too-perfect ending confirms the suspicion that the daughter is not a real person but a narrative trope.[51]

Considering that both Santini and Tavernini are part of a women's writing group connected to the Libreria delle donne di Milano, the Comunità di storia vivente (Community of living history), it is very likely that the proposed dialogue is in fact not a real dialogue but a constructed text that furthermore enacts the relationship of *affidamento* that was theorized and promoted by the very feminists of the women's bookshop. Hence, the daughter is a passive listener or, at best, a timid interlocutor, who befits the role of the trustee and whose predominantly absent voice is symptomatic of that conceptualization of time as linear and, accordingly, 1970s feminism as the hegemonic model, the collective voice of a revolution that can continue only in a similar relationship of trust. Hence agency lies with the older generation, while the younger generation is no more than a recipient of this legacy.

A completely different effect is obtained in *Fra me e te: Madre e figlia si scrivono: Pensieri, passioni, femminismi* (Between you and me: Mother and daughter write to each other: Thoughts, passions, feminisms). It is a real letter exchange, which took place over the period of a year, between the late feminist journalist and politician Mariella Gramaglia and her thirty-some-thing feminist daughter Maddalena Vianello. Like *Mia madre femminista*, this dialogue again offers a personal account of feminist, lived experience, but its aim is not to transmit feminist legacies to new, uninformed genera-tions who have yet to see the light.

Its purpose is more authentic and intimate, and the dialogue more real and concrete, not just because we now actually have two real interlocutors. More importantly, a true conversation is going on where mother Mariella and daughter Maddalena reflect on the achievements and failures of the mother's feminist revolution and, in particular, the impact of these achievements on their personal lives and roles as mother, daughter, and (working) women.

Inevitably this produces a more critical confrontation, which at times sees the daughter in an accusing role, where she occasionally evokes a nostalgia for feminism that she ascribes, however, to her mother's generation. For example, while recalling the libertarian education she had received from her progressive parents, Maddalena acknowledges the fact that they nevertheless taught her to value her body and never to use it to obtain privileges. She bitterly contrasts this valuable life lesson with the contemporary sexual (self-)exploitation of women, and projects her criticism of the failure of second-wave feminism on to her mother by evoking a sense of nostalgia that she attributes to the second-wave generation of her mother:

> A volte ripenso a tutto questo e provo molta tenerezza. Non ti aspettavi che sarebbe andata così, vero? Credevi fermamente che le donne dovessero essere apprezzate, valorizzate, rispettate. E che fosse anche loro preciso impegno smarcarsi con intelligenza da inutili ambiguità. Povera, povera mamma. [52]

> (At times I rethink all this and I feel much tenderness. You didn't expect things to go this way, did you? You firmly believed that women had to be appreciat-ed, valorized, respected. And that it was also their specific effort to break free, with intelligence, from useless ambiguities. Poor, poor mom.)

This implicit yet poignant finger pointing at the failures of her mother's generation, however, touches the mother's pride especially in those last three, pitying words, and Mariella's reaction is in fact defensive. She con-fesses feeling rather slighted by this observation, counters it by listing a number of gains obtained by second-wave feminism (such as the increased presence of leading women in traditionally male jobs), and eventually puts her daughter back in her place by reminding her that she is not a survivor of any (feminist) battle: "Non sei una reduce dal fronte"[53] (You are not a war veteran). Nevertheless, Maddalena opens Mariella's eyes to the reality of a new generation of feminists who face a whole new set of challenges, for which the feminist revolution of the 1970s has no solutions on hand:

Il cestino dei regali per le nuove generazioni—l'emancipazione nelle profes-
sioni, la libertà nella famiglia, i diritti, la freschezza e la profondità delle
relazioni fra donne che noi da ragazze non conoscevamo, di cui in passato mi
sentivo tanto fiera, mi appare terribilmente inadeguato, i fiocchi sgualciti, il
contenuto impolverato e vecchio. [54]

(The gift basket for new generations—work emancipation, freedom in the
family, women's rights, the freshness and profoundness of relations between
women which we as girls have never known, of which I had been so proud in
the past, now appears terribly inadequate, the bows all creased, the content
dusted and old.)

Rather than a teacher who transmits the feminist revolution to a successor,
she realizes that it is *she* who needs to start learning again: "È come se, dopo
aver creduto di superare brillantemente l'esame di maturità, dovessi tornare
in prima elementare a far le aste, a imparare ancora tutto da zero in un mondo
che non decifro"[55] (It is as if, after thinking I had brilliantly passed my final
school exam, I had to go back to primary school and learn how to write, to
learn everything from scratch again in a world I can't decipher).

In her response to her mother's proud list of feminist achievements, Maddalena places emphasis on current economic problems and the challenges of
an everyday life where women continue to be discriminated in their jobs and
limited in their life choices:

Non vi renderò mai abbastanza grazie per le conquiste per cui avete lottato,
quelle che nella mia vita sono acquisizioni da difendere. Mai abbastanza. Solo
che qui la situazione è sconfortante e noi sopravviviamo. Non è un bel vedere.
Perdona questi toni, ma sono molto arrabbiata. Anche con te. Mi avevi raccon-
tato che il mondo era diverso, che essere donna era una cosa diversa. E io ti
avevo creduto. Mamma, il cestino dei regali è talmente impolverato da sem-
brare vuoto. [56]

(I will never thank you enough for the achievements that you fought for, and
which in my life are acquisitions that need to be defended. Never enough.
Except that the situation here is discouraging and we are surviving. It's not a
pretty sight. Forgive these words of mine, but I am very upset. With you as
well. You told me that the world was different, that being a woman was
something different. And I believed you. Mom, the gift basket is so dusted that
it seems empty.)

Nostalgia for feminism has no place here: the progress made by Mariella's
generation is old and dusted, and it is pointless to lament it now, much less
teach it to younger women who are facing different challenges. Instead, the
solution lies in a unity between women, without competition and without
division:

Ma possiamo immaginare che sia arrivato il momento di abbandonare i cavilli, di smetterla di sottolineare chi ha fatto quanto e quando? Smetterla, smetterla, smetterla di condannarci da sole a essere divise. Possiamo immaginare una nuova fase in cui le donne con le loro differenze possano accompagnarsi per mano, chi con esperienza, chi con entusiasmo, ciascuna con le proprie idee, ma uguali a quelle della donna che le sta a fianco, e andare avanti? [57]

(Can we imagine that the time has come for us to drop the quibbles, to stop underlining who did what and when? Stop, stop, stop condemning and dividing ourselves. Can we imagine a new phase where women can walk side by side with all their differences, who with experience, who with enthusiasm, each with her own ideas but equal to those of the woman that stands beside her, and move on?)

A FUTURE WITHOUT NOSTALGIA

In this chapter we have seen that memories and histories of second-wave feminism often contain loss narratives, which imply a nostalgia for feminism as they require that we see history in terms of linear time and graduated progress, with a hegemonic feminist model—the 1970s women's movement—making important gains but subsequently suffering from backlash and amnesia, substituted with the politics of equality and emancipation while gender discrimination and violence continue, and established rights (such as abortion) are put at risk. A return becomes necessary, which is only possible through the transmission of lived experiences to successive "waves" of feminism who are no more than successors to this lost legacy, continuing a battle that was temporarily suspended by absorbing the lessons of the previous generation.

I have argued against this idea of graduated progression, which underestimates the value of previous and intermediate generations of feminists, and—more importantly—fails to see that different problems and challenges arise in different times, and that a simple continuation of the feminist revolution is not enough. Other than economic problems and job insecurity, the rise of queer feminism has also created a short-circuit between generations.

This conflict is illustrated in the testimonies of a young feminist collective that was published in a recent photographic book on the feminist gesture of the vagina. Although the latter obviously represents an important symbol of feminist subjectivity and activism, for these younger feminists it is felt as exclusive: "Trovo che questo gesto sia invecchiato, legato al passato, che in qualche modo non ci appartiene" (I find that this gesture has grown old, linked to the past, which in some way doesn't belong to us); "Se vent'anni fa il gesto della vagina ha rappresentato delle istanze di libertà, di riconoscimento e sorellanza, mi rendo conto che ora costringe nel determinismo biologico" (If twenty years ago the gesture of the vagina represented instance of freedom, recognition and sisterhood, I realize that today it compels us to biological determinism); "Oggi penso che il soggetto del mio femminismo non è una donna biologica, ma è una varietà di corpi queer più o meno nomadi"[58] (Today I think that the subject of my feminism is not a biological woman, but a variety of queer and more or less nomadic bodies).

What we need, then, is a reactivation of the feminist potential, which takes place not by looking back to the past and hoping for a return of something that is expired, but by "recollecting forwards," which is possible only where there is no one teacher or passive listener, but where both interlocutors listen and learn from each other. Contrary to *Mia madre femminista*, which attempts to transmit the past through a one-directional movement (old → young), *Fra me e te* contains a more interactive dialogue (old ↔ young). This is not to say that older generations of feminists are stuck in a nostalgic mechanism of preservation; on the contrary, this is often discarded by those same generations. Indeed, some historical feminists are extremely adamant about creating dynamic relations with younger generations, and once again Emma Baeri's experience (of her collaboration with a younger archivist) may very well offer the winning solution:

> Durante quel lungo e appassionato parlare di spazi urbani e luoghi politici del Movimento femminista a Catania era cresciuta tra noi una relazione inusitata, per la quale io avevo sentito ben presto che il piacere di raccontare quella storia mia e nostra, di trasmettere eventi e forme del Movimento, si arricchiva di un gusto nuovo e imprevedibile, quello di ereditare la passione di Sara di ascoltare e di ricevere, il suo sguardo avido, critico e affettuoso insieme, su di me insegnante e sulla mia storia di femminista.[59]

> (During that long and passionate discussion about urban spaces and the political places of the feminist movement in Catania, between us an uncommon relation had developed, thanks to which I had quickly felt that the pleasure of telling mine and our story, of transmitting events and forms of the movement, was enriched by a new and unforeseen flavor, that of inheriting from Sara the passion to listen and receive, her eager look, critical and affective at once, at me as a teacher and my history as a feminist).

Perhaps it is time to simply stop thinking about the legacy of feminism in terms of failure and loss, as reflected in this comment by a participant in the national protest demonstration against gender violence, on November 27, 2016: "La cosa più bella, per noi che eravamo in piazza negli anni Settanta, è la vivacità di questo corteo, la concretezza senza nostalgie." (The most beautiful thing, for those of us who were out on the streets in the 1970s, is the vivacity of this demonstration march, the concreteness without nostalgia).

Funding Acknowledgement

This work was supported by the British Academy [grant number pf130101].

NOTES

1. On the definition of the 1970s as "years of lead" see Andrea Hajek, "Teaching the History of Terrorism in Italy: The Political Strategies of Memory Obstruction," *Behavioral Sciences of Terrorism and Political Aggression* 2, no. 3 (2010); Andrea Hajek, *Negotiating Memories of Protest in Western Europe. The Case of Italy* (Basingstoke: Palgrave Macmillan, 2013).

2. Enrico Franceschini, *Avevo vent'anni: Storia di un collettivo studentesco 1977–2007* (Milan: Feltrinelli, 2007).

3. *Volevamo solo cambiare il mondo: Romanzo fotografico degli anni '70 di Tano D'Amico* (Napels: Edizioni Intra Moenia, 2008).

4. Nanni Balestrini, Franco Berardi Bifo, and Piero Sansonetti, "Perché non possiamo fare a meno di quegli anni," *"70," gli anni in cui il futuro incominciò* 1 (2007): 4.

5. On these militant memories and progressive nostalgia among contemporary, radical left activists, see Hajek, *Negotiating memories*, 139–42.

6. Kate Eichhorn, "Feminism's *There*: On Post-ness and Nostalgia," *Feminist Theory* 16, no. 3 (2015): 255.

7. Eichhorn, "Feminism's *There*," 257.

8. Michael Pickering and Emily Keightley, "The Modalities of Nostalgia," *Current Sociology* 54 (2006): 920.

9. Fred Davis, "Nostalgia, Identity and the Current Nostalgia Wave," *Journal of Popular Culture* 11, no. 2 (1977): 420.

10. Pickering and Keightley, "The Modalities of Nostalgia," 921.

11. Eichhorn, "Feminism's *There*," 258.

12. Eichhorn, "Feminism's *There*," 254, 259.

13. Victoria Browne, "Backlash, Repetition, Untimeliness: The Temporal Dynamics of Feminist Politics," *Hypatia* 28, no. 4 (2013): 918.

14. See, for example, Jonathan Dean, "Who's Afraid of Third Wave Feminism? On the Uses of the 'Third Wave' in British Feminist Politics," *International Feminist Journal of Politics* 11.3 (2009): 334–52; and Claire Hemmings, *Why Stories Matter: The Political Grammar of Feminist Theory* (Durham-London: Duke University Press, 2011).

15. Victoria Browne, *Feminism, Time, and Nonlinear History* (Basingstoke: Palgrave Macmillan, 2014), 1–2.

16. Browne, *Feminism*, 2.

17. Browne, *Feminism*, 11.

18. Deborah Withers, *Feminism, Digital Culture and the Politics of Transmission: Theory, Practice and Cultural Heritage* (London: Rowman & Littlefield International, 2015), 29. Moreover, a similar temporal delineation of feminist generation also implies a spatial or geographical restriction, in that this hegemonic model risks reinscribing a specifically Euro-American feminist historiography as hegemonic. Dean, "Who's Afraid Of Third Wave Feminism?," 335.

19. Hemmings, *Why Stories Matter*, 3.

20. *Why Stories Matter* offers a critique of the way Western feminist history since the 1970s is narrated by feminist scholars. Drawing on a select number of feminist journals, Hemmings argues that the development of Western feminism in these accounts is told through narratives of progress, loss, and return.

21. Rita Felski, "Telling Time in Feminist Theory," *Tulsa Studies in Women's Literature* 21, no. 1 (2002): 22.

22. Hemmings, *Why Stories Matter*, 64.

23. Hemmings, *Why Stories Matter*, 77.

24. Hemmings, *Why Stories Matter*, 73.

25. Hemmings, *Why Stories Matter*, 87.

26. Browne, *Feminism*, 18.

27. Erin Matson, "On Nostalgia in Feminism." Accessed November 28, 2016. https://erin-tothemax.com/2015/03/04/on-nostalgia-in-feminism/.

28. Alessandra Gribaldo and Giovanna Zapperi, *Lo schermo del potere: Femminismo e regime della visibilità* (Verona: Ombre Corte, 2012), 92.

29. The term "autocoscienza" is usually not translated into English because it is highly characteristic of the Italian feminist movement, but it is comparable to the concept of self-awareness. On the Femministe Nove see Andrea Hajek, "'We Are Not Heiresses.' Generational Memory, Heritage and Inheritance in Contemporary Italian Feminism," in *Protests and Generations: Legacies and Emergences in the Middle East, North Africa and the Mediterranean*, ed. Mark Ayyash and Ratiba Hadj-Moussa (Leiden: Brill, 2017).

30. In its common meaning, a "staffetta" or courier is someone who takes over the torch, while the historical reference here is to the female partisans of the anti-Fascist resistance, usually referred to as simple "staffette" (i.e., carrying messages or objects to male partisans in combat) rather than as the more correct "partigiane," female partisans. The wordplay then implies a rejection of the idea that the Femministe Nove are simply taking over the torch from older feminists and is at the same time a proud self-identification as partisans.

31. Chiara Martucci, *Libreria delle donne di Milano: Un laboratorio di pratica politica* (Milan: FrancoAngeli, 2008), 19.

32. "Il tema," *Memoria: Rivista di storia delle donne* 19/20 (1-2, 1983): 3.

33. Emma Baeri, *Dividua: Femminismo e cittadinanza* (Padua: Il Poligrafo, 2013), 15.

34. See, for example, Elda Guerra, "Femminismo/femminismi: Appunti per una storia da scrivere," *Genesis* III/I (2004): 87–111; Anna Rossi-Doria, "Ipotesi per una storia che verrà," in *Il femminismo degli anni Settanta*, ed. Teresa Bertilotti and Anna Scattigno (Rome: Viella, 2005), 1–23.

35. Nadia Atia and Jeremy Davies, "Nostalgia and the Shapes of History," *Memory Studies* 3, no. 3 (2010): 181.

36. Think, for example, of the sexist behavior of former prime minister Silvio Berlusconi throughout the years of his government, but we could also mention the continuous undermining of self-determination rights (e.g., abortion), gender discrimination, and stereotyping, and increasing violence against women.

37. Maria Schiavo, *Movimento a più voci: Il femminismo degli anni Settanta attraverso il racconto di una protagonista* (Milan: FrancoAngeli, 2002), 8.

38. Schiavo, *Movimento a più voci*, back cover.

39. For examples of these see Rossi-Doria, "Ipotesi per una storia che verrà."

40. To my knowledge only two publications, in 1976 and in 2014, focus exclusively on photographic representations or narrations of feminism; Paola Agosti et al., *Riprendiamoci la vita: Immagini del movimento delle donne* (Rome: Savelli, 1976); and Ilaria Bussoni and Raffaella Perna (eds.), *Il gesto femminista: La rivolta delle donne: Nel corpo, nel lavoro, nell'arte* (Rome: Derive Approdi, 2014)

41. See Hajek, *Negotiating Memories*, 35–53.

42. Eichhorn, "Feminism's *There*," 254, 255.

43. Teresa Bertilotti and Anna Scattigno, "Introduzione," in *Il femminismo degli anni Settanta*, ed. Teresa Bertilotti and Anna Scattigno (Rome: Viella, 2005), xii.

44. In an interview published in *La Repubblica* on November 23, 2016, for example, the outgoing director of the women's documentary center in Bologna observed how one of the things that remain to be done in Italy is a "generational transmission."

45. Hemmings, *Why Stories Matter*, 148.

46. Santini and Tavernini, *Mia madre femminista*, 13.

47. Santini and Tavernini, *Mia madre femminista*, 14.

48. The book is divided in four thematic sections that discuss the themes of women's writing and language, body and sexuality, women's spaces, and work.

49. Santini and Tavernini, *Mia madre femminista*, 14.

50. Santini and Tavernini, *Mia madre femminista*, 231.

51. This suspicion is further enhanced by the fact that the idea for the book, as explained in the foreword, originated from questions directed at the two editors by a group of Milanese school children after visiting an exhibition on feminism in 2008.

52. Gramaglia and Vianello, *Fra me e te*, 13.

53. Gramaglia and Vianello, *Fra me e te*, 16.

54. Gramaglia and Vianello, *Fra me e te*, 18.

55. Ibidem.

56. Gramaglia and Vianello, *Fra me e te*, 22.

57. Gramaglia and Vianello, *Fra me e te*, 32.

58. Collettiva XXX, "A ciascun* il suo gesto," in *Il gesto femminista*, ed. Ilaria Bussoni and Raffaella Perna (Rome: DeriveApprodi, 2014), 106, 109, 111.

59. Emma Baeri, "Noi, utopia delle donne di ieri, memoria delle donne di domani," in *Inventari della memoria: L'esperienza del Coordinamento per l'Autodeterminazione della Donna a Catania (1980– 1985)*, ed. Emma Baeri and Sara Fichera (Milan: FrancoAngeli, 2001), 18.

WORKS CITED

Atia, Nadia, and Jeremy Davies. "Nostalgia and the Shapes of History." *Memory Studies* 3, no. 3 (2010): 181–86.

Baeri, Emma, and Sara Fichera. *Dividua: Femminismo e cittadinanza*. Padua: Il Poligrafo, 2013.

———. *Inventari della memoria: L'esperienza del Coordinamento per l'Autodeterminazione della Donna a Catania (1980–1985)*. Milan: FrancoAngeli, 2001.

Balestrini, Nanni, Franco Berardi, and Piero Sansonetti. "Perché non possiamo fare a meno di quegli anni." *"70," gli anni in cui il futuro incominciò* 1 (2007): 3–5.

Bertilotti, Teresa, and Anna Scattigno. "Introduzione." In *Il femminismo degli anni Settanta*, edited by Teresa Bertilotti and Anna Scattigno, vii–xviii. Rome: Viella, 2005.

Browne, Victoria. "Backlash, Repetition, Untimeliness: The Temporal Dynamics of Feminist Politics." *Hypatia* 28, no. 4 (2013): 905–20.

Browne, Victoria. *Feminism, Time, and Nonlinear History*. Basingstoke: Palgrave Macmillan, 2014.

Collettiva XXX. "A ciascun* il suo gesto." In *Il gesto femminista*, edited by Ilaria Bussoni and Raffaella Perna, 97–111. Rome: DeriveApprodi, 2014.

Davis, Fred. "Nostalgia, Identity and the Current Nostalgia Wave." *Journal of Popular Culture* 11.2 (1977): 414–24.

Dean, Jonathan. "Who's Afraid of Third Wave Feminism? On the Uses of the 'Third Wave' in British Feminist Politics." *International Feminist Journal of Politics* 11, no. 3 (2009): 334–52.

Eichhorn, Kate. "Feminism's *There*: On Post-ness and Nostalgia." *Feminist Theory* 16, no. 3 (2015): 251–64.

Felski, Rita. "Telling Time in Feminist Theory." *Tulsa Studies in Women's Literature* 21, no. 1 (2002): 21–28.

Femministe Nove. "#manifesto di femministe nove." Accessed November 28, 2016. https://femministenove.wordpress.com/2014/02/06/manifesto-di-femministe-nove/comment-page-1/.

Gribaldo, Alessandra, and Giovanna Zapperi. *Lo schermo del potere: Femminismo e regime della visibilità*. Verona: Ombre Corte, 2012.

Gramaglia Mariella, and Maddalena Vianello. *Fra me e te: Madre e figlia si scrivono: Pensieri, passioni, femminismi*. Milan: Et al. edizioni, 2013.

Guerra, Elda. "Femminismo/femminismi: Appunti per una storia da scrivere." *Genesis* III/I (2004): 87–111.

Hajek, Andrea. *Negotiating Memories of Protest in Western Europe: The Case of Italy*. Basingstoke: Palgrave Macmillan, 2013.

————. "Teaching the History of Terrorism in Italy: The Political Strategies of Memory Obstruction." *Behavioral Sciences of Terrorism and Political Aggression* 2, no. 3 (2010): 198–216.

————. "'We are not heiresses.' Generational Memory, Heritage and Inheritance in Contemporary Italian Feminism." In *Protests and Generations: Legacies and Emergences in the Middle East, North Africa and the Mediterranean*, edited by Mark Ayyash and Ratiba Hadj-Moussa, 224–44. Leiden: Brill, 2017.

Hemmings, Claire, *Why Stories Matter. The Political Grammar of Feminist Theory*. Durham-London: Duke University Press, 2011.

"Il tema." *Memoria: Rivista di storia delle donne* 19/20 (1–2, 1983): 3.

Lussana, Fiamma. *Il movimento femminista in Italia: Esperienze, storie, memorie*. Rome: Carocci editore, 2012.

Martucci, Chiara. *Libreria delle donne di Milano: Un laboratorio di pratica politica*. Milan: FrancoAngeli, 2008.

Matson, Erin. "On nostalgia in feminism." Accessed November 28, 2016. https://erintothe-max.com/2015/03/04/on-nostalgia-in-feminism/.

Pickering, Michael, and Emily Keightley. "The Modalities of Nostalgia." *Current Sociology* 54 (2006): 919–41.

Rossi-Doria, Anna. "Ipotesi per una storia che verrà." In *Il femminismo degli anni Settanta*, edited by Teresa Bertilotti and Anna Scattigno, 1–23. Rome: Viella, 2005.

Santini, Marina, and Luciana Tavernini (eds.). *Mia madre femminista: Voci di una rivoluzione che continua*. Padua: Il Poligrafo, 2015.

Schiavo, Maria. *Movimento a più voci: Il femminismo degli anni Settanta attraverso il racconto di una protagonista*. Milan: FrancoAngeli, 2002.

Withers, Deborah. *Feminism, Digital Culture and the Politics of Transmission: Theory, Practice and Cultural Heritage*. London: Rowman & Littlefield International, 2015.

Chapter Twelve

Transnational Nostalgia in an All-Female Italian Facebook Group and Cooking Blog

Incoronata (Nadia) Inserra

Writing about Italian-American cookbooks, historian Donna Gabaccia states, "Among Italian Americans, food and cooking are powerful expressions of our ties to the past and our current identities. They also say much about how America has responded to us and our foods."[1] Food habits among Italian migrants abroad have in fact been studied in relation to larger concerns of cultural and national identity, especially considering the role played by foodways as "not simply celebrations of what we eat" but also as "vehicles for the public and private construction, negotiation, and manipulation of identity."[2]

Given the importance of food habits among previous generations of Italians migrated abroad, it becomes natural to ask what role foodways play in the lives of Italian nationals who have recently left Italy to reside in the United States or elsewhere in the world. On July 7, 2015, the Italian newspaper *IlSole24ore* reported that in 2014 the number of Italian nationals migrated abroad was over one hundred thousand, the largest number since 2004.[3] According to another 2015 report, in 2014 the number of Italians migrating abroad has grown faster than the number of foreign immigrants to the country and for the first time since 1994.[4]

These numbers lead to considering the impact of the new wave of international migration on Italian culinary culture. An analysis of foodways among Italians currently migrating abroad can thus help us address larger questions of cultural transmissions and transformation, as well as of national and cultural belonging; it also compares this new migration experience with previous ones. For example, how do recently migrated groups define themselves as "Italian" through their foodways? How do they portray Italian cuisine for other cultural groups with which they interact and how do they negotiate between this image of Italian cuisine and the global image of Italian cuisine that is popular outside of Italy?

This chapter engages with the questions above by exploring the role of social media, as they reflect, enhance, and potentially influence the food experiences of recently migrated Italians. Social media play an important role in the transmission of both individual and collective values associated with food culture, given their ability to create a transnational community[5] and to encourage intimacy between writers and their transnational readers.[6] Indeed, online cooking blogs tend to allow more room for discussing cultural topics than print cookbooks do.[7] Cooking blogs have even been considered "a new form of memoir, written and read by women"[8] and examples of "culinary autobiographies,"[9] given their strong use of personal and cultural anecdotes. The fact that blogs are often paired with Twitter accounts or Facebook pages turns them into "ideal platforms for engendering this kind of relationship,"[10] since social networking platforms "help to generate an even greater sense of immediacy and proximity."[11] This element of intimacy makes both food blogs and Facebook groups particularly relevant to discourses of migration and cultural identity, since both writers and readers are inclined to share so much about their personal experiences and cultural beliefs beyond eating and cooking.

My interest in this topic began in the spring of 2015 when I joined the all-female Facebook group "Le Ambasciatrici del Buon Gusto: Donne Italiane nel Mondo" and was immediately struck by the group's extremely active Facebook page. The Facebook group was created on October 22, 2013; as of January 8, 2017, the group included 1,836 members with active members coming from various countries in Europe, North America, East Asia, and the Middle East. However, since the administrator, two of the four official bloggers, and many active members in the group live in the United States, Anglo-American readers constitute the main audience for the group. In addition, both the blog and the Facebook page are administered by and explicitly geared toward Italian women. The age of most active members, between thirty and fifty years old, fits with the recent migration model, unlike its geographical distribution[12]; in fact, most Italian regions are represented in the group from north to south and the Sardinia region is largely represented in the group, probably thanks to its Sardinian administrator. While no second-generation Italian features among the active group members, probably because of the language barrier, Italian-proficient MCH was born in Naples, Italy, but has lived in the United States for many years; her participation has certainly contributed to widening the scope of the group, although most of the recipes posted by her can be considered Italian rather than Italian American.

As I set out to observe the group, my goal was to investigate its representation of Italian food and cooking traditions and to explore the self-portrayals of the bloggers as Italian female expatriates. Since my initial observation, it was evident that foodways reflect not only these women's personal and shared experiences as professional and nonprofessional cooks, mothers, and wives, but also a collective experience that is based on national and cultural belonging; the latter is often discussed in explicit ways within the group, therefore confirming Anne Murcott's observation that "food as a means of communication is another way of transporting the concept of a national identity."[13]

For the purpose of this study, it is also important to note that both blog and Facebook pages are closely intertwined, which allows the administrator and the other co-bloggers to use the Facebook page as an advertising tool for the blog, while also granting the blog a much higher visibility; at the same time, the Facebook page remains the group's main reference point, as well as a forum in which group members can freely voice their opinions and share their photos, even if their posts are monitored by the administrator. Accordingly, while this study is based on my continued observation and analysis of members' postings and interactions on the Facebook page, along with my questionnaire responses from the food bloggers and some of the most active group members, I also weigh this perspective against a close reading of food and cultural descriptions contained in the blog. Since the bloggers play a key role in controlling the group's "meanings and representations of [Italian] food,"[14] it becomes important to analyze these descriptions, especially as they endorse well-known stereotypes about Italian food culture.

Moreover, my study illustrates that, like in many other experiences of migration, the collective Italian identity represented through the group's foodways is the result of daily negotiations between regional, national, and global images of Italian cuisine,[15] as well as between these women's places of origin and their adopted communities. Beyers recommends that we look at these "different Italian styles" not as "fixed recipes," since "Italian traditions [are] (re)invented in accordance with the changing social, economic and political circumstances."[16] However, even if these acts of negotiations are evident from Facebook members' daily posts and comments, the food discourse employed by Le Ambasciatrici's group administrator and official bloggers indicates a willingness to hold on to a fixed idea of Italian cuisine and of Italian culture, one that resonates with popular images of Italian cuisine outside of Italy and especially in the United States.

In turn, this fixed notion of Italian food draws on a larger discourse of nostalgia, which clearly emerges from the blog and, to some degree, from the Facebook group. Memory and nostalgia do seem to play an equally important role for these women expatriates as they did for previous generations of migrated Italians,[17] even as social media grants them a much closer interaction with their families and communities of belonging. I argue that these feelings of nostalgia not only work as a unifying force among group members but also help convey the ideology of Italian food as peasant food,[18] which well fits the expectations of both national and international readers. The constant tension between cultural nostalgia and cultural creativity, both in these women's kitchen and online, ultimately reveals the complexity of asserting Italianness through social media and within the current context of Italian migration abroad.

MEETING UP IN THE ONLINE KITCHEN

The group dynamics emerging from Le Ambasciatrici's Facebook page show how over time, the group has come to function as an online community sharing similarities with Meetup and other online social networking portals that are geared toward specific groups. Unquestionably, even if food-centered group interactions constitute the bulk of the Facebook posts, there is another level of interaction occurring on the Facebook page, which includes the sharing of meaningful personal or family moments, often but not necessarily through food—such as one's children's first day of school, being in bed with the flu, a special meal cooked for family or friends, applying for a local job, or teaching Italian abroad. Similarly to many women's food blogs, the group functions as "a female community of writers and readers that is mutually supportive and who enjoy corresponding with one another about making food they love, caring for family, friends, and themselves."[19] While this atmosphere of intimacy is already present in cooking blogs, social media certainly amplifies it, as suggested by Le Ambasciatrici's offline meetings and their posts about the experience on the Facebook page. As a matter of fact, the use of personal details is not surprising when it comes to social networks; yet, in the close-knit environment of this Facebook group, the sharing of personal stories seems to be particularly encouraged. The social value of the group is confirmed by several members I contacted through my questionnaire; for example, BM mentioned "Friendship, camaraderie, moral support." As professional cook and blogger Rosa Mariotti from Eugene, Oregon also puts it, "[the group] is a virtual family."

More importantly, the Facebook page provides a space for these women to share their thoughts and feelings about their own personal experiences abroad. For example, when I first joined the group, I was also struck by numerous self-introductory posts by group members; many of them included personal details, such as age and marital status, while some mentioned personal problems. But what truly piqued my interest was the realization that each of these posts included the writer's reasons for leaving Italy and moving abroad. Thus, the social bond among these women is possible thanks to their common experience as Italian female expatriates. Surely, the group's Facebook page provides a safe space for Italian nationals and Italian-speaking women to share their experiences of migration and to help each other locate resources useful for other expatriates. Recurring post topics include not only local availability of Italian ingredients or tips on how to replace hard-to-find Italian ingredients with local alternatives, but also survival-abroad tips and job information for Italian expatriates, or information about Italian cultural programs in the host countries. Another common post topic concerns the first successful home-cooked Italian meal in a new living context or recent adaptations of family dishes based on local ingredients.

The importance of the migration experience for the group as a whole is not only echoed but also amplified by the bloggers' need to "be in close contact with our home lands which will always remain in our hearts," and of "rediscovering the importance of our culinary tradition, as a way to introduce our Paese (country) to the peoples who host us." The use of the term "Paese" with a capital p is particularly symptomatic of a strong attachment to the idea of an Italian nation, as has often been the case for many Italian migrants in the United States and elsewhere[20]; on the contrary, recent migrants, who most often leave Italy as professionals in search of better living conditions rather than to escape poverty, "are more likely to eschew attachments to *paese* or specific places, preferring to define themselves as world citizens."[21] Viewed in this light, the explicit reference to the mother country in Le Ambasciatrici's blog contrasts strikingly with the general trend among recent migrants, thus suggesting a willingness to underline these women's positions as migrated Italians, rather than simply as cosmopolitan citizens, and to look for an emotional connection with other Italian expatriates.

This somewhat nostalgic representation of Italian culture taps into a larger discourse of nostalgia that is displayed both by the blog and the Facebook page, and that is strictly connected to these women's experiences as Italian expatriates. Here the representation of Italian food often passes through cultural memory and cultural loss, as these women strive to re-create Italian culinary traditions within their new living contexts. When introducing the group, for example, the administrator explains, "This group was created because of a willingness to keep alive true Italian cuisine in our houses far away from Italy. And we know how difficult it is sometimes to find many of the ingredients required in the recipes. I have lived in California for almost twenty years and I had to learn to recreate at home many things that in Italy you can easily find at the supermarket." The blog's introduction page further confirms that the bloggers' main goal is to "keep alive our culinary traditions...and to teach our culture to our local friends." An undertone of nostalgia from home and from Italian culture is evident from both these statements and also evident from the bloggers' bios. Blogger Irene, for example, writes about herself: "Migrated to France 16 years ago...over time, and especially after her daughter was born six years ago, she felt an increasingly strong desire to rediscover aromas and flavors from home, savors of when she was a child, traditional family dishes, and also to rediscover all the cultural abundance of our regions, and to transmit them to her daughter."

Naturally, memory and nostalgia are to some degree encouraged by group interaction, as the group gradually extends from a food-centered group to an online community, in which these women can communicate, meet, and support each other beyond their food and cooking interests. At the same time, the increasingly global availability of Italian recipes, ingredients, and cooking tools, along with transnational access to culinary and cultural support from other Italian women via social media, helps these women move beyond the nostalgia for cultural loss, as well as toward new ways of transmitting Italian cultural values among Italian nationals living abroad, those who have never left Italy, and those who have returned.

Indeed, while the blog highlights the women's national bond, by participating in online conversations about Italian foodways and Italian culture on a daily basis, Le Ambasciatrici get to navigate a mediatic space that helps them build "transnational lines of connection"[22] with other Italian women living abroad, those living in Italy, and also previous generations of migrants. In doing so, they are able to create "rhizomatic connections with others in the diaspora and beyond, thereby disrupting older notions of diasporic alienation and insularity."[23] In other words, daily mediation between two different representations of Italian culture, national and transnational, seem to be constantly at play within the group. An example of successful transnational communication concerns the earthquake relief campaign promoted by Facebook and other social networks in the summer of 2016, following a disastrous earthquake that devastated several areas in central Italy. In particular, the earthquake destroyed the historic town of Amatrice, a well-known tourist destination and also the birthplace of the popular "amatriciana" pasta dish. As social media promoted the fundraising campaign, group members immediately joined the call by preparing *amatriciana* in their home kitchens and by posting a picture with the hashtag #leambasciatriciperAmatrice (Le Ambasciatrici for Amatrice). As a result, the event became a great opportunity for group members, both in Italy and abroad, to express their emotional connections to Italy and to Italian culture during a moment of crisis and also to share these connections within the group.

NEGOTIATING ITALIANNESS

The model of Italian cuisine that is available to Italian migrants within their new living contexts is often a complex one; it includes the juxtaposition of the increasingly globalized Italian culinary tradition, the popular image of

Italian cuisine in Italy, and migrants' own regional and local culinary traditions.[24] This mediation between different cultural traditions is evident from Le Ambasciatrici's blog and Facebook pages; for example, a major post category concerns the sharing of regional and local specialties or regional variants of well-known Italian dishes, such as eggplant parmigiana with bread, a tradition from the Lombardy region, or without it. From an Italian-national's perspective, exchanging notions of nationality largely means sharing ideas of regionalism, a major topic of discussion when it comes to both Italian culture in general and Italian food in particular.[25] In addition, while allowing group members to discuss local and national cuisine, the Facebook page also allows them to "cross over their own traditional cultural boundaries and engage with other foodways."[26] Many Facebook posts describe both the bloggers and other group members experimenting with different culinary traditions or with fusion dishes, such as Vietnamese summer rolls or mac and cheese with *ragù*. Moreover, one of the group's most active member, chef and blogger Rosa Mariotti, is well-known for her unique take on Italian cuisine and her fusion recipes.

Nevertheless, these daily acts of mediation are often de-emphasized, especially by the bloggers, in favor of more generalized expectations about both Italian cuisine and other cuisines with which the first interacts. The bloggers' note about food unit conversions is a clear example of this type of rhetoric; the note announces: "Some recipes, since they are being used in the United States, have different units of measure than the ones we are used to. Here they use cups, spoons, and teaspoons. Not very precise!" So, Italian cuisine is also defined for international readers by comparison with the Anglo-American one, supposedly less precise when it comes to units of measure—and yet, the very act of adopting Italian recipes to the Anglo-American context testifies to the translated space that these women inhabit, and embrace, in their everyday lives. This food discourse reminds us that food can function not only "as an expression of identity," but also "as a means by which communities both construct their own identities" and also "define the boundaries between themselves and others,"[27] in this case between Italian food culture and the other local food cultures with which these women interact on a daily basis. Indeed, while experimenting with Italian food on a daily basis, group members often betray a similar attitude though their posts, for example by sharing what they consider horrifying examples of Italian fusion dishes or Americanized Italian dishes. In other words, since online food-centered groups "perform their identities through the recipes they choose to cook, photograph, and share with their readers,"[28] posting about non-authentic Italian food dishes that are popular outside of Italy helps group members confirm and strengthen their own roles as Italian nationals outside Italy's national borders.

Naturally, holding on to the authenticity of one's culinary tradition represents a popular strategy when it comes to food writing; a concern for authenticity appears in much food discourse in popular culture both online and offline, especially following the process of globalization; as Karaosmanoglu puts it, "[e]ven though the local is produced by global and foreign resources, it is equated with authenticity (in contrast to the global, which is presumed to be inauthentic)... [hence,] local culinary practices are celebrated as sites of tradition and authenticity in a globalized world."[29] This appeal to authenticity is evident from the bloggers' reference to "true Italian cuisine" (la vera cucina italiana), which suggests that only Italian nationals are able to discern what Italian cuisine is or should be, as opposed to Americans, for example. After all, the very name of the group can be read as the creators' willingness to function as ambassadors, and therefore authoritative representatives, of Italian cuisine online. Charged with such an important task, the bloggers end up employing more or less stereotypical notions of Italianness to draw in their global readers. "Italians in the world," they explain, "love to sit at the table and lose track of time while enjoying conversation and eating well." The importance of sitting around the table together—a central component of Italian food culture both in Italy and in the diaspora and one that international food chains often capitalize on[30]—is here combined with the less flattering notion that Italians love "perdersi in chiacchiere," literally "losing themselves in conversation." In this way, the bloggers are able to respond to their readers' international expectations by projecting an image of Italian culture that fits well within the Anglo-American perspective illustrated by the media, for example through such popular films as *Under the Tuscan Sun* (2003) or *Eat, Pray, Love* (2010).

Since the bloggers play an active role on the Facebook page and since their professional-looking recipes and photos tend to attract more attention on the Facebook page, one may go as far as concluding that this conservative image of Italian food culture emerging from the blog represents the group as a whole. At the same time, member interactions on the Facebook group often tell a different story, as suggested by the recent debate over the group's name. In a post dated October 8, 2015, the administrator responded to several group members' inquiries regarding recent member additions; the problem was that some group members had invited their foodie relatives and friends who live in Italy to join the group. The administrator responded that the presence of "some women who live in Italy [or have returned to Italy after being abroad] enriches us and keeps us tied to our roots and besides it does not diminish the value of the group"; this response initiated a long list of comments that explicitly engaged with identity politics—one of the members wrote, for example, "We are still all Italian." As a result of this debate, the administrator decided to change the second part of the name from "Italian women abroad" to "Italian women in the world" to reflect a more inclusive definition of Italianness. This incident ultimately suggests that the idea of being Italian is up for discussion within the transnational context of social media and, potentially, within the current context of Italian migration. Likewise, this renaming introduces a more dynamic idea of Italianness, which includes Italian-born women who have lived abroad most of their lives and might include second-generation Italians in the future; in this sense, this group has at least the potential to contribute to "reshuffl[ing] the ways in which the nation, its diaspora and globality intersect."[31]

ITALIAN WOMEN AND CULTURAL NOSTALGIA

A popular notion of Italian cuisine adopted by the bloggers is that of Italian food as simple and genuine, a notion that is very common to identify Italian food both in Italy and abroad[32] and that has become even stronger in recent years with the emergence of the Slow Food movement.[33] A clear example of this rhetoric is given by the bloggers' choice of a traditional Italian staple, *panino con la mortadella*, to represent the essence of the Italian culinary tradition and thus to introduce themselves as both consumers and makers of simple food such as *mortadella*: "A mortadella sandwich and it all began! And what could unite us more than food?" This idea is shared among several other group members, as confirmed by my questionnaire responses. When asked "What sets Italian cuisine apart from other cuisines?" group member AT from San Diego replied, "Genuine ingredients and their simplicity." Furthermore, in reply to my question, "How did your passion for cooking start?" the group administrator states, "All started from that feeling of missing the genuine things that we have in Italy and the desire to reproduce them abroad." Finally, SP from Los Angeles replies, "The attention to detail, the tradition, the quality of the ingredients."

Likewise, Le Ambasciatrici's posts often reflect on the difficulty of cooking in the same genuine way as their mothers did, as well as on the differences between the Italian context, in which cooking a locally sourced meal is mostly considered still possible, and the international context, particularly the fast-food-centered American culture. Some of my questionnaire replies are very explicit in this regard; for example, for VM, who lives in San Francisco, Italian cuisine is different "because it is healthier and richer of fresh ingredients and not processed and, I believe, also without much sugar, in other culinary cultures you find sugar and corn everywhere." Defining one's own position toward local food and the local communities which these women embrace outside of Italy can become a way to continue the Italian tradition of eating healthy within a new sociocultural context. Chef Rosa Mariotti's goal, for example, is "to transmit the incredible gratitude and appreciation [she] ha[s] for the source of everything [she] eat[s], whether it comes from an animal or the hard labor of a farmer. Only then, will [she] feel[s] that [she] ha[s] served this local community, while also making [her] parents and grandparents really proud of the childhood traditions and respect for food they have given [her]."[34]

The recurrence of this discourse both on the Facebook page and in my questionnaire responses reflects the resilience of the myth of Italian food as earthy food among Italians today. However, this global myth is ultimately contrasted by the reality of a cuisine that in its most developed form is very far from its peasant version.[35] As for Le Ambasciatrici, it is important to note that both the blog and the Facebook page are filled with gourmet recipes and professional-looking photos by the bloggers in the group or by other blog links shared by group members. This appeal to simplicity thus becomes a marketing tool that is used, more or less consciously, by both the bloggers and other group members, to endorse a popular image of Italian cuisine; as it turns out, this strategy is successful since it helps attract to the group less-experienced cooks who post about their children's school lunch boxes or even share their latest recipe failure.

This dwelling on the simplicity of a home-cooked meal becomes especially problematic when it is employed by Le Ambasciatrici to define themselves as Italian women. Since people choose certain dishes not only because of who they are but also because of who they want to be,[36] by holding on to the myth of Italian food as peasant food, Le Ambasciatrici are able to convey the image of Italian women who cook every day for their families and friends, even when in reality many of them work as chefs. In turn, this image reflects long-standing notions of femininity in relation to the Italian context, given that the Italian food culture is still largely centered on traditional notions of family life.[37]

Viewed in this light, the image of the "trattoria" (rustic restaurants) that is often associated with Italian cuisine ultimately functions as "a bastion of the local and a form of resistance against the global, in which female cooking becomes professional."[38] Remarkably, reclaiming this old-time home cooking tradition is also made possible by the latest kitchen technology that is globally available; for example, when asked where her passion for cooking comes from, the administrator writes, "from the desire to eat well, to cook like my mum used to do." Even so, she adds that her passion for cooking deepened once she bought a Bimby (the Italian equivalent of KitchenAid). In other words, these women seem to be holding on to the traditional role assigned to women in the Italian kitchen, which is strictly intertwined with Italy's still strong local cultural traditions, while at the same time exploring their own freedom to express themselves as either amateurs or professional cooks, as well as redefining gender dynamics in the kitchen.

As a matter of fact, several of these women were able to reinvent themselves, both personally and professionally, outside of Italy thanks to their passion for cooking. Group and blog administrator Stefania Pisanu left Italy after high school and moved to the United States where she studied chiropractic medicine, inexistent in the Italian context at the time; however, once she got a job as a nanny, she started paying attention to the food she cooked, which ultimately led her to rediscover her family and national food traditions and to create a Facebook group on the topic.[39]

CC, instead, worked for twenty years as a graphic designer before she moved to Tokyo with her Japanese husband. In Tokyo, she is a teacher of Italian cuisine, particularly traditional cooking from Sardinia. AT also left Italy for love, but she ended up reinventing herself as a chef once she moved to the United States. This storyline—very common among Italian women expatriates to the United States, especially for accompanying spouses with limited employment opportunities—illustrates these women's determination to adjust and to succeed professionally in a foreign context, even as Italian patriarchal ideology still provides them with a conservative role model to follow.

These considerations suggest that we look at Le Ambasciatrici's group as a mediated community of expatriates, in which both bloggers and other group members variously contribute to confirming, negotiating, and to a certain extent redefining established cultural values and gender roles associated with Italian food, a community that, through its tension between cultural nostalgia and creativity reveals today's complexity in asserting identity.

NOTES

1. Donna Gabaccia, "Food, Recipes, Cookbooks, and Italian-American Life: An Introduction," in American *Woman, Italian Style: Italian Americana's Best Writings on Women*, ed. Carol Bonomo Albright (New York, NY: Fordham University Press, 2011), 121–22.

2. Lucy M. Long, "Introduction." *Journal of American Folklore* 483 (2009): 3.

3. Sergio Nava, "Lavorare all'estero: Nel 2014 oltre 100mila in fuga dall'Italia." *Il-Sole24Ore*, March 23, 2015, accessed March 3, 2017. http://www.ilsole24ore.com/art/notizie/ 2015-03-23/lavorare-estero-2014-oltre-100mila-fuga-italia-103109.shtml?uuid=ABJX9dDD& refresh_ce=1.) The article also warns that the actual number of Italians requesting a visa in foreign countries is often much larger than the number registered by the Registry of Italians Resident Abroad (A.I.R.E).

4. Programma Integra, "Dossier IDOS—UNAR: Dopo 20 anni gli italiani all'estero crescono più degli immigrati." July 7, 2015. Accessed January 16, 2017. https://www. programmaintegra.it/wp/2015/07/dossier-idos-unar-dopo-20-anni-gli-italiani-allestero-crescono-piu-degli-immigrati/.

5. Radha S. Hegde, "Food Blogs and the Digital Reimagination of South Asian Diasporic Publics," *South Asian Diaspora* 6 (2014): 89.

6. Signe Rousseau, "Food for Sharing." In *Food and Social Media: You Are What You Tweet*, 1–16. Blue Ridge Summit, PA: AltaMira Press, 2012, 8.

7. 7 Stefan Diemer, Marie-Louise Brunner, and Selina Schmidt, "Like, Pasta, Pizza and Stuff'—New Trends in Online Food Discourse." *Cuizine: The Journal of Canadian Food Cultures / Cuizine: revue des cultures culinaires au Canada* 5, no. 2 (2014).

8. Paula M. Salvio, "Dishing It Out: Food Blogs and Post-Feminist Domesticity." *Gastronomica: The Journal of Food and Culture* 12, no. 3 (2012): 32.

9. Salvio, "Dishing It Out," 31.

10. Rousseau, "Food for Sharing," 9.

11. Ibidem.

12. According to Nava, over half of the expatriates are twenty to forty years old and most of them come from the central and northern regions of Italy, particularly the Lombardy region, contrary to previous migration waves that included large numbers of Southern Italians.

13. Kerstin McGaughey, "Food in Binary: Identity and Interaction in Two German Food Blogs," *Cultural Analysis: An Interdisciplinary Forum on Folklore and Popular Culture* 9 (2010): 82.

14. Long, "Introduction," 6.

15. Leen Beyers, "Creating Home: Food, Ethnicity and Gender among Italians in Belgium since 1946," *Food, Culture & Society* 11 (2008): 18.

16. Ibidem.

17. Within the Italian-American context, for example, "food expresses the nostalgic connection with the past and the land of origin, as well as the relevance of family ties and affection." Fabio Parasecoli, "We Are Family: Ethnic Food Marketing and the Consumption of Authenticity in Italian-Themed Chain Restaurants." In *Making Italian America: Consumer Culture and the Production of Ethnic Identities*, 244–55. Edited by Simone Cinotto. New York: Fordham University Press, 2014.

18. John Dickie, *Delizia!: The Epic History of the Italians and Their Food*. New York: Free Press, 2008, 5.

19. Salvio, "Dishing It Out," 34.

20. Donna R. Gabaccia, *Italy's Many Diasporas*. Seattle: University of Washington Press, 2000, 3; Loretta Baldassar and Donna R. Gabaccia, *Intimacy and Italian Migration: Gender and Domestic Lives in a Mobile World*. 1st ed. Critical Studies in Italian America. New York: Fordham University Press, 2011, 176.

21. Baldassar and Gabaccia, *Intimacy and Italian Migration*, 178.

22. Hegde, "Food Blogs," 89.

23. Hedge, "Food Blogs," 90.

24. Beyers, "Creating Home," 23.

25. Alberto Capatti and Massimo Montanari, *Italian Cuisine: A Cultural History*. New York: Columbia University Press, 2003, xiii. (Italian ed. 1999.)

26. McGaughey, "Food in Binary," 82.

27. Long, "Introduction," 7.

28. McGaughey, "Food in Binary," 75.

29. Defne Karaosmanoglu, "Authenticated Spaces: Blogging Sensual Experiences in Turkish Grill Restaurants in London," *Space and Culture* 20 (2013): 5.

30. Parasecoli, "We Are Family," 253.

31. Hedge, "Food Blogs," 90.

32. Davide Girardelli, "Commodified Identity: The Myth of Italian Food in the United States." *Journal of Communication Inquiry* 28, no. 4 (2004): 308.

33. Dickey, *Delizia!* 4–5.

34. Mariotti's bio was featured on Our Stories: Immigrants of America's Facebook page on December 10, 2016.

35. Dickey, *Delizia!*, 5.

36. McGaughey, "Food in Binary," 81.

37. Francesco Buscemi, "Television as a Trattoria: Constructing the Woman in the Kitchen on Italian Food Shows," *European Journal of Communication* 29 (2014): 307.

38. Ibidem.

39. Stefania Pisanu, Facebook message, January 17, 2017.

WORKS CITED

Baldassar, Loretta, and Donna R. Gabaccia. *Intimacy and Italian Migration: Gender and Domestic Lives in a Mobile World.* 1st ed. Critical Studies in Italian America. New York: Fordham University Press, 2011.

Beyers, Leen. "Creating Home: Food, Ethnicity and Gender among Italians in Belgium since 1946." *Food, Culture & Society* 11, no. 1 (2008): 7–27.

Buscemi, Francesco. "Television as a Trattoria: Constructing the Woman in the Kitchen on Italian Food Shows." *European Journal of Communication* 29, no. 3 (2014): 304–18.

Capatti, Alberto, and Massimo Montanari. *Italian Cuisine: A Cultural History.* New York: Columbia University Press, 2003. (Italian ed. 1999).

Dickie, John. *Delizia!: The Epic History of the Italians and Their Food.* New York: Free Press, 2008.

Diemer, Stefan, Marie-Louise Brunner, and Selina Schmidt. "Like, Pasta, Pizza and Stuff"— New Trends in Online Food Discourse." *Cuizine: The Journal of Canadian Food Cultures / Cuizine: revue des cultures culinaires au Canada* 5, no. 2 (2014).

Gabaccia, Donna. "Food, Recipes, Cookbooks, and Italian-American Life: An Introduction." In *American Woman, Italian Style: Italian Americana's Best Writings on Women*, edited by Carol Bonomo Albright, 121–22. New York, NY: Fordham University Press, 2011.

Gabaccia, Donna R. *Italy's Many Diasporas.* Seattle: University of Washington Press, 2000.

Girardelli, Davide. "Commodified Identity: The Myth of Italian Food in the United States." *Journal of Communication Inquiry* 28, no. 4 (2004): 307–24.

Hegde, Radha S. "Food Blogs and the Digital Reimagination of South Asian Diasporic Publics."
South Asian Diaspora 6, no. 1 (2014): 89–103.

Karaosmanoglu, Defne. "Authenticated Spaces: Blogging Sensual Experiences in Turkish Grill Restaurants in London." *Space and Culture* 20, no. 10 (2013):1–15.

Long, Lucy M. "Introduction." *Journal of American Folklore*, 122, no. 483 (2009): 3–10.

McGaughey, Kerstin. "Food in Binary: Identity and Interaction in two German Food Blogs." *Cultural Analysis: An Interdisciplinary Forum on Folklore and Popular Culture* 9 (2010): 69–95.

Murcott, Anne. "Food as an Expression of National Identity." In *The Future of the Nation State: Essays on Cultural Pluralism and Political Integration.* Edited by Sverker Gustavsson and Leif Lewin. London, UK: Routledge, 1996.

Nava, Sergio. "Lavorare all'estero: Nel 2014 oltre 100mila in fuga dall'Italia." *IlSole24Ore* March 23, 2015.

Parasecoli, Fabio. "We Are Family: Ethnic Food Marketing and the Consumption of Authenticity in Italian-Themed Chain Restaurants." In M*aking Italian America: Consumer Culture and the Production of Ethnic Identities*, 244–55. Edited by Simone Cinotto. New York: Fordham University Press, 2014.

Programma Integra. "Dossier IDOS—UNAR: Dopo 20 anni gli italiani all'estero crescono più degli immigrati." July 7, 2015. Programma Integra S.C.S. Accessed January 16, 2017. https://www.programmaintegra.it/wp/2015/07/dossier-idos-unar-dopo-20-anni-gli-italiani-allestero-crescono-piu-degli-immigrati/ .

Rousseau, Signe. "Food for Sharing." In *Food and Social Media: You Are What You Tweet*, 1–16. Blue Ridge Summit, PA: AltaMira Press, 2012.

Salvio, Paula M. "Dishing It Out: Food Blogs and Post-Feminist Domesticity." *Gastronomica: The Journal of Food and Culture* 12, no. 3 (2012): 31–39.

Index

211

Contributors

Adele Bardazzi is currently completing her D.Phil. at Christ Church, Oxford. In her thesis she explores the notion of "shadow" in relation to Montale's poetry. Her research interests lie in the field of modern Italian lyric poetry, with a particular focus on loss and mourning, and questions of gender and artistic authority. In 2015 she created the Gender & Authority Research Network, funded by the Oxford Research Centre in the Humanities.

David W. Ellwood is senior adjunct professor of European studies at the Bologna campus of the Johns Hopkins University's School of Advanced International Studies. His latest book is *The Shock of America: Europe and the Challenge of the Century* (2016), a major historical work dedicated to America's impact on the politics of change in Europe. Ellwood is a frequent contributor to academic journals, policy forums, and news outlets. He was president of the International Association for Media and History (1996–2002).

John Foot is professor of modern Italian history at the University of Bristol. His publications include *Italy's Divided Memory* (2009) and *The Man Who Closed the Asylums: Franco Basaglia and the Revolution in Mental Health Care* (2015). His book *The Archipelago: Italy since 1945* will appear in Italian and English in 2018.

Torunn Haaland is associate professor at Gonzaga University where she teaches Italian language and culture. She has published several articles on modern Italian literature and cinema and is the author of *Italian Neorealist Cinema* (2012). Her current research explores literary and cinematic representations of traumatic memories and liminal states.

Andrea Hajek obtained her doctorate degree from the University of Warwick. She is the managing editor for the *Memory Studies* journal, and an associate editor for *Modern Italy*. She is also a founding member of the Warwick Oral History Network and an associate fellow of Glasgow's *Centre for Gender History*. Her research interests include memory studies, women's history, European protest movements, contemporary Italy, and oral history.

Incoronata (Nadia) Inserra is assistant professor in the department of focused inquiry at Virginia Commonwealth University. She received her Ph.D. from the University of Hawaii at Mānoa (UHM) with a specialization in transnational Italian cultural studies, folklore, and performance, along with translation and adaptation studies. Her book *Global Tarantella: Reinventing Southern Italian Folk Music and Dances* is forthcoming (2017). She has also published peer-reviewed articles, reviews, and translations in Italian and Italian-American journals and volumes. Her current interests include transnational migration in Europe and the Mediterranean and digital Italian folklore studies. Currently, Nadia teaches in both LLEA and English departments at UHM.

Charles L. Leavitt IV is lecturer in Italian studies at the University of Reading. He studies postwar Italian literature and cinema in a comparative context. Leavitt earned his Ph.D. in literature from the University of Notre Dame, where he was Presidential Fellow in Humanities, Annese Fellow of the Nanovic Institute for European Studies, and a postdoctoral research fellow.

Martin McLaughlin is Agnelli-Serena Professor of Italian at Oxford, and a fellow of Magdalen College. He has published widely on Italian literature from the Middle Ages to the present, including *Literary Imitation in the Italian Renaissance* (1995), *Italo Calvino* (1998), and *Leon Battista Alberti: La vita, l'umanesimo, le opere letterarie* (2016). He has coedited and contributed to a number of volumes, including *Image, Eye and Art in Calvino: Writing Visibility* (2007) and *Biographies and Autobiographies in Modern Italy* (2007). He has also translated works by Umberto Eco—*On Literature* (2005); and Italo Calvino—*Why Read the Classics?* (1999), *Into the War* (2011), and *Letters 1941–1985* (2013).

Sandra Parmegiani is associate professor of European studies and Italian at the University of Guelph. Her research focuses on eighteenth-century English-Italian literary relations and on twentieth-century Italian literature. She is the author of *Ugo Foscolo and English Culture* (2011) and the editor of